"Outstanding . . . The exercises for developing intuition are clear, effective, and safe. This is the all-around best guide for anyone who wants to begin activating his or her intuitive ability."

—John White, author of *What Is Enlightenment?*

"You can be assured that the keys to intuition presented by Rosemary Ellen Guiley will work magic in your life—even if you do not believe this could happen for you. Rosemary . . . has transformed her life and thousands of others who have been touched by her books."

—Jeffrey Mishlove, Ph.D., author of *The PK Man*

"Offers a rich array of exercises and approaches to developing intuitive ability. There is something here for everyone."

—Belleruth Naparstek, author of *Invisible Heroes*

The Tao
of
Dreaming

Rosemary Ellen Guiley, Ph.D.
and Sheryl Martin, O.M.D

B
BERKLEY BOOKS, NEW YORK

THE BERKLEY PUBLISHING GROUP
Published by the Penguin Group
Penguin Group (USA) Inc.
375 Hudson Street, New York, New York 10014, USA
Penguin Group (Canada), 10 Alcorn Avenue, Toronto, Ontario M4V 3B2, Canada (a division of Pearson
Penguin Canada Inc.)
Penguin Books Ltd., 80 Strand, London WC2R 0RL, England
Penguin Group Ireland, 25 St. Stephen's Green, Dublin 2, Ireland (a division of Penguin Books Ltd.)
Penguin Group (Australia), 250 Camberwell Road, Camberwell, Victoria 3124, Australia (a division of Pearson
Australia Group Pty. Ltd.)
Penguin Books India Pvt. Ltd. 11 Community Centre, Panchsheel Park, New Delhi—110 017, India
Penguin Group (NZ), Cnr. Airborne and Rosedale Roads, Albany, Auckland 1310, New Zealand (a division of
Pearson New Zealand Ltd.)
Penguin Books (South Africa) (Pty.) Ltd., 24 Sturdee Avenue, Rosebank, Johannesburg 2196, South Africa

Penguin Books Ltd., Registered Offices: 80 Strand, London, WC2R 0RL, England

This book is an original publication of the Berkley Publishing Group.

PRINTING HISTORY
Berkley trade paperback edition / August 2005

Library of Congress Cataloging-in-Publication Data

Guiley, Rosemary
     The Tao of dreaming / by Rosemary Ellen Guiley and Sheryl Martin.
         p.   cm.
     Includes bibliographical references (p. 303).
     ISBN 0-425-20280-1
         1. Dream interpretation.   2. Taoism.   I. Martin, Sheryl.   II. Title

     BF1091.G85 2005
     154.6'3—dc22

                                                        2005042002

PRINTED IN THE UNITED STATES OF AMERICA

10   9   8   7   6   5   4   3   2   1

Contents

Introduction

The Tao, once a concept and word unfamiliar in the West, has become quite fashionable. "Tao" prefaces almost everything imaginable: the "Tao of gardening," the "Tao of miniature train railroading," or the "Tao of computer programming." The implication of the word is it implies a secret to these crafts. *Tao*, which means "the way," may lead one to believe that the way presented is the *only* way. When we chose the title to this book, *The Tao of Dreaming*, we did not feel that we held the keys to the kingdom of dream deciphering. We merely wanted to present another "way" or method of dream exploration that utilizes a different contextual framework than has been presented before.

This book is unprecedented by offering a means to explore dreams using both Taoist philosophical principles and Chinese Medicine principles blended with Western dream techniques. We are adding an "arm" to the study of dreams by helping individuals not only to see their dreams as a means of gaining insights into mental challenges and concerns, but also see them as a means of gaining insights into potential physical health imbalances. Beginners in the field of dream study will find that the book is written in such a manner that both the novitiate and the sage dream explorer can benefit.

In Chapter 1 we introduce readers to the history and benefits of personal dream study. We discuss important preparations that will make dream exploration an easier undertaking. We stress the importance of keeping a dream diary as a means to mental and spiritual development; however, one can start work immediately with a single written dream. We also discuss cultural and historical perspectives of how, from the beginning of time, humans have sought to understand their dreams, and how they have utilized dreams for personal, social, political, and medical purposes.

In Chapters 2 and 3 we provide an introduction to Taoism and give examples of how Taoist thinking pervades our culture, sometimes assisting modern-day psychotherapists and other medical practitioners in health care.

Chapter 4 discusses yin and yang theory, which is at the core of Taoist and Chinese Medicine thought. We demystify this basic theory of how the universe works by bringing it into modern-day language. The readers will be able to identify what things in the world are basically yin and what are basically yang, and will learn how to recognize how they use these principles in everyday life. We then guide dream explorers into a specific dream process that utilizes the interplay of yin and yang to gain more insight into the meaning of their dreams.

In the final chapter, Chapter 5, we further explore the ancient Chinese Medicine principles of the Five Elements. We first cover historical perspectives and discuss in detail each of the Five Elements. Readers who have not been previously exposed to this line of thinking will have a new blueprint, enabling them to see their dream world in a whole new light. Each section that discusses the individual elements will cover some of the mind/body perspectives of elemental imbalances and how they might be identified in dreams. There are also a variety of Five Element charts, tables, and diagrams to help readers who are novice to these principles. These diagrams and charts act as visual aids to better comprehend what may be completely new material.

In both Chapters 4 and 5 there are dream samples with step-by-step guidance on how to use both the yin/yang and the Five Element dream processing. Each individual element is highlighted in the samples with explanations of how to decode what seems to be a cryptic dream message. There is also discussion on what to do about vague dreams and how to handle those dreams that tend to stump most dreamers.

At the end of the book we've included an extensive glossary that provides commentary on hundreds of common dream images. The glossary is an excellent tool for the serious dream explorer. Like other aspects of this book, it is unprecedented with its blend of Eastern and Western associations. Available translated Chinese texts provide brief explanations to meanings of certain dream images, but these are certainly culturally biased and very limited in their ability to help the modern-day student of dreams. Our glossary provides more than just Taoist cultural perspectives and draws on the ancient Western dream traditions as well. Most entries in the glossary are categorized according to the image's nature of being either yin or yang. They also have a Five Elements designation. Some entries have more commentary than others, depending on their complexity.

To explore these ancient theories, allow time for thoughts to digest each step of the way on this journey. If you are that novice who has never been exposed to Taoist thought, you might find it helpful to take in the information a little at a time. Meditate on it, ponder it more, and allow the sages from a time nearly forgotten to whisper in your ear, furnishing you with the ability to fully comprehend. Then go about your day, identifying yin and yang, and each of the Five Elements in your environment. See how they apply to your everyday activities. Identify yin and yang in things and personalities. See how they apply to your health and relationships. Identify objects and people with Wood, Fire, Earth, Metal, or Water Element characteristics, and then review with the charts in this book to see those Five Element interrelationships. Once you have a good handle on how the principles apply in waking life, it will become more apparent to you how they apply in your dream world.

If you are that dreamer with prior exposure to the yin/yang and Five Element theories, you may also need to expand your thinking just a little beyond what you originally learned about these theories. Most of you who are students of Taoism and Chinese Medicine were not taught about how these ancient principles apply to your dreams. The little information that is currently available in Taoist philosophy books or in translated Chinese medical texts is, as previously mentioned, limited and culturally biased. It's important to realize that meanings of dream images are very individualized. A certain image to one person will convey a meaning that may be quite different from the meaning another person receives from the same image. Of course, there are images that have universal connotations and are not limited by a certain culture or era. These universal meanings are usually clear and apparent; for example, the image of the ocean will most likely convey the same meaning to people of all cultures, throughout all ages. The only individual meaning that might be realized is that one person who dreams of an ocean might feel fear, and another might feel safe and peaceful. Messages from dream images are dependent upon a person's prior personal experience with that image.

This book will be most beneficial when the chapters are studied in sequence—don't be tempted to jump ahead. Just as one cannot build a house starting with the roof, you cannot go directly to the instructions on dream processing to understand how it works. An important foundation is laid in the progression of chapters that is needed for building a productive dreamwork program.

We hope you find that this innovative and unique approach to dreamwork brings many blessings into your life.

—Sheryl Martin and Rosemary Ellen Guiley

The Tao

of

Dreaming

CHAPTER 1

Introduction to Dream Study

P EOPLE have paid attention to their dreams and sought to understand them for thousands of years. In ancient cultures around the world, dreams were seen as divinely inspired or gifts of the gods that brought important messages. Professional and priestly dream interpreters and oracles worked for emperors, kings, and other royalty, seeking to know the future or get guidance on important matters of state.

Gudea, a Sumerian king who ruled circa 2200 B.C. is one of the earliest known historical figures who was guided by dreams. The king intended to build a temple to honor the god Nin-Girsu. He had a dream sent by Nin-Girsu in which a large human figure appeared, wearing the headgear of a god but possessing the wings of a bird. The figure was accompanied by two lions. Then Gudea saw a rising sun, a woman looking at a tablet that showed "favorable stars," and a warrior drawing the outline of the temple on a tablet of lapis lazuli. A basket for carrying earth and a brick mold with a brick in it were placed at Gudea's feet, and a donkey pawed the ground in front of the winged figure.

The king could not understand the dream, so he underwent incubation rituals to ask a goddess, Gatumdung, to interpret it for him. She told him that the winged figure was Nin-Girsu and the donkey was the impatient Gudea. She also explained other elements in the dream.

Gudea then appealed to Nin-Girsu for a clearer message. The god appeared in a dream and said he would give the king a sign when the time was right to start the construction of the temple.

The Egyptians considered dreams to be a "revelation of truth" and thus attached great divinatory significance to dreams, looking to dreams alone for omens. Dreams retained an importance throughout the history of ancient Egypt, even into its declining years. A surviving account tells about the pharaoh Tanuatamun (ruled 664–656 B.C.), an Ethiopian ruler during the decline of Egypt, who had a dream in which he was holding two snakes, one in each hand. When he awoke, he saw there were no snakes. He asked for an interpretation and was told:

> Upper Egypt belongs to thee, take to thyself, Lower Egypt. The Vulture and Ureaus goddesses have appeared on thy head, and the land is given to thee in its length and breadth, and none shall share with thee.

The dream seemed to address his ruling over both Upper and Lower Egypt—represented respectively by the Vulture and Ureaus (fire-spitting cobra)—which he subsequently accomplished. On the stele upon which this story is recorded, Tanuatamun stated, "Lo, the dream is true! It is profitable for him who sets it in his head, evil for him who understands it not." In other words, it is good if a dream is correctly understood, and bad if it is misunderstood or ignored.

The early Hebrews placed great importance on dreams; the Bible contains many references to significant and prophetic dreams of the patriarchs and great prophets.

The Greeks especially valued dreams for their healing power as well as for their divination importance. The Greeks discovered that not only can dreams aid healing once a person is ill, but dreams also can forecast the onset of illness, sometimes early enough to prevent a serious illness. Such forecasting dreams are called "prodromal dreams." The great depth psychiatrist Carl G. Jung observed prodromal dreams in his own patients. Illness warning dreams continue to be reported in the medical literature today.

The Greeks, and the Romans, who absorbed their traditions, built hundreds of temples throughout the classical world. Pilgrims traveled to the temples to seek dreams of healing from the gods—or at least information that would enable them to be healed. Christianity integrated this tradition with churches and shrines dedicated to the healing ministrations of archangel Michael.

Similarly, the ancient Chinese realized that dreams played an important role in the diagnosis and maintenance of physical health. The understanding of dreams is deeply embedded in Taoism, a system of mysticism and philosophy and the only indigenous religion of China. From a Taoist perspective, dreams can play a prodromal, or forewarning, role by alerting the dreamer to physical and psychical imbalances, which, if not rectified, are likely to cause or contribute to significant health problems and illness.

Everywhere, dreams have played a prominent role in the health, well-being, and fortunes of people and in the affairs of state. Dreams have been used to discern the future, gain divine guidance, and restore health and wholeness. Numerous systems and procedures of interpretation have been developed.

In many cultures, including the Chinese culture, dreams have maintained a fairly unbroken role in human well-being. In the West, we have been less fortunate. Dreams have suffered under the influence of the Christian church, and Aristotelian philosophy and science. The Christian church—even though it allowed the Michaelean healing churches and shrines—sought to reduce the influence of pagan gods by denigrating dreams. Aristotle's philosophy, promoted by St. Thomas Aquinas in the thirteenth century as the underpinning of

Christian theology, maintains a separation of mind and body—a fundamental of Western science. From that perspective, dreams can have no real influence over the material world.

Western outlook began to shift in the nineteenth century, as we will see in the next chapter. We are now much less rigid in our views on the existence and interplay of mind and body. We increasingly have recognized the validity and importance of dreams as part of that interplay. We are returning to a more holistic view of life and of creation—a perspective that has been at the core of Eastern philosophy and science for millennia.

Today, dreamwork is pursued around the world in professional therapy and medical treatment, and also in lay dreamwork for personal improvement and self-awareness. Dreamwork is productive and rewarding. Dreamwork is also fascinating, taking us on an incredible journey into ourselves and our place in the scheme of the Tao/Universe. Both Eastern and Western approaches to dreams have a wealth of help to offer. In *The Tao of Dreaming*, we've sought, in true Taoist fashion, to integrate both to provide lay dreamworkers and professionals alike with a holistic dreamwork system.

CHAPTER 2

Introduction to Taoism

TAOISM is based on the *Tao Teh Ching*, a slim work dated to the fourth century B.C., but attributed to the legendary mystic Lao Tzu, who was born about two hundred years earlier, around 604 B.C.

Tao means *The Way*. Taoism was expanded upon by various sages. It provided a metaphysics that was lacking in Confucianism and facilitated the emergence of neo-Confucianism during the Sung Dynasty from 960 to 1279. It also helped the entrance of Buddhism into China and the development of Ch'an (Zen) Buddhism. With Confucianism, Taoism forms the foundation of Chinese thought.

Little is known about Lao Tzu. Whether or not he even existed is controversial among scholars. According to the biographer Ssuma Ch'ien (145–86 B.C.), Lao Tzu came from the southern state of Ch'u, which is now the provinces of Hunan and Hupei. His family name was Li, his personal name was Erh, his courtesy name was Po-yang and his posthumous name was Tan. He worked as custodian of the imperial archives of the Chou House in the city of Loyang. He reportedly granted an interview to Confucius, who was some fifty years younger and came to him with questions about rituals.

Lao Tzu's cultivation of Tao allegedly enabled him to live for more than two hundred years, outliving Confucius by 129 years, according to Ssuma Ch'ien. He retired from his job when the Chou House began to decline. As he took the pass westward, Hsin Yi, the warden of the pass, asked him to write a book for his enlightenment. Lao Tzu agreed, and wrote a two-part book on the meaning of the Tao (The Way) and the Teh (Virtue or Power), totalling 5,350 words. Initially, the book was called *Lao Tzu*. The name was changed to the *Tao Teh Ching*, or "Classic of the Way of Its Virtue," sometime during the Western Han dynasty, 202 B.C. to A.D. 9.

Approximately one thousand commentaries have since been written on the *Tao Teh Ching*, the most notable by Han Fei Tzu (died 233 B.C.), Chuang Tzu (369–286 B.C.), Ho Shang Kung (died 159 B.C.), and Wang Pi (A.D. 226–249). Ho Shang Kung's commentary was the first in detail and comprehensiveness and was a major influence in the later development of the religion of Taoism.

Key Principles of Taoism

Taoism is permeated with mysticism, which makes it an ideal medium for dreamwork. Tao is the Absolute Truth, the Ultimate Reality, the Eternal Ground of Being. It is the origin of all temporal phenomena, including the One, which is the creative principle of Tao and preceded all other things. Unlike Logos, the personal Godhead of Christianity, or Heaven, the remote but purposeful Supreme Being of Confucianism, Tao is impersonal. Tao has a dual nature. The Eternal Tao is unnameable, indescribable, and beyond discussion. It is the mysterious essence of the universe, unborn, nonbeing, above and beyond heaven, above and beyond the universe. Manifest Tao is the named, the being.

YIN AND YANG

Within Tao are two complementary principles, the *yin,* or passive/female/earth principle, and the *yang,* or active/male/heaven principle. Yin and yang are in constant interaction, ebb and flow, and their balance governs the harmony and well-being of all things. To be "in the flow" of the Tao, one shifts in accordance with the ebb and flux of yin and yang, both in terms of one's interior life and one's exterior life.

This key principle of Taoism is expressed in its symbol, the T'ai Chi T'u ("Diagram of the Supreme Ultimate"): two fishlike figures, one black and one white, contained in a circle. The white figure represent yang and the black figure represents yin. Within each figure is a dot of the opposite color, the lesser yang and lesser yin, demonstrating that each opposing force contains its opposite. The figures are separate yet originate from each other and flow into each other in a perpetual cycle. The T'ai Chi T'u shows that these fundamental forces are in continual opposition and interaction, which nourishes all things. The T'ai Chi T'u also represents the human being, who is comprised of light and dark.

According to legend, the symbol originated in prehistoric times, though there is no evidence to support that contention. The earliest written description of yin and yang is found in the *I Ching,* which tells of the Great Primal Beginning generating two primary forces, which in turn generate four images, which in turn generate the eight trigrams upon which the *I Ching* is based. Lao Tzu was inspired by the *I Ching* in his writing of the *Tao Teh Ching.*

Diagrams to express the concept yin and yang appeared by the time of the Sung Dynasty. An important work was the *T'ai chi t'u shuo* ("The Diagram of the Supreme Ultimate Explained") of the neo-Confucian philosopher Chou Tun'i (1017–1073), who said the diagram symbolized the production and evolution of all things.

More about yin and yang and how they are expressed in dreams is discussed in Chapter 4, "Balancing Your Yin and Yang."

TEH

Teh, the virtue or power of Tao, is expressed in *Wu-Wei,* which is nonaction in terms of noninterference. Nature is spontaneous and effortless, and Wu-Wei constitutes going with the flow. Thus in Taoism, one avoids aggression and challenges, and instead seeks passivity. Toughness and aggression may be overcome with softness, gentleness, meekness, and humility: yang is countered and balanced with yin.

Tao is often identified with Nature, and the same passive principle is applied. One does not seek to control Nature, but to have respect for it and bend to its forces.

SPIRITUAL PURIFICATION

Spiritual purification in Taoism comes through purity of heart and avoidance or elimination of desires, which enable the seeker to embrace the One. The best way to accomplish this is through meditation. Taoist meditation is characterized by several features: 1) concentration; 2) breath control; 3) purification of heart and mind; 4) practice of Wu-Wei in daily life; and 5) the ability to play the female, or yin, role during mystical union with Heaven, the yang principle.

Breath control is of great importance, as it is in yoga. Lao Tzu favored natural breathing, which induces tenderness, the essential characteristic of life (as opposed to rigidity, the characteristic of death). Lao Tzu considered the infant to be the perfect symbol of Tao and said it was highly desirable to breathe as an infant does. Later Taoists advocated "fetus breathing," which is so faint that it is nearly extinguished, and which when done precedes the mystical state of *samadhi.*

The return to a newborn state as a way to Tao is expressed in Taoist yoga, which advises (for men) the sublimation of the vital male force at age sixteen, when it is at its apex of strength, into *hsien t'ien,* the prenatal vital force, which leads to spiritual immortality.

Lao Tzu wrote that he saw immortality in spiritual terms, but some later Taoists looked for physical immortality. From the time of

Chuang Tzu to the century following, there was great interest in alchemy and in the search for an elixir or yoga of immortality. The elixir specialists, *Fang Shih*, enjoyed great prestige.

East Influences West

Eastern philosophical concepts made a significant merge with Western philosophy in the nineteenth century in the Transcendental movement in the West. The New Thought movement embodied the holistic idea that mind and body affect each other. Ralph Waldo Emerson, a Transcendentalist, observed that "We become what we think about all day long." The Science of Mind movement founded by Ernest Holmes underscores the concept that purifying one's thoughts will bring about dramatic changes in health and external circumstances. We can make the extrapolation that one's dreams are a part of the inner landscape of thought and feeling; thus dreams, too, are interwoven in the complexities of health and well-being, fortune and adversity.

CONTRIBUTIONS BY CARL G. JUNG

Carl G. Jung (1875–1961), the Swiss psychiatrist who founded depth psychology, was a significant influence on the merging of Taoist and other Eastern and Western philosophies. Carl G. Jung's introspection of man's inner realms was fueled to a large extent by his own personal experiences involving dreams, visions, mythological and religious symbolism, and paranormal phenomena. He took Sigmund Freud's knowledge of the unconscious and brought it into spiritual realms. His psychology has Taoistic elements, in that he perceived the dual nature of the psyche, and the flow, balances, and imbalances that occur in the quest for wholeness.

Jung also viewed dreams as tools for individuation—the attainment of one's "personal best" by leaving behind habitual, unproductive methods of problem solving. He emphasized dreaming's role in finding wholeness of self and how different aspects of the personality will appear in dreams based on what is needed to achieve that wholeness. Jung worked with the concepts of *animus* and *anima,* the female and male essences of us, respectively, which is another way of expressing the yin and yang of Taoism. They are halves in each individual, which must be balanced for happiness and wholeness.

Another expression of duality in Jungian psychology shows up in dreams: the persona and the shadow. The persona represents the dreamer's "surface" self—brighter, simpler, and often the way we like to see ourselves and wish others to see us. The shadow self is darker—harder to recognize, more complex, and represents aspects of ourselves that we would rather not see, and do not wish others to see.

Both male/female and persona/shadow parts of a person show themselves in dreams, said Jung, and thus reveal which parts need to be softened or strengthened. This is why dream analysis is crucial to personal growth, he said.

Jung became intensely interested in alchemy, which at the time was a lost art or science, and in Eastern thought. Eastern philosophy especially influenced his development of the concept of synchronicity, or "meaningful coincidences."

Jung was fascinated with patterns and divination systems such as the *I Ching.* In 1928, he collaborated with the Sinologist Richard Wilhelm on studies of the Chinese Taoist alchemical text, *The Secret of the Golden Flower,* about the attainment of immortality. His commentary on this text, published in 1929, is another of his major works.

East-West Integration Today

The twentieth century saw more influences of Eastern thought upon Western science, psychology, and medicine.

SCIENCE

The concept of the Tao is expressed in quantum physics: everything is interconnected, and everything affects, and is affected by, everything else.

The land of dreams, or dreamscape, is not an imaginary place concocted from our fantasies. It incorporates the world we know, but extends far beyond into reaches we may not even comprehend. It exists beyond the limits of time and space, incorporates past, present, and future simultaneously, and is peopled with both persons familiar to us and strange to us—strange because they belong to the dreamscape itself.

In the terms of quantum physics, the dreamscape emerges from the implicate order. According to physicist David Bohm, the implicate ("enfolded") order is the seamless whole of the universe, the unbroken continuum of all things. Like the aboriginal dreamtime, it is a deep level of reality that contains all time and yet is timeless. It holds all potentiality. It is fluid. From the implicate order comes the explicate ("unfolded") order, which is what we know as material reality. There is a constant flow of energy between the two orders. There is no cause and effect, but rather influences that give rise to the acausal connections of synchronicity.

The implicate order is the realm of the mystics: a state of being that is eternal. We can gain direct knowledge of this realm through spiritual discipline, such as meditation and prayer. We also gain knowledge of it through our dreams. Our dreams take us into the implicate order, where we have access to potentiality, and thus can bring it into manifestation.

PSYCHOLOGY

In psychology, Taoist concepts have become absorbed into many Western therapeutic approaches. Many, including Jungian techniques, emphasize dreamwork based on the Taoist principles of interconnectedness.

Transpersonal psychology especially includes both Eastern and Western methods of working with the consciousness, including traditional Western methods such as dream analysis and imagery, Eastern meditation and yoga, behavioral medicine, bodywork, and the transpersonal experience of altered states of consciousness as a means of achieving higher states. The groundwork for transpersonal psychology was laid at the turn of the twentieth century by William James, but was not developed for some fifty years. In transpersonal psychotherapy, ego is illusion, something to be transcended so that the individual can identify with the total self. Body and mind are not separate, but subsystems of each other. Transpersonal psychology assumes everyone has the capacity for self-healing. The consciousness is expanded to overcome space and/or time to identify with other consciousnesses, phenomena, or states.

MEDICINE

In medicine, Chinese Medicine is increasingly sought as a treatment along with Western allopathic medicine. Research into "complementary medicine" and "intentionality" provides increasing scientific evidence for concepts known and accepted by the ancient Chinese: our health is a holistic picture of our physical, mental, emotional, and spiritual conditions. Our states of mind, conscious and unconscious, including our intentions about whether or not we will be healthy or sick, influence the body.

What's more, our dreams give us honest information about all of those states of mind and being. By paying attention to our dreams, we can better keep ourselves in balance in all areas.

Dreamwork in Chinese Culture and Medicine

The dreamwork of Taoism-steeped Chinese culture expresses attitudes still found in dreamwork today: dreamwork is beneficial, instructive, and healing in nature. Early Taoist literature makes numerous references to dreams. The ancient Chinese, like other ancient peoples, compiled and published dream dictionaries and articles, dream diaries, and paintings and woodcuts of dreams in progress. Magical spells against nightmares and bad dreams proliferated. Dream incubation— the solicitation or self-programming of dreams for a specific purpose— was widely practiced by artists in China, who would dream to receive inspiration for their paintings and music.

Like others in the ancient world, the Chinese had a dream god, who could be petitioned to grant certain types of dreams. The *Compendium of Literary Allusions (Shih-lei t'ung-pien)* refers to a dream god called *Chih-li,* a name that probably was adopted from foreign sources. Chih-li could be invoked for productive dreaming by reciting a mantra or charm seven times before sleep.

Many of the old dream texts, from early times to medieval years, are still in modern circulation, and have been translated into other languages and studied by scholars and dream researchers.

The Chinese text *Meng Shu* of the seventh century A.D. sees dreams as teaching tools; therefore the correct interpretation is necessary if the dreamer is to learn how to improve his or her life. The *Meng Shu,* while it encourages the dreamer to look "inside" for interpretations of his or her dreams, also acknowledges the influence of the external world, including astrological forces.

Other dream texts feature lists and dictionaries of dream signs organized by categories. In addition to astrological forces, there are features of the natural landscape, tools and weapons, cosmetics, marital relationships, and other topics related to daily life. Professional diviners used these texts, but they were also used and readily understood by the general public. Lay dreamwork—the ability of ordinary people to interpret and understand their own dreams—was popular in China long before it took hold in the West.

DREAM LITERATURE RELATING TO DIAGNOSIS

Classical medical literature attests to the importance of dreams as a diagnostic tool. Few of these texts survive, but they reinforce the concept of dream diagnosis and they borrow heavily from each other. All dreams, pleasant and unpleasant, are produced by imbalances in the body. Thus, by understanding the images and symbols in dreams, one could know the state of one's physical and mental health and gain understanding on remedies for correcting the imbalances. Unlike traditional Western Medicine, which separates mind and body, Chinese Medicine makes no clear distinction between the two; like the interplay of yin and yang, one affects the other.

Dream diagnosis is featured in one of the oldest and best-known medical texts, *The Yellow Monarch's Book of Medicine* (*Huang-ti nei-ching su-wen*). It lays out the basics of dream diagnosis according to each of the Five Agents, which are the vital organs: heart, liver, spleen, lungs, and kidneys. The content and images in dreams are determined by the balance of yin and yang in each organ and in general regions of the body. Yin relates to water and yang to fire. If there are excesses in any of the vital organs, dreams will relate to the emotions governed by them: the liver governs anger, the lungs govern grief, sadness, and flying, and so on. An excess of both yin and yang do not balance each other, but clash with each other.

Similarly, deficiencies in the vital organs produce specific dream images. For example, a depleted heart produces dreams of flames, hills, and mountains, while depleted lungs yields dreams of flying and things made of gold and iron.

Numerous relationships between physical and mental health and dream imagery are given, such as the following. The term "thrives" refers to the condition of excess:

Thus do we know that when the Yin thrives, one dreams of wading through great [bodies of] water in fear. When the Yang thrives, one dreams of great fires burning and scorching. And when both Yin and Yang thrive, then occur dreams of killing and maiming each other. When the upper [pulse or portion of the body] thrives, one dreams of flying. When the lower [pulse] thrives, one dreams of falling. Overfed, one dreams of taking. When the breath of the liver thrives, one dreams of being angry. When the breath of the lungs thrives, one dreams of crying. An abundance of short worms [in the bowels] brings about dreams of gathering a throng. An abundance of long worms causes dreams of beating and hurting each other.

Information in *The Yellow Monarch's Book of Medicine* was adapted into an important text of the second century A.D., *The Book of the Divine Pivot (Ling-shu ching)*. Other examples of dreams relating to imbalances are given, such as:

When the breath of the heart thrives, one dreams of being prone to laughter or of fear and timidity. When the breath of the spleen thrives, one dreams of song and music, or of one's body growing heavy and unwieldy. When the breath of the kidneys thrives, one dreams that the waist and backbone are loose and disjointed.

The Book of the Divine Pivot gives other dream symbolisms related to health and correlated to the Five Elements of water, wood, metal, fire, and earth; some are taken from *The Yellow Monarch's Book of Medicine:*

When the impeding breath (*chueh-chi*) [deficiency] dwells in the heart, one dreams of hills, mountains, smoke and fire; in the lungs, objects of gold and iron; in the liver, of forests and trees; in the spleen, of hills and great marshes, and of winds and rain destroying houses; in the kidneys, of verging on a chasm, or of being submerged in water; in the bladder, of traveling; in the stomach, of drinking and eating; in the large intestines, of fields and the wilds; in the small intestines, of villages and towns, and of roads high and low; in the gall bladder, of fights and litigations, or of disembowelling oneself; in the genitalia, of being beheaded; in the legs, of walking but not being able to move forward, and of living in a caved-in place or a sunken garden; in the thighs and forearms, of performing ceremonies which involve kneeling and rising; and in the mucous membrane of the bladder, of urinating.

Sometimes the texts personify the deficiencies as dream demons and ghosts that invade the body. Chinese medical texts also acknowledge the influence of external stimuli on the content of dreams. For example, sleeping on a belt may produce a dream of snakes.

Dreams remain important in the practice of modern Chinese Medicine. Practitioners assess a patient's dreams as part of a holistic diagnosis.

Dreams provide an excellent medium for the integration of Eastern and Western concepts and therapies for healing. Each has its distinct characteristics and subtle nuances, but both ultimately arrive at the same place: an assessment of imbalances in a person's life, and what to do to remedy the imbalances. *The Tao of Dreaming* presents such an integration.

Before we enter the techniques of *The Tao of Dreaming,* let's look at the basics of dreamwork itself.

CHAPTER 3

The Importance
of Dreamwork

W HY should we pay attention to our dreams? If they're
meaningful, why are dreams fragmented, strange, and
often confusing? Actually, our dreams are quite straight-
forward: they speak in the plain and blunt language of image and
symbol, a language that can be understood universally. Our dreams
are honest. They tell us "like it is." They do not sugarcoat life or
practice avoidance, as we often do in waking life. Jung viewed dreams
as a part of nature that has no wish to deceive.

Much of dream interpretation is a subjective art. If two persons
were to have exactly the same dream, each would interpret it somewhat differently, based upon his own unique experiences, beliefs, and
worldviews. Though the ancients relied upon professional dream interpreters, they also recognized that the meaning of a dream is not
necessarily fixed, but open to multiple interpretations. A dream seldom has just one message. Because symbols are intuited rather than
defined, they can be read in different ways. A dream is likely to have
a primary message, but also have one or more secondary messages as

well. The messages may all relate to the same situation, or may address multiple things going on in your life.

Our dreams are highly emotional and give us feedback on how we are dealing with life situations emotionally. Working with dreams gives us insight into how we can deal with stresses, limiting belief patterns, obstacles, stressful situations, and so on. From the Taoist perspective, when we learn about our imbalances of yin and yang, we also get insight into how to restore balance in life.

Why Dreams Are Important

Here are five key thoughts about dreams:

1. Our dreams are experiences that have just as much meaning to us as our experiences in waking consciousness. They take place in their own reality and speak their own language, primarily through symbols and images and also through emotions and intuition. Many symbols and images have roots in universal meanings; others are unique and personal.

2. Our dreams are primarily about us and reflect how we think we are doing in the world. They reveal our anxieties and true feelings, and help us see what we need to change and heal.

3. Our dreams provide a clear screen for intuitive and spiritual guidance and can be invaluable in helping us sort through difficulties, make decisions, and take needed action.

4. Our dreams help us heal, sometimes quite spectacularly. Through dreams, we can make brilliant leaps in creativity. We can have deeply spiritual, even mystical, experiences in dreams.

5. Our dreams also carry us into other realms, in which we encounter "others," including spirits, angels, spiritual helpers and

teachers, and the dead. These "encounter" dreams are real and not imagined.

Dreamwork manuals such as this book provide a road map. It will take you where you need to go, but the routes you choose will vary depending on your unique assessment of your dreams. In an East-West approach, there are certain fixed meanings, such as relations to the Five Elements and the Five Agents. The fixed meanings are shaded with subjective interpretations.

The open-ended nature of dream interpretation is a great strength, providing considerable latitude in which to explore a dream and discover its truth. An interpretation is right when it rings true to you.

Dreamwork Fundamentals

Any program of dreamwork requires a commitment of your intent, time, and energy. In the beginning, you will spend more time on dreams. As you become more familiar with your dream landscape and language, the process becomes easier. As time goes on, you will become more selective, recording and working with the dreams that seem charged with the most energy.

We've provided numerous worksheets and charts in this book to help you along the process and to use for continuing productive dreamwork.

Here are five basic and simple fundamentals of all dreamwork.

1. **Make a commitment to your dreams.** A commitment sets your intent to pay attention and respond to the information in your dreams. Intentionality sets powerful spiritual forces in motion. The resources of the Tao/Universe organize on your behalf to make dreamwork a powerful ally and tool.

2. **Honor your dreams.** They're part of you—the deepest part of you, in fact. When you take your dreams seriously, your dreaming life will undergo a dramatic change. Your dreams will give you more and more help. A tenet in modern Western dreamwork is that our dreams do not ask us to deal with anything beyond our inner resources or capabilities. Rather, our dreams are under the guidance of the Higher Self, which is concerned with our path of fulfillment and wholeness.

3. **Record your dreams.** Dreams evaporate quickly once we awaken, no matter how strongly we think we will remember them "later." The only way to avoid nearly instant "dream memory loss" is to record dreams as quickly as possible. Write it down or record it on tape. Even repeating a dream, either to yourself or another person, will help to set it in memory, at least until you can get it written down. If you're traveling or pressed for time, put your dreams on a tape recorder and transcribe them later. The written record is important, and you will need written accounts to work with the Tao dreamwork techniques in this book.

4. **Include all details.** Record all the details, no matter how bizarre or unimportant they may seem. Often it is the "little things" that prove to be the most important factors in interpretation. Include emotions, colors, sensations, "atmosphere," and numbers. Do not edit as you go, or make judgment calls on whether or not certain details "fit."

Dreams involving activities from the previous day or days— called "day residues"—are not just rehashes of life, but rather use our activities as ways of getting across information.

Likewise, dream fragments are important, too. Dreams do not have to be like stories, with a beginning, a middle, and an end, in order to have meaning. In fact, most dreams are not complete, but seem to start and stop in the middle of a "story."

5. **Set aside time to work on your dreams.** Do at least a little dreamwork daily if possible; if not, then as frequently as possible. Work on

a dream while it is fresh. Then let it set for a while and go back to it later. You are likely to be surprised at the additional insights you get from a new approach. Perhaps other dreams you will have had in the interim will also shed new light on a dream.

Dreamwork is an ongoing "life process." Sometimes profound new meanings of a dream come to light even years later. Some dreams keep unfolding like chapters in a book—the Book of Life. Each chapter brings a different insight.

Sometimes a specific dream recurs over a period of time, even a lifetime. A recurring dream can be the same dream, or a core dream with variations, or dreams that are similar with the same theme. It's especially important to pay attention to recurring dreams, because they often address repressed material and unresolved emotions. When the underlying issues are addressed, the recurring dreams usually stop.

Dream Interpretation Basics

In Chapter 5, "The Five Elements," we provide a blueprint for Tao dreamwork and a step-by-step process. There are five basics to keep in mind for all dreamwork techniques:

1. **Dreams have multiple layers of meanings.** A dream usually has one dominant message and one or more secondary messages. For example, you may find that a dream strongly addresses a single issue of imbalance in your life. But perhaps some of its imagery and theme will deal with related issues, perhaps things from the past, or other concerns on the edges of the primary issue—perhaps ongoing anxieties or patterns of behavior when you react to certain stresses.

Dreams also can simultaneously address our different "bodies"—physical, mental, emotional, and spiritual. In this fashion, dreams are extraordinarily holistic.

2. Pay attention to your emotions. Your emotions in a dream and upon awakening—how you react to the dream and feel about it later—all provide important information to the dream's interpretation. Do not be afraid to honestly examine negative emotions, such as fear and anxiety. Imbalances create upsets, the very things which need healing.

3. Follow your intuition. When working with the interpretation blueprints and techniques in this book, pay attention to your intuition—thoughts and feelings that arise spontaneously from within. The intuition always takes the truest—and often the shortest—path to revelation. For many people, the intuition makes itself known through the body and through feelings: something "feels" right or it doesn't. Pay attention to your physical cues—body responses such as tightening, tingling, and so on—when working with dreams.

4. Pay attention to outside cues and clues. The Tao works externally as well as internally. We often get information from the outside world through synchronicities, the "meaningful coincidences" that Jung talked about. We may suddenly get answers and insights into dreams while going about our affairs in daily life. We may see or read something that facilitates a "pop." Other people may say something to us that suddenly makes the message in a dream clear.

Synchronicities can come at any time. They are part of "the flow," the eternal and natural ebb and flux of the Tao. To be in the flow of the Tao, we must recognize that things unfold in their own perfect time, way, and place. We are always given what we need to know when we need to know it. Synchronicities cannot be rushed or "made" to happen. However, when we put ourselves in a mindful state of "the flow," synchronicities will increase.

5. Persist. Sometimes dreams seem to defy our understanding, even after we've worked on them. When that happens, don't give up on a dream. Let it rest. The flow of the Tao will shift at the right time, and the dream will untangle. Go back to difficult dreams later. You may find that suddenly they are crystal clear.

Sometimes the external world needs to shift, or other dreams need to occur, before a dream is fully understood. Trust the process.

Improving Dream Recall

From time to time, you may have difficulty recalling your dreams. This is natural; our ability to remember dreams can be affected by external stresses, energy levels, travel, medication, changes in sleeping and eating habits, and a host of other reasons. It is not unusual to go through dry periods. Dream recall restores itself at the appropriate time.

Keep in mind also that individuals vary significantly in their dream recall. Some people seem to dream long and involved dreams every night—and remember every little detail. Others recall sketchy fragments. Don't feel you have to imitate another person's dream recall in order to be a "successful" dreamer. Remember, amazing information can come from a fragment or even a feeling about a dream.

There are many techniques, some of them ancient, for encouraging better recall. Here are five that work for many people, and may help you end a dry spell.

1. During the day, frequently imagine yourself remembering, recording, and interpreting your dreams with great enjoyment. This conditions the waking mind to be receptive to the dreaming mind.

2. Establish a daily habit of meditation, quiet time or prayer, which strengthen your ability to perceive inner messages. At bedtime engage in prayer or meditation to still and center the mind. As you go to sleep, repeat: "I will remember my dreams." This is an incubation technique of programming the dreaming mind to respond.

3. When you awaken, hold the body still while you remember all you can, even fragments. It may be helpful to return to a favorite position. As soon as we start moving around, dream recall can vanish.

4. Think about people, animals, and objects familiar to you in waking life, which may trigger dream recall.

5. Try backward recall. As you go to sleep, recall in reverse order the things you did during the evening and day. As you awaken, do likewise: "I am awake, and before that I was dreaming . . ."

Let's move now into a deeper discussion of the yin and yang of dreams.

CHAPTER 4

Balancing Your Yin and Yang

DID you know that you use the principles of yin and yang every day? Did you know that your body's physiologic functions are following natural physical laws that the ancient Chinese called the laws of yin and yang?

In this chapter, you will learn just what these Chinese words mean, and you will be able to recognize how you unconsciously are applying the laws of yin and yang in your everyday activities without being aware that you are doing so. You will become familiar with the things in the world that are inherently yin and the things that are yang. You will also understand how yin/yang philosophy can help you to make sense of a nonsensical world. Our goal is to demystify Chinese Medicine and enable you to use the Taoist approach in your dream explorations.

Introduction to Yin/Yang Theory

In order to understand how to use the Taoist concepts for dream exploration, you must first understand the principles of yin and yang. Then you must develop a familiarity with things that correspond with yin and things that correspond with yang.

From the Tao, the universal oneness of all things, emerges the yin and the yang. Although the literal translations of the words are the "shady side" (yin) and the "sunny side" (yang) of the mountain, most people today refer to them as the two polar opposite forces that evolve from the oneness. Yin is the word used to denote negative energy, and yang is the word used for positive energy.

All things seen and unseen in this universe are either inherently yin or inherently yang in nature; however, within a yang thing resides its yin opposite that creates a balancing force. For example, within the yang light is an apparent yin aspect that keeps light from being too hot or too blinding, and within the yin darkness resides an apparent light that keeps the darkness from being too black or too cold. If we examine the yin/yang symbol, you can see this illustrated. The white side represents the yang, or light energy, and within that light is a small dark circle of yin, black, representing the darkness. On the other side of the symbol the black represents the yin, and within that, a small circle of yang white.

YANG

Let's begin to describe those things that are yang. Bear in mind while reading about yang that yin things are the absolute opposites.

Yang energy is energy building and expanding, radiating outward from a center. Light and radiant heat from the sun are yang. Other yang energetic functions or movements are: additions, constructions, explosions, fire, lightening, giving, delivering, depositing. In all of these examples, something is adding, building, or expanding outward, upward and away from itself. Males are yang because they are more warriorlike. Historically, men left the hearth to hunt and find food for the family. They used their might and strength to fight battles, and assert their beliefs in the pulpits, temples, and political arenas. Males have their sexual organs outside their body, and their role within the procreative act is to deposit sperm to the "palace of the child," the woman's womb. This yang, male energy is pushing forth to accomplish and fulfill its energetic role.

Things that are etheric, hot, invisible, and light are yang in nature. The closer to the heavens something resides, the more yang it is. The tops of trees, shrubs, and plants are considered the yang aspects. Poison ivy that climbs and strangles is considered a yang plant. The rash that becomes visible after exposure to poison ivy is red and hot to touch, a yang condition. The top of the head is the yang aspect of the body in humans. The Qi (vital force), the breath, and the hollow organs, such as the bowels are yang. Other examples are: winds, air, electricity, and atomic energy.

YIN

Yin energy is negative. Negative energy moves toward itself. It is a contracting, destructive, diminishing, imploding, receiving energy.

The yin earth, with its gravitational force, sucks and pulls things toward its center and keeps all of its residents from floating off into outer space. Other words that describe the nature of yin are: darkness, water, winter, coldness, contemplation, and meditation. People with yin qualities have soft voices and are more introverted. They may be content, have a warm, receptive demeanor and enjoy staying at home. Women are yin because they are nesters. They have their reproductive organs protected inside their bodies. In the act of procreation, they receive the yang male energy. New life originates within.

Things that are more material are yin. The more substance, the more yin they are. The more heavy, the more turbid, the more opaque, and the denser something is, the more yin it is. The closer to the earth something is, the more yinlike it is. The roots of a tree or plant lie within the earth and yin. A tree's sap also is yin. It is thick and viscous, and flows in the interior, just like the blood flowing within all creatures.

The Interplay of Yin/Yang Forces

The polar opposite forces of yin and yang are mutually dependent on each other. They are nothing in and of themselves. For example, light is nothing without the presence of darkness. One cannot conceive of light if darkness did not exist. Heat cannot be understood without the presence of cold, and so forth. The interplay of the yin and yang forces is what comprises the whole, or the Tao. In Chapter 22 of *Chuang Tzu,* an important Taoist text, it is said, "The way of life is the blended harmony of yin and yang."

There are five principles of yin and yang. They are:

1. **All things have two aspects: a yin aspect and a yang aspect.**
Examples are:

	YIN	YANG
TIME:	night	day
PERSON:	female	male
PLACE:	earth	heaven
THINGS:	material	ethereal
	solid	hollow

2. Any yin or yang aspect can be further divided into yin and yang.
For example, temperature that is divided into cold and hot, can be
further divided. Cold is basically yin, but can be further divided into
icy cold (yin), and cool (yang). Thus there are subtler qualities of yin
within yin or the yang within yin. An illness may be classified as either yin or yang. Illness that has symptoms of heat and hyperactivity
(yang) combined with weakness and mucoid secretions (yin) exhibits
yin within yang.

3. Yin and yang mutually create one another. Although yin and
yang can be distinguished, they cannot be separated. One is created
by the other. A wave in the ocean is yang but cannot be separated
from the water, which is yin. The yin creates the yang. A thing that
exists creates or gives meaning to its opposite merely by its existence.
We need to have the presence of darkness to comprehend light, and
we need to have cold to comprehend heat. We need to have downward movements to understand upward movements, winter to understand summer, ugly to appreciate beauty, and war to know peace.
Yin or yang by itself cannot exist, for it has no purpose or meaning.
As Lao Tzu says, "When all in the world understand beauty to be
beautiful, then ugliness exists; when all understand goodness to be
good, then evil exists."

Another way to describe the phenomenon of mutual creation is to think of a pencil portrait of a face. The portrait is composed on the white (yang) paper. The black (yin) pencil is sketched in such a way so that definition of the individual can be accomplished. The lines and contours are drawn and smudged so that the stark contrast between the whiteness of the paper and the blackness of the pen create the picture that is desired.

4. **Yin and yang control each other.** Water (yin) controls fire (yang). Wind (yang) controls air stagnation (yin). If yin is excessive, then yang will have an apparent weakness. For example, a heavy fog is a yin excess. When fog is present, there is a weakness or deficiency of the yang sunshine. If sun's heat increases, the fog will burn off. This is yang controlling excess yin.

Another example of yin excess is obesity. This condition causes a lack of yang energy or vitality. If we increase aerobic activity, this controls the growth of fat, a yin substance.

An example of yin controlling yang is water controlling fire. This occurs in the body with the natural production of sweat. When body heat builds, water is produced to cool the body to prevent the heat from burning vital tissues.

5. **Yin and yang transform into one another.** This principle depicts the natural course of revolving cycles within nature, both in the external world and in internal organic processes. In the night (yin), darkness falls until it is the darkest it can get, and then suddenly darkness makes the leap to become light. An old saying, "The darkest hour is just before dawn," exemplifies this principle.

Yin and yang are dynamic forces. They are mutable and revolve until they transform into one another. Consider the contraction of the heart. From the moment we are born until the hour of our deaths, the dance of yin and yang creates continuous, harmonious movements in this vital organ. These opposing forces act intelligently through both contractive and expansive movements of the heart muscle. The squeeze of the muscle ejects all of the blood, then contraction transforms to expansion as the muscle relaxes and allows itself to be full once again with new blood. The inhalation and exhalation of the breath also demonstrates this contraction/expansion transformation.

Transformation processes can be natural and harmonious, but can also occur because of disharmonious situations. Let's examine an example of a disharmonious transformation:

Two people are married. They each have personality characteristics that are radically opposite. One person is extremely passive (yin) and the other is extremely aggressive (yang). The passive individual is continually bullied and abused by the aggressive partner. Being so passive, she can't speak up for herself. She is defenseless and becomes numbed by the onslaughts. Then, one day, she snaps and waits at home with an axe in hand, ready to pounce on her aggressor. Passivity suddenly transforms into aggression. This is a prime pathological example of the yin transforming into the yang.

The chart below gives some examples of yin/yang associations. Read it carefully before proceeding farther into the chapter. Think about why the words belong in their specific categories. Thus you will understand their controlling and transformative principles explained above. If you read from top to bottom in chronological order, you will see the basic characteristics of yin and yang. This will help you to identify dream images as yin or yang.

YIN	YANG
Negative	Positive
Dark	Light
Night	Day
Cold	Hot
Winter	Summer
Earth	Heaven
Material	Ethereal
Water	Fire

Internal	External
Female	Male
Receiving	Giving
Passive	Active
Contraction	Expansion
Down	Up
Disintegration	Construction
Depression	Expression
Full	Empty
Order	Chaos
Peace	War
Beautiful	Ugly
Solid	Hollow

Yin/Yang Balancing Act: The Natural Thing to Do

The principles of yin and yang serve as a template for examining aspects of our lives. We can use it to understand thoughts, actions, relationships, events, nature, and, of course, dreams.

Let's look at a few examples of how you employ the principles of yin and yang in your everyday activities.

Think of what you do when you draw a bath to relax. Intuitively, you go to the tub and turn on the two opposing spigots for hot (yang) and cold (yin) water. You blend the streams to obtain the desired warm water temperature. Warm is what you know will bring about the solace you seek. It will generate relaxation. It will bring you into the comfort zone. Now, let's say you've drawn the bath and the water is too hot. You don't even think about it. Instinct takes over. If the water is too hot, you automatically know that you use hot's opposite, cold, to balance it, and vice versa. This is an example of how we use yin to control, or remedy, excessive yang.

Let's say that you have entered a room. The room is too dark. What do you do? You take the opposite of dark, which is light, and you add light to the room, whether by flipping a switch or opening a shade on the window. Without any conscious thought, you are using the yin/yang principle to bring about a balance of the two polar opposites to remedy the problem. This is an example of using yang to balance excessive yin.

You are dressing for work, and you put on your shoes. The shoes are too tight. The natural impulse is to loosen them to fit. What you are doing, by sheer instinct, is balancing looseness and tightness, the two yin/yang forces governing this situation.

Now your awareness of yin and yang is sharper. Think of more examples of how you are using these principles each day. Look at nature and see the myriad ways that you can see the forces of yin and yang in action.

Think of August, the month of heat and humidity. The air is stagnant and seemingly immovable. You've probably thought, "I wish I could get a big fan and just blow this humidity out of here!" Then suddenly nature provides a thunder squall. The trees sway as air movement is initiated. Water falls from the sky. The fiery, yang heat is controlled by the cool yin water. The humidity, which is stagnation of water molecules, is controlled by wind, the opposite of humidity. Hurricanes usually happen at this time of year. Though hurricanes are destructive, their wind and water are necessary to control the equally destructive forces of heat and humidity.

Balancing yin and yang is the most natural thing to do. As illustrated above, we balance the forces of yin and yang in our lives by instinct. Unconsciously, we know exactly what to do to remedy simple problems such as making water temperate or illuminating a room just to the point of comfort. Practitioners of Chinese Medicine take it a step further. They are trained to make more intellectual decisions of how to balance yin and yang bodily functions, how to recommend a meal plan that will be medicinal, or how to engage their patients in certain mental and physical exercises to remedy yin/yang deficiencies or excesses.

The Yin and Yang of Thought: Religion vs. Science

Religion and spirituality belong to the realm of the abstract. Science belongs to the realm of the concrete. They are yin/yang opposites. Religious leaders explain the world of the immaterial, and scientists explain the world of the material. Let's take a closer look at these two opposing realities of thought.

As Westerners, we tend to look at concrete things and abstract concepts as two separate entities. Within the realm of the concrete, fire and water are opposites. In the world of the abstract, joy and sorrow are opposites. The ancient Taoists studied the nature of both the concrete and the abstract. They observed that although the concrete and abstract were distinct opposites, they were part of the same whole. Within each separate realm were other phenomena with opposing forces, and those opposites were just as inseparable. The Taoists observed a dynamic interplay between two seemingly opposite phenomena. This dynamic force led them to conclude that you could never observe something by itself. The only way to explain the ways of the universe was to observe them in the context of the whole.

Many Chinese mystics have spoken about the inseparability of these two opposing forces. Experiences in thought and feeling are only possible because of the existence of both yin and yang. In our normal state of consciousness, it is difficult to accept that cold and hot or good and evil are different aspects of one unified phenomena, so we tend to relate to the world by accepting one and rejecting the other. In social settings, we accept people who are responsible, benevolent, and productive, but we reject those who are irresponsible, malevolent, and lazy. We don't give conscious thought to the fact that these opposing characteristics are part of an abstract unified whole, necessitating that both exist. *Tao* is the Chinese word to define this unified oneness.

Like Taoism, Buddhism gives no thought to the world of separate opposites. Buddhism holds that humanity will experience spiritual transcendence into the realm of the absolute when a person is able to see that polar opposites are merely two sides of the same reality, and when there is no judgment cast upon one or the other. Joy (yang) and sorrow (yin) are emotions springing forth from the same stream. Joy and sorrow are two contrasts within an abstract idea of "heart" (not to be confused with the physical heart organ). Someone has "heart" when they are able to express both joy and sorrow, without judging that joy is good or sorrow is bad. You may remember someone who was heartfelt toward you. They celebrated with you when times were good and cried with you when times were bad. They helped you to see the positive things from a negative experience, and they also helped you to see potential problems that could arise from a good experience.

You wouldn't use the word "heartfelt" to describe someone who rejoices with you only during victorious moments and leaves you high and dry when you've been victimized. You'd probably call that person a "fair weather friend." Since joy and sorrow are opposing emotions of the same universal reality of "having a heart," it follows that the person who is heartfelt is one who can see the purpose and meaning behind the existence of both. Isn't it interesting that we use the word "wholesome" to describe this type of person? Being "whole-some" may be as close as we can all get to the experience of spiritual transcendence, or being one with the Tao.

In scientific circles, the unification of opposites can be seen at the subatomic level. Physicists have come to realize that the world of the concrete really is not so concrete. Looking at subatomic particles, they have found that electrons, normally considered to be tiny particles, will transform from matter into a wave. In Taoist terms, this is yin transforming into yang. Matter is the visible, definable stuff that has a fixed location (yin), yet a wave is invisible and indefinable (yang) and is spread out in space. Defining an electron only as a particle is impossible. For many centuries, Sir Isaac Newton's theories of how the world operates dominated science. Newtonian thought is based on knowledge that the world is absolute. Space and time are unchangeable. Space is fixed and is mathematically and geometrically measurable in three dimensions. Time is a constant, always marching on from the past to the future.

Quantum physics has rendered these concepts obsolete. Albert Einstein's theory of relativity demonstrated to the scientific community that space is not three dimensional and time is not a separate entity. Both time and space are unified and form a fourth dimension of "space-time." The concrete thinking of scientists and the abstract thinking of the mystics are unified in the fourth dimension. The old and the new are not separate, but are part of a unique "whole" that is unfathomable. In a way, science and religion are lost without each other. God and man are inseparable. God is the yang, the invisible, deified entity, and humanity is the visible, substantive yin entity. God and humanity are opposite, yet are similar beings communing together.

The Yin/Yang Approach to Dream Interpretation

Now that you have some background knowledge about the nature of yin and yang, let's begin to examine how we can understand our dreams using Taoist principles. Dream images can be described as being basically yin or yang in nature—but to separate them would not embrace the Tao of the dream. We cannot separate these two opposites, as they are part of the whole. Ultimately, in all things yin and yang need to be balanced. As we've seen, we do this instinctively.

To apply Taoist principles to your dreams, see them as stories. Dreams inhabit the realm of the abstract. The human psyche invokes impressions with the five senses to bring dreams into tangible form, but to say what a story is, or what a dream is, is like trying to harness the wind. Although intangible, stories are powerful. There are many accounts in history of how nations made decisions about conquest and property based on a dream or a story told by a famous, well-revered leader. The morality tales of Moses, Jesus, Muhammad, and

Buddha have shaped the course of world history. Is it possible that their teachings had root in their own dreamwork?

Many old stories developed from the dreams of our predecessors. The darkness of dreams germinates the seeds of creative endeavors that unfold a future. Fairy tales, folktales, and legends are eternal because they highlight the universal issues that man encounters. They are very dreamlike. They have images, events, and landscapes that help to concretize the realm of the abstract. As children, we loved hearing those stories our parents read to us at night. We never wanted them to stop reading and always asked to hear them over and over again.

In the old fable of Goldilocks and the Three Bears, a young girl finds herself in the woods. She happens upon a house inhabited by strange bears that are humanlike. They eat from bowls, sit in chairs, and lie in beds. Goldilocks explores the house and discovers choices of three everywhere she goes. She finds three bowls of porridge. One is very hot, one is very cold, and the other is just right. She sees three chairs in the living room: one soft, one hard, and one just right. She tries out three beds. One bed is too big, one too small, and one just right. The things that are just right have the perfect balance of yin and yang.

Metaphorically, this story could typify any one of us, who suddenly find ourselves in darkness (the woods). We see many things in life where there are stark contrasts. Something is either too hot or too cold, too hard or too soft, too big or too little. We encounter the unknown (the humanoid bears). The place of feeling "just right" will be where each opposing force is balanced with its counterpart. Goldilocks instinctively recognizes the place of well-being. The story ends with her being awakened by the Three Bears and returning to her own home. She saw the choices of three and realized that contentment exists by experiencing both the yin and the yang opposites. What an astute thinker was Goldilocks! She intuitively knew about balancing her yin and yang!

Now it is time for you to try Taoist principles of yin and yang balancing in your own dream. See your dream as a story. Write it down as if you were writing a story. Begin with "Once upon a time . . ."

Write it in the third person. For example, instead of saying, "I was going for a walk in the woods, when suddenly . . ." say, "*Someone was taking a walk through the woods, when suddenly . . .*"

After you have written the dream out in story form, examine each of the images and categorize them as yin or yang. Remember, yang things are always going to have a little yin in them, and vice versa. Look for the predominate energy. Contemplate the images as parts of an encompassing whole.

Then take each image and ask yourself what other kinds of yin or yang things are like this image. You can refer to the chart on pages 31–32 or check the glossary for help. Here's an example from a dreamer's dream diary:

> *I was living at some house where the entire yard was filled with piles and piles of old seashells. There were many small pieces and chips of shells. Some were still in their whole form, resembling large conch shells that you find on the beach. I saw a very large shell among the debris. It looked like a giant clam. I went over to lift it up and there was a dead baby under it. I wasn't sure if it was really dead, and I took a stick to poke it. When I did, the image of the baby turned into a rubber doll.*

For dreamwork, the dreamer rewrote the dream as a story in third person: "*Someone was living in a house with a yard full of piles and piles of old seashells . . .*" Then she identified the images: the seashells and the rubber doll. Because rubber was the main descriptor of the doll, she focused on rubber. She asked herself, "What are seashells and rubber like? Where do they come from?" She determined that they are yin images because a shell comes from creatures that live in water and rubber is a thick, gooey substance found in the core of a rubber tree.

She then asked, "How do seashells get broken down?" The question conjured an image of the ocean and surf, which breaks down shells. The surf is not seen in the dream and thus is only implied. The surf is yang because it is an active force, even though water is essentially yin. Surf out of balance with the little seashell can disintegrate the shell.

The dreamer extrapolated this insight to her life: yang energy was causing a disruption, a breaking apart. Remember, in most cases each image or action in the dream speaks about the dreamer herself, so in this example, the dreamer uses the seashell as an image of self. She then asked herself, "What yang or active forces could be causing my body to break down?" The dreamer realized her dream was speaking to her about her level of activity: her overactive lifestyle threatened to take a toll on her body. Like the seashell, her body might be broken into little pieces—if she didn't make changes.

You might ask whether or not the dreamer was already aware of those conditions in her life. Did she really have to write down her dream in story format and analyze the images as yin or yang to come to that conclusion? The answer for this dreamer was clear. She was having a lot of physical complaints, yet kept trying to find something outside herself that was causing the problems. She thought she might have an undiagnosed illness. Going within and doing Taoist dream work enabled her to clearly see what was the cause of her physical problems. Her dreamwork made clear the message that she needed to take a break from work.

Like a story, a dream tells you what you wanted to know, what struggle you went through, and what realization you got out of it. When you set out on a journey toward a goal, you encounter hardships and struggles along the way. Dreams tell you the unfoldment of this journey—your life's story.

In the fairy tale of Cinderella, a young and impoverished girl dreams of being a princess, but as she embarks on this path she encounters abuse by her ugly stepsisters and stepmother. Her resolve comes from an encounter with a fairy godmother who assists her so that the negativity in her world transforms, and she then experiences the joy of going to the ball, ultimately meeting the prince and living happily ever after. If this story were a dream, the overabundance of yin negativity in Cinderella's life (her daunting tasks of slave labor to her stepsisters and mother) was overcome when she encountered an angel from the spirit realm. The message to that dreamer might be to practice more spirituality in order to get to a desired result of life happily ever after.

Now that you have gotten a handle on identifying yin and yang and can see the interplay of yin and yang energies, you can pinpoint where there are excesses of yin or yang in your life, and take corrective action.

The goal of this book is to teach you how to use your dreams to help you balance your life. Let's review the five steps:

1. Write down the dream as a story.

2. Identify the major images.

3. Associate yin or yang energy with the images.

4. See where there are excesses/deficiencies of yin and yang energies.

5. Devise an action plan for restoring balance.

Let's look at another dream example and yin/yang analysis. The dream is:

I am in a building at least three hundred floors high. I ride the elevator down from the three hundredth floor with a man. I remark that I have never done something like that before, ride down three hundred floors. The elevator goes very fast, then slows for a while, and then picks up a little more speed before coming to rest on the ground floor. It seems maybe other people get on somewhere in the lower floors.

The three-hundred-story building is definitely yang; however, the main action in the dream is the rapid descent in the elevator, which shows yang energy being rapidly diminished. To make a physical association of this dream, the dreamer might ask herself, "What does the top floor represent in my body?" Naturally, the top floor would be associated with the head. Further self-questioning might help her to see that some energy in the head is rapidly diminishing. When this dreamer was guided in the yin/yang dream study process, here were her comments:

This dream occurred after I had finished a long period of intense mental activity related to work. I literally was up in an airy mental tower. When it was over, I had to reintegrate myself in the world—thus the descent to the realm of matter. The speed of the elevator indicates that this is an uneven process. It's always hard to come down. I think the man on the elevator is another symbol of yang mental energy. He symbolizes that part of myself that needs to come down. The dream reminded me not to resist, but to facilitate the coming down.

Not all dreams will be so clear, so we will now give an example of one that is more difficult to decipher. The dreamer writes:

I was driving an eighteen-wheeler, but was standing up driving. There was no seat in the truck. I was trying to negotiate the truck over a narrow mountain dirt road. I remember being somewhat fearful that I wouldn't make it to my destination, yet I wasn't sure where I was going. I don't remember any cliffs, just narrow passages, and a bumpy dirt road that was hardly a place for an eighteen-wheeler to be.

The dreamer wasn't sure where to begin with this one. She could identify only two dominant images, the eighteen-wheeler truck and the bumpy, narrow dirt road over mountainous terrain. At first she wasn't certain whether they were yin or yang, and she consulted her dream glossary. She saw that "automobile" is yang, and that this applied to trucks as well. As for the narrow, mountainous dirt road, she considered what was more pronounced—the hilly, mountainous nature or the dirty, narrow nature. She felt the dirty, narrow nature was more vivid, and the mountainous nature was more implied than seen. She reviewed the yin/yang charts and could see that narrow is a yin quality.

She proceeded to the next step of the process and asked the question, "What is yang in my life that is trying to make its way through narrow passages?" She looked at a few possibilities of what this dream could be telling her, from both a physical and a psychological perspective.

The dreamer's comments were:

I recognized the conflict in the dream once I just reduced the dream images and sequences down to basic yin and yang. Instead of trying to figure out why there was an eighteen-wheeler in the dream, or why was I standing up instead of sitting, I consulted the yin/yang charts and glossary, and saw that the image of the truck was representing something yang, and the image of the narrow road was representing something yin. I got a feeling that there was a conflict between the two. The yang thing was having difficulty mobilizing through some yin thing. I asked myself what were some physical associations with "narrow roads," and thought it might be blood vessels or breathing passages. I said to myself, "If there was something yang passing through blood vessels or through breathing passages, what would it be?" Then I knew the yang thing must represent air. Immediately after making this association, I could see that the dream was about some thought I was having about fears of respiratory problems. Even though I already had fleeting thoughts of needing to make some changes in my lifestyle to improve my respiratory health, doing this yin/yang approach and seeing the dream as an inner message of some potential respiratory imbalance helped me to take more direct action. I made a decision and took the necessary steps to exercise more to increase my lung capacity and to improve my cardiac health.

When we asked the dreamer to also examine her dream from a yin/yang approach for psychological perspectives, she said:

I asked myself, "What is a yang emotion?" because in the dream something yang is trying to make its way through something narrow. I saw the following emotional states as being yang: creativity, joy, excitement, and anger. I took each one and said, "Something creative is trying to make its way through a narrow passage; something joyful is trying to make its way through a narrow passage; something exciting is trying to make its way; something angry is trying to make its way." It then resonated with me. The dream was speaking to me about difficulty experiencing joy. The yang joyful energy in my life was being obstructed by something very yin and narrow. I recognized that my thinking at the time was narrow, and one-way. I was entertaining a lot of negative thinking at the time.

Now let's use this same dream to illustrate another method of using the yin/yang dream analysis. The dreamer rewrites the dream in terms of opposites. Instead of driving the truck on a narrow, mountainous dirt road, she drives on a wide, flat, paved road, and does so sitting rather than standing. She then examines her feelings in light of the new images. Perhaps she feels relief and loss of fear. Or she might see a conflict previously unknown to her. Standing while driving is yang, and the truck also is yang. Thus the dream energy is not balanced.

The dreamer might feel tension in this imbalance, which she could then extrapolate to situations in her life: "Something that is tense prevents something that is yang from traveling on open smooth spaces." The dreamer has already recognized that she needs to exercise to open up air passages and blood vessels, and now the new perspective alerts her to tensions in her thoughts. Changing her thinking may remedy those tensions and ultimately remedy her physical concerns.

Summary of the Yin/Yang Dream Analysis Process

First begin with a recorded dream. It is imperative that you write the dream down before attempting to analyze it. Select a simple dream, one or two paragraphs in length, which is preferable dream length for learning this process.

Now follow these five simple steps:

1. **Identify the basic conflict.** This is the only part of the dream that you will work with. Your goal is to identify a particular problem in your life, and use the yin/yang dream analysis process to help resolve it, or to help clarify decisions you are trying to make.

2. **Once the conflict of the dream is highlighted, look at the images and determine if they are yin or yang.** Here is a dream conflict example to help. In all of the remaining steps we will use this dream example.

> *I was driving an eighteen-wheeler standing up. I was trying to drive on a narrow dirt road in the mountains. I feared I wouldn't be able to keep the truck on the road.*

Eighteen-wheeler is *yang*.   Narrow dirt road is *yin*.

3. **Interject the words *yin* and *yang* into the sentence using impersonal pronouns and similar verbs.**

> *Big yang energy is trying to move through too narrow yin energy.*

4. See how your results may relate to a particular health concern.
Ask yourself what body function/s might be relative to the conflict.
Check the chart in Appendix B, "Dream Images and Physical Correspondence," if necessary to see what types of dream images are related to certain body parts.

For example, a yang function is breathing, running, heart pulsating, and so on. The dreamer could ask, "Is my breathing trying to move through narrow dirty air passages?"(metaphorically similar to the narrow dirt road). She could also ask, "Is my heart pulsation trying to move through narrow arteries?" This phrase also is a metaphoric interpretation of what the narrow dirt road could mean.

5. After doing step 4, there may already be a revelation about the dream, but if not, pursue applying the principle of opposites to the dream imagery. Rewrite the conflict, using an *opposite image* that will help you to feel a sense of resolve. Remember, the law of opposites is a natural law that is applied to all things in an effort to restore balance. For example, if something is too hot, you use cold, its opposite, to find the happy medium.

I am driving the eighteen-wheeler sitting down through a wide, paved road that is flat.

This is the opposite statement of the conflict. The dreamer then gets the confirmation that she needed to resolve her conflict—to create open arteries in her body by taking action to do more cardio exercise.

Remember, balancing your yin and yang comes naturally. You do this in all things every day. Your body/mind intelligence does this without your conscious awareness. In a sense, your unconscious self actually uses dreams to do more yin/yang balancing even without your conscious intervention. If this process becomes too difficult to grasp at first, just let it go and relax in the knowing that your inner intelligence is already taking care of things. Don't let dreamwork become a stressor—it's supposed to be fun.

This dreamwork process shouldn't be used in place of medical attention if there are health concerns, and one should not see their dreams as ultimate diagnosticians of problems to be remedied. Remember, energy is always in motion. Energetic conflicts and imbalances use a universal intelligence to work things out. Sometimes when we see these conflicts, we are viewing that process of resolution in action, and it is possible for us to muck things up, so to speak, by our feeble interventions. If the process is not clear on any dream you are trying to resolve, and if it seems as if it is too difficult to figure out, use this old remedial saying to help you decide what to do: "When in doubt, leave it out."

In the next chapter we will discuss one of the other major tenants of Chinese philosophy and medicine, called Five Element Theory.

CHAPTER 5

The Five Elements

T HE word "element" is defined as a substance that cannot be broken down or reduced to other elementary substances by ordinary chemical means. The ancient Chinese first identified five basic elements in the physical world; however, modern reductionistic science has now identified that there are 110 basic elements. (Interestingly, this is a number evenly divisible by five). These five elements were once thought to be the fundamental elements of nature, but now they can be further reduced to more elementary particles.

The term "Five Elements" was the translated term assigned to the Chinese phrase *Wu Xing* from the *Nan Jing,* an ancient Chinese medical text, which actually means "five phases." The theory of five elements was most likely conceived in or around the Warring States Period (476–221 B.C.) by a man named Zou Yen. It was used as a basis for understanding the way certain elements in nature relate to each other. Yin/yang theory speaks about general characteristics of two opposing forces such as light and dark, or hot and cold. Five Element Theory is an expansion of yin/yang thought to give more distinction and individuation to the various shades and characteristics of yin and yang and to the phases of yin and yang energy movements. An understanding of the five elements forms the basis of Chinese Medicine, astrology, government, psychology, spirituality, and many other disciplines. The five basic elements of nature serve as metaphorical blueprints for understanding both external and internal energetic forces.

All things organic and inorganic in the cosmos have an inherent characteristic. Man recognizes the myriad of things set apart from each other because these characteristics are distinct and different. Something is either black or white, or it is a variation of contrasting opposites. If one were to ask if a tree trunk is closer to black or closer to white, the answer would depend on subjective associations. For example, one might answer black if one thinks of an old oak, or white if one thinks of a birch. A person given a set of crayons to draw a tree most likely would select a brown crayon to draw the trunk. By most standards, brown is closer to black than to white, but it is not black or white. It is distinctly different. Because of these differences in nature, the Chinese sages needed to identify and classify things according to more than just their yin and yang characteristics.

These ancient sages observed Mother Nature and described her multiple characteristics and individuated all her functions. They quickly identified that between the white light (yang) and the black darkness (yin), there was a rainbow of colors. In other words, the presence of light and dark yields five distinct variations of color. This is an illustration of how the advent of Five Element Theory may have taken place.

In ancient days, humans lived closer to nature and spent more time on such observances. These early theorists were able to identify five basic constituents of all things natural, which became the Five Elements of Chinese Medicine: wood, fire, earth, metal, and water. The Chinese realized that in addition to yin and yang descriptions, all things in nature could also be described as having either a basic wood, fire, earth, metal, or water quality.

Other cultures besides the Chinese identified basic elements of nature and documented how these elements pervaded all things. For example, the ancient Tibetans talked about five elements as well, but they called them fire, air, earth, water, and space. They theorized that these elements, although basic, actually evolved from even subtler energies in space. They called them the "Five Lights." The Five Lights are considered aspects of primordial luminosity, and are the subtlest level of the Five Elements.

In ancient Greece, a concept of four elements was developed between 490 and 430 B.C. by Empedocles of Agrigentum, but the credit was given to Aristotle during his lifetime (384–322 B.C.). Aristotle was the academic successor of Plato and was known as a great organizer of Greek ideas. His philosophical writings had a profound impact on all subsequent Western thought. He said that all matter was made up of four elements: fire, earth, water, and air. He postulated that the elements arose from the working of two opposing properties of hotness and coldness, and dryness and wetness, upon some original unqualified primitive matter. It is interesting to see how his thinking correlated to the Chinese yin and yang theory.

Although the Chinese, Tibetans, and Greeks have a few differences in the way they systematized the basic elements of the natural world, their similarities are astonishing. It is difficult to determine which culture can be given the credit for originating this thought. It is as though the theories developed simultaneously around the world. Perhaps these early forefathers unconsciously tapped in to the great ocean of the collective unconsciousness, bringing forth this knowledge so that all peoples could know their connection to nature.

Within the Five Element Theory is the Five Phase Theory. All things in nature are not only identified by one of the five elemental characteristics, but are seen functioning harmoniously in relationship with each other through five energetic movements, or transitional phases. The sages observed that within the whole of nature were many changes and cyclic movements such as from the direction of activity to rest, from light to dark, and from creation to destruction. In between were distinct phases, each with its unique characteristics.

The terms "Five Elements" and "Five Phases" have been used interchangeably in texts to educate students of Eastern philosophies and medicine. They both are the yin and yang aspects of what we know as Five Element Theory. The term "Five Element" by itself implies stasis. Something remains static in a certain elemental characteristic. It is what it is, and does not ever change. Water is water, is water, is water. Stasis is a yin quality. The term "Five Phases" implies movement. There is activity within the element that enables energy to transition from one phase to another. For example, water becomes vapor and eventually transitions back into a pure yang energetic state.

There also are five energies relative to the Five Elements. Fire energy is like the spark of creativity. Like the sun, fire is always warming, and is promoting all physiologic functions in nature. Earth energy is nutritive. Like the soil, earth energy is always giving, feeding all of nature's creations. Metal energy is sustaining. It works with precision to ensure that nature's workings are on time. Water energy is cooling and soothing, allowing reflection and quietude, so that the desire for new growth exists. Like a tree, wood energy is rooted, strong, and protective. It contains the urge to grow, and asserts itself with a yang force that eventually becomes fuel to ignite the fire of new creations.

As was noted in the chapter on the theory of yin and yang, one of the basic tenets of Taoist philosophy and also of Chinese Medicine is that man is a microcosm of the macrocosm. The external workings of nature have internal counterparts. In other words, the basic elements in nature have internal correspondences. The external world is an amalgam of the Five Elements. It functions because of the harmonious relationships between their five energies. Each of our body's organs and functions are said to be amalgamated manifestations of these primordial energies of the Five Elements. The precept of Chinese Medicine is that when the five energies of the Five Elements are in harmony with one another, then health will abound. We are all aware that in a perfect world harmony and balance exists, but in this imperfect world, balance and harmony are captured in brief moments. The rest of the time, we are working consciously to restore that which has become out of sync.

This chapter discusses in more detail each individual element and highlights some of both the internal and external correspondences to each. It mentions both physical and psychological correspondences to the Five Elements. Examples of illnesses relating to imbalances in an element, as well as behavioral characteristics and changes occurring as a result of a certain elemental presence, are also presented. There are several charts included at the end of the chapter that have various categorizations such as organs, body parts, emotions, and so forth, as they correspond with the Five Elements.

Once you have read, contemplated, and then assimilated both the yin/yang and the Five Element philosophical principles, you will be able to apply them directly to your personal dream study. The beauty of this philosophy is that it has so many applications in everyday life. Many people around the globe who have come to learn these principles have applied them not only to their own personal emotional, mental, and philosophical aspects of living, but have also successfully utilized them in business and in politics.

The Yin and Yang of the Five Elements: The Creative and Destructive Cycles

THE YANG CREATIVE CYCLE

According to the yin/yang theory, there is the yang creative cycle of energy and there is the yin destructive cycle. Things wax and wane. They grow and die. They appear and disappear. The Five Elements themselves are forever static, but the five energetic phases of them are always in flux. For example, the Water Element exists and never goes away, but its form changes. Knowing the relationships between the Five Elements will help you understand the reason behind certain external and internal, physical and psychological, states of existence.

Figures 1 and 2 illustrate the yang creative cycle of energy within

The Five Elements—Creation Cycle

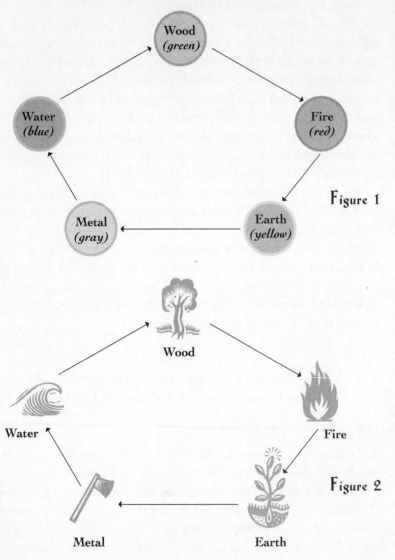

Figure 1

Figure 2

Creation Cycle
The cycle of life begins with water. Out of the
water springs forth wood and all things.
Wood creates the fire. Fire creates the earth.
Earth brings forth the metal.
Metal melts to become liquid, giving birth to water.

the Five Elements. Follow the arrows on the chart around in a clockwise direction, beginning with the Water Element. The cycle of life begins with water. It is from the blackness of the void that all things are born. The wood drifts up from the depths. It asserts and seeks new growth, then ignites, creating fire. The fire in turn generates the creation of earth, which then brings forth the metal. Metal then melts to become liquid, and thus water is born. You may see this relationship in nature, but how does it translate to your internal environment?

One example is this: The Water Element enables us to ponder and reflect. From out of the void of no thought comes new thought. When we empty our minds in meditation, we enter into a waterlike state of being. Only when we have emptied our minds can we then assert and determine our life's strategy and take on a woodlike nature to create new growth of ideas. Once these ideas have been asserted, fiery passion takes over and creativity abounds. When all our creations have manifested, it is then time to be like Mother Earth and nurture those creations, always being loyal and steadfast, seeing each of them to their end of time. When our earthiness has reached a fullness, we then need to have sharp distinction and define our boundaries so that we aren't consumed by our loyalties to so many things. We put on our metal suit of armor. With precision, we become disciplined and have discernment over what will be and what won't be. And when we've redefined our boundaries, we can then go to that soothing, cool place and reflect once again, emptying our minds, returning back to the watery void.

THE YIN DESTRUCTIVE CYCLE

Follow the arrows in the center of Figures 3 and 4 to understand the destructive cycle of the Five Elements. Water that flows downward extinguishes fire that flames upward. Proliferation of wood erodes the earth. Intense heat of the fire melts metal. Excess earth will diminish water. The sharpness and definition of the metal chops the wood.

The Five Elements—Destructive Cycle

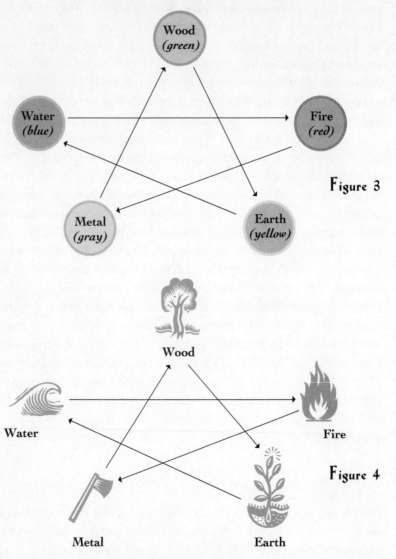

Figure 3

Figure 4

Destructive Cycle

Proliferation of wood erodes the earth.

Excess earth diminishes the water.

Intense heat will melt the metal.

The sharpness and definition of metal chops the wood.

Now let's see how this cycle of energy translates to man's internal environment. Being too long in the watery, meditative space disables fiery creativity. If we are asserting, developing strategies, and continuously building, woody tension will erode our ability to nurture ourselves, and subsequently others. When we are trying to be Mother Earth taking care of everyone and everything, we diminish the ability to fluidly express ourselves and exert our will.

The Myriad of Organic Expressions

Figure 5 shows how the creative and destructive cycles of the Five Elements relate to many other things, both internal and external. For example, the seasons of nature illustrate the creative cycle. The coldness of winter (water) reaches its fullness, then gives birth to the spring (wood), when the winds carry the seeds of new growth. The warmth of spring (wood) builds till summer (fire) is born. The heat of the fiery summer (fire) then results in the dampness and humidity of late summer (earth), nature's way of tempering the fire. The humidity dries from the heat of late summer (earth) until the next season of autumn (metal) comes about with its dry, falling leaves. The dryness (metal) generates energy and makes the quantum leap giving birth to the cold winter (water).

Tastes are an example of the destructive cycle. Salty taste controls bitter taste, sour taste controls sweet taste, bitter taste controls spicy taste, and so forth.

Clinicians who practice Chinese Medicine may use these principles of the creative and destructive cycles of the Five Elements when prescribing herbs. Herbs are classified according to the five tastes, each of which has five basic energies. For example, the sour taste causes one to pucker. On a cellular level sour is an astringent, moving energy in a yin direction inward toward the center. The spicy taste, on the other hand, is yang, causing the rapid movement of molecules, producing heat, and moving energy away from the center. The clini-

Five Element Correspondences—Creative and Destructive Cycles

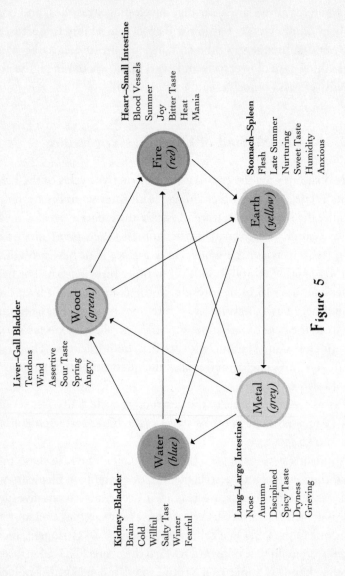

Liver–Gall Bladder
Tendons
Wind
Assertive
Sour Taste
Spring
Angry

Heart–Small Intestine
Blood Vessels
Summer
Joy
Bitter Taste
Heat
Mania

Stomach–Spleen
Flesh
Late Summer
Nurturing
Sweet Taste
Humidity
Anxious

Kidney–Bladder
Brain
Cold
Willful
Salty Tast
Winter
Fearful

Lung–Large Intestine
Nose
Autumn
Disciplined
Spicy Taste
Dryness
Grieving

Fire
(*red*)

Earth
(*yellow*)

Wood
(*green*)

Metal
(*grey*)

Water
(*blue*)

Figure 5

cians will diagnose a condition, decide which of the elements are out of balance, and will then formulate herbal prescriptions to restore balance. They select herbs for their energetic function. For example, if someone has low energy, is pale, has slow body movements, and has a posture that seems to be collapsing downward and inward, a clinician may prescribe a formula that has spicy herbs in it. The intent is to cause the movement of Qi to go upward, which brings more blood into the head.

Figure 5 also shows the organ associations to the Five Elements. For practitioners of Chinese Medicine, understanding the physiology of how the body works requires understanding the energetic relationships of the Five Elements. In Western Medicine, some of the body's systems are viewed as separate systems and may not have a direct relationship to another system. Western practitioners may recognize that there is a direct relationship between the liver and the gall bladder, for example, but they may not see a direct relationship between the liver and the kidneys. They may not see a direct correspondence of the kidneys to the brain, and so forth. But in Chinese Medicine, there is a direct relationship. For example, the kidneys are the "mother" of the liver. It is a Water Element organ, and the liver is a Wood Element organ. According to the creation cycle of the Five Elements, water (kidneys) begets wood (liver). Subsequently, the liver is the "son" of the kidneys. If a problem exists in the liver, the true origin of the problem might be in the kidneys. Metaphorically, the mother may not be feeding her son. In other words, the energy of the kidneys is not being delivered to the liver.

An analogy that might be helpful to understand the distinct differences between a Western Medicine approach to a problem and a Chinese Medicine approach is this: You are an innocent bystander on the street. You see a child who looks very emaciated. The child's cheeks are sunken, the belly is rotund, the eyes are darkened, and the skin around his lips is cracked. You'd say, "Here is a very sick child. We need to get this child to the hospital." The child goes to the hospital and certain blood tests are performed. He is fed intravenously for several days. Soon the child gets better because of the medical intervention and is ready to be sent home. The only problem is that the true underlying cause of why the child is sick is that the mother was not feeding the child. Sending the child back to that mother will only result in the child returning to a sickly state. The way you remedy the problem for good is to remedy the relationship of the mother to the child.

In Chinese Medicine, we evaluate the relationship of one organ system to another. In other words, we try to find the elemental culprit and restore balance and harmony so that health prevails. We can assess an element to be deficient, meaning not enough energy is allotted to a particular element, in which case there will be a problem. Using the example above, if the problem is in the liver, the root cause may be from lack of kidney energy. If a mother is deficient, meaning she lacks energy herself, then she cannot feed her son. We can also assess an element to be in excess. If an element's energy is in excess, then conceivably it will affect another element as well, much the same way that if one child in a family has more things than another child does, conflict will arise. You may even think of the five major organ systems in the body with their elemental correspondences being similar to five siblings in a family. If the parents are showing favoritism to one, there is rebellion, and consequential outcomes for other members of the family.

People who have consulted practitioners of Chinese Medicine find that their approach to treatment is holistic. Western Medicine and Chinese Medicine, like the East and the West, are yin/yang opposites. Western Medicine is more fragmented and specialized, while Chinese Medicine is more unified and holistic. Humorously speaking, in Western Medicine a person may go to one doctor for the left ear and another doctor for the right ear. If a person has the symptoms of knee pain, ringing in the ears, frequent urination, and a lower back problem, and he went to Western doctors, he might have to see a neurologist for the back problem, an orthopedist for the knee problem, an ear, nose, and throat doctor for the ringing in the ears, and a urologist for the frequent urination. If the patient went to a Chinese Medicine practitioner, the holistic diagnosis might be a deficient Water Element (kidney) condition. The practitioner would prescribe an herbal formula, do an acupuncture treatment, and make some lifestyle recommendations to strengthen the Water Element within. When the kidney energy is strengthened, the whole cluster of symptoms may disappear.

Going to a practitioner of Chinese Medicine for multiple health issues can be like one-stop shopping. In the long run, it may be cost effective, preventing the need to see many expensive specialists.

In Figure 6, you can see that the Five Element overlay can be applied to the personality and to the emotional body as well as to the physical body. Follow the creative and destructive cycles on the diagram to help understand how one emotion can control another, and how one can foster the growth of another. For example, look at the Water Element diagram according to the creative cycle. You can see that the personality of the element is to be conservative in expression and to be strong willed. When one has a healthy amount of this element, water energy moves forward and creates a woodlike character, strongly rooted, asserting its expressions. Now look at the destructive cycle between water and fire. You can see that conservative expression overcomes joyful expressions. The nature of people with strong water element tendencies will cause them to have difficulty expressing joy.

In Chinese Medicine, we pay a lot of attention to one's emotions and to one's constitutional tendencies, not just physically, but also psychologically as well. People have a predisposition to having either a weakness or a strength in a certain element. Knowing those situations helps the practitioner assess a health condition. Certain emotions are elementally associated with an organ. If one experiences either too much of a certain emotion or too little of that emotion, the organ system having the same element will show an impact. For example, too much grief or not enough grief will affect the lung. Anger may harm the liver, and worry may cause ulcers in the stomach.

Five Element Personality and Behavioral Characteristics

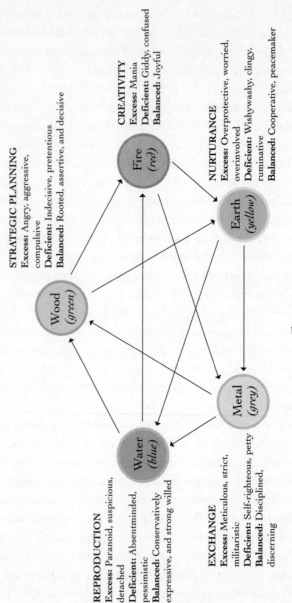

STRATEGIC PLANNING
Excess: Angry, aggressive, compulsive
Deficient: Indecisive, pretentious
Balanced: Rooted, assertive, and decisive

CREATIVITY
Excess: Mania
Deficient: Giddy, confused
Balanced: Joyful

NURTURANCE
Excess: Overprotective, worried, overinvolved
Deficient: Wishywashy, clingy, ruminative
Balanced: Cooperative, peacemaker

REPRODUCTION
Excess: Paranoid, suspicious, detached
Deficient: Absentminded, pessimistic
Balanced: Conservatively expressive, and strong willed

EXCHANGE
Excess: Meticulous, strict, militaristic
Deficient: Self-righteous, petty
Balanced: Disciplined, discerning

Wood (*green*)

Fire (*red*)

Earth (*yellow*)

Metal (*grey*)

Water (*blue*)

Figure 6

The Five Element system gives practitioners of Chinese Medicine excellent skills for identifying the root of a certain problem in the body. They ask a lot of interesting questions that to the untrained person may seem very silly and trivial. One of the things they might ask is about dreams. Elemental imbalances may show themselves in dream imagery, as well as in waking life experiences. A Water Element imbalance may show itself in the form of fluid retention in the ankles. A dream of water accumulation in the basement of your house could be an earlier clue that would alert the astute dreamer of this potential outcome.

If we examine the order of how things begin and evolve, we see that things start small and grow bigger. For example, atoms come together to form molecules, and molecules come together to form cells. Then cells organize together to form tissue, which in turn organizes to form an organ. Organs then come together in such an arrangement to make up the human body. In a similar fashion, dreams are the atoms of the psyche. They come together to produce ideas. Ideas then are acted upon through intention, which creates forms, which creates experience. Working backward, we can postulate that if a person has aberrant behavior, there was before that an elemental imbalance in her psychological state, which before that manifested in her dream state.

From the perspective of the physical plane, an imbalance in an organ is preceded by an imbalance in the cellular fields, and before that in the molecular fields, and even before that in the atomic or pure energetic fields.

Many people today practice some form of energy medicine, among them Reiki, Qi Gong, Healing Touch, and many others. Each has its own approach and rituals, but each is oriented toward making an assessment of a person's subtle energies. An imbalance may be diagnosed, followed by an active manipulation of the energy by the practitioner upon that person. Most energy medicine disciplines have their roots in Chinese Medicine. Some have evolved from other Eastern cultures that have philosophies and medical practices based on subtle elemental energies as well. If we were to examine dreams as a subtler form of energy and approach dreamwork as a type of energy medicine, we might find it has more to offer than we previously thought.

There are numerous accounts in ancient texts of how spiritual and government leaders used dream interpreters to help make not only personal decisions, but decisions that would involve the masses. The desire to understand dreams is basic to all humanity, and these desires compelled leaders to hire dream interpreters. Many decisions and strategic movements in a society were based on the dreams of their kings and queens. One well-known biblical figure is Joseph, the great-grandson of Abraham. The name Joseph actually comes from an Egyptian word meaning "discoverer of hidden things." He is the same Joseph known for his "coat of many colors." Perhaps his colorful coat was a metaphor for a person innately possessing a healthy balance of the Five Elements. He was welcomed to the court of the pharaoh of Egypt because of his amazing ability to interpret the hidden meanings in dreams.

We don't really know how our dream-interpreting biblical forefathers like Joseph actually processed a dream. They all most likely had their own unique system. Could it be possible they used a yin/yang approach? If so, they most likely would have used concepts using words such as "God" and "Devil" to illustrate what in reality may have been the positive and negative energies of yin and yang. Is it also possible they had knowledge of the five elemental orders of nature, but they used a different language and a different conceptual framework to illustrate them? These questions are merely conjectural, but they are great food for thought.

We will now get into the meat of each element, so you can become more intimate with each of their natural characteristics. By the end of this chapter, you should have enough familiarity with each of the elements, and then will be ready to use a Five Element system to process and interpret your own dreams.

WOOD

In some of the ancient cultures, the Wood Element was not described as an element in and of itself. The ancient Greeks, for example, only spoke of four elements, which were water fire, earth, and air. The Chinese, on the other hand, conceptualized that all material forms originated from the earth, so they extracted one of the components of earth—wood—and gave it its own recognition as a basic element.

External Correspondences

The Chinese character for wood is *mu,* which means "tree." Think of the characteristics of a tree when contemplating the Wood Element. The following are a few words and phrases that are descriptive of trees: sturdy, firmly rooted, expansive, grows upward, protective. The season that is associated with the Wood Element is spring. The full potential of the Wood Element is experienced in springtime. The tree, which has been storing energy throughout the winter season, awakens and reaches out to burst forth with new growth. Before the actual appearance of growth, tension builds because of nature's anticipation to display the first signs of its creative potential. The movement of the new growth energy is upward and outward toward the crown and the branches, producing a show to all of nature's observers, while still dispersing downward, firmly rooting itself and connecting to the earth.

The climatic correspondence to the Wood Element is wind. When one thinks of springtime, one thinks of the wind. The new seeds, spawned by rapid growth and the expansion of foliage, need to be carried by the wind to begin their own cycles of growth. Springtime gives birth to the wind and commissions it to carry out its natural duty. To remember this association, just gaze into your mind's eye and listen to the sound of trees. When the wind is not present, they are silent. It is the wind acting upon the trees that helps us to hear their voice.

The colors of the Wood Element are green, turquoise, and brown. Green is more associated with the Wood Element's youth, and brown the color most associated with its maturity. The tender shoots of new green grass that arise from the ground help us realize spring has arrived. The brown and brittle woody growth informs us that the energy of wood has reached its maximum potential and is ready for its transition.

The direction associated with the Wood Element is the east, which relates to morning and sunrise. It is in the dawning of a day when new growth begins. Yesterdays are forgotten. Similarly, with the birth of spring, the darkness of winter fades to a fleeting memory, and the perennial cycle of new growth commences. The morning is when all of nature begins its new daily cycle. According to the Five Element creation and destruction cycles, wood is produced by water, is weakened or diminished by fire, and is controlled by metal. Here is an analogy to understand this principle: Rain nourishes and helps the trees to grow. Fire reduces wood to ash. The metal axe cuts the trees and controls their growth.

Internal Correspondences

The Wood Element within is the liver and gall bladder. They are yin/yang paired organs, working harmoniously together, sending energy in all four directions, just like the tree. Together as a team, they are responsible for directing the metabolic strategies. It is interesting to note that the bile manufactured in the liver is green, and the biliary system has been called the "biliary tree." The character of the liver/gall bladder team is assertive, decisive, and wise. Just like the tree that takes nourishment from the soil and reaches out to grasp the wind, they are ready for action with well laid plans for how to handle both what is nutritive and what is toxic to the body.

In Chinese medical literature, the liver has been called "the General." The General has the responsibility to develop strategies for war, keeping the troops properly trained, exerting tension to be prepared for every possibility. The General asserts his authority, using cunning decisiveness, to see that there is a smooth flow of Qi throughout the body and that all movements of the troops (Qi) are harmonious and purposeful.

In addition to maintaining strategic physiologic workings, the internal Wood Element is about growth and balance. It provides coordinated activities of growth and expansion giving us the ability and the flexibility to grow and mature. In nature, trees and forests grow, naturally providing a sense of order and structure. In gardening and landscaping we sometimes plant in perfect rows and use woody shrubs to define boundaries. A healthy Wood Element within us dwells in the chaos, yet provides this same order and structure.

Other parts of the body related to the Wood Element are the tendons, muscles, fingernails, and eyes.

Physical Problems

The following are physical manifestations of Wood Element problems: biliary disease, digestive disorders, eye diseases, chronic tension, fertility problems, fibromyalgia, migraine headaches, menstrual disorders, and musculoskeletal problems.

Psychological Problems

As mentioned before, the Wood Element season is the spring, when there is new growth and the reemergence of life in the trees and flowers after the somnolence of winter. The essence of the Wood Element is renewal and rebirth. This element, when balanced, gives us the ability to see life anew and to have a sense of hope. It allows us to be firmly rooted in the past, stand tall in the present, and have vision for the future. When we have a balanced Wood Element, we have the ability to initiate thoughts and actions. We can venture forward into the unknown, following an instinctual direction. We are tempered when we encounter obstacles on our path, and then we follow hunches to take a different path to the same destination. This is seen in nature when a plant encounters an obstacle in its path. Its healthy Wood Element enables the plant to send out shoots in another, unencumbered direction. The obstacles themselves, though binding and constricting to the strong assertive powers of the plant to "do its own thing," enable the plant to take on unique forms and shapes, thereby giving it its own unique identity. People with strong Wood Element characteristics are able to forge through life asserting and striving toward identified goals. They have the ability to see obstacles as springboards rather than as chains. They recognize these obstacles as the "pruners" and "weeders" of some of their misguided plans, rather than see them as the capturers that will render them prisoners and unable to continue on a desired path. They also are able to maintain order amongst the chaos. They know their roots, from where they came, and they stay connected to the ancestral energy that gave them life. They are assertive, even tempered, decisive, self-directed, and self-assured. They are good organizers and planners.

The emotions and behaviors relative to problems in the Wood Element are: anger, disorganization, frustration, and indecisiveness. One feeling chronically stressed or tense, especially because of the inability to assert one's beliefs or opinions, could be considered weak, or deficient wood. One who is consistently bullying others, using belligerent or violent force to express their nature, would be considered strong, or excess wood. Drug abuse and control issues are related to Wood Element imbalances.

Wood Element People

People who are wood types usually have olive-colored skin and are either tall and angular like trees or short and energetic like bushes. They have muscular arms and legs and strong eyebrows or jaws. They can also be thin and sinewy. They are assertive and direct with lots of drive. A healthy Wood Element person will exemplify good judgment and planning. They are assertive, firmly rooted, and secure socially. They always seek avenues for new growth. If their wood element is undernourished, they can become very frustrated people with a tendency toward passive aggression. In extreme undernourishment of wood, they can exhibit suicidal or self-destructive behaviors. If overnourished and uncontrolled, they can have strong tempers, be loud and belligerent, and have tendencies toward violence. Some examples of famous Wood Element people are: Abraham Lincoln, Henry Thoreau, and George S. Patton Jr.

Dream Associations

The Wood Element can be seen in dreams where wooden objects are the props in the dream play, or where flora and fauna are visible in the dream landscape. The characters in the dream play will have Wood Element qualities as previously described. A Wood Element characteristic might show itself in people who are: well motivated and organized, scrupulous planners, self-employed or directors of a company, and accustomed to having things mapped out ahead of them. The dream character could be a general or a military leader, a successful owner of a company, or a strong muscle man. Wood Element dream characters are also people who like to be pushed and who like their abilities tested and stretched. They are totally dedicated to everything they pursue, whether it be for work, play, or family life—even to the point where someone would lay down his life for a cause. An example in history is St. Joan of Arc, who was totally dedicated to what she believed in and gave her life for it.

Other examples of dream images that correspond with the Wood Element are green objects, budding flowers, paper money, and mushrooms. Dreams with the emotions of anger, inability to express concepts, frustration, feeling wimpy, and violence demonstrate an imbalance in this element.

For more image correspondences see the glossary in the back of this book.

FIRE

Fire is the creative, spiritual principle. This yang energy is the source of all life. Aboriginal peoples once worshipped fire and the fires of the sun as their God, perhaps because they may have imagined that a world without a sun and without warmth would be cold, lost, and incapable of existing.

External Correspondences

On planet earth, the sun is our true source of warmth and heat. It is like the perpetual flame that is never extinguished. In daily cycles, it rises and sets in the sky, and in quarterly cycles it changes its orientation to the earth. This sun/fire energy promotes the heat and light so that all of nature can exist. Nature absorbs this fire energy and utilizes it for perpetual motion. Without this yang energy, motion ceases, stagnation occurs, and progression of life in viable form is halted.

The fire Qi moves in all directions. It spreads. It is radiant and hot. Radiant energy moves away from its center. According to the creative cycle of the Five Elements, fire is produced by wood, and at the same time exhausts wood. It is controlled by water.

The season corresponding to the Fire Element is summer. The yang fire energy of the sun abounds. The days are longer. The sun is closer to earth. All of nature is active. Growth of plants, shrubs, and trees is plentiful. Both fauna and flora are engaged in the creative dance of life, proudly displaying reproductive capabilities, and extending nature to its fullest potential.

The color associated with the Fire Element is red. A fiery yellow is associated, for this is the color of the sun, and of the flames seen in an actual fire. The climatic corresponding to the Fire Element is heat, and the direction is the south. According to the principles of feng shui—the Chinese art of placement for the maximizing of Qi and natural forces in one's environment—the southern rooms of a home should display Fire Element images to attract the creative, perpetual moving energy that brings abundant growth.

Internal Correspondences

The Fire Element organs in the body are the heart and the small intestine. Just like the sun/fire energy keeps nature moving and growing, the heart is the perpetual yang energetic pump that keeps our blood pumping, and brings all the nutrients manufactured by the small intestine to all our cells ceaselessly from birth to death.

The organ extensions related to the Fire Element are the blood vessels. The tongue and bitter taste also are Fire Element Correspondences.

Physical Problems

Physical ailments corresponding to the Fire Element generally are conditions associated with a heart or small intestine imbalance. Cardiac arrythmias, difficulty sleeping, feeling hyperactive, panic attacks, and restlessness are all Fire Element problems. In Chinese Medicine, a person with these conditions is said to have "hyperactive heart fire." Difficulty digesting or assimilating food can be another example of a Fire Element problem, because this is the role of the small intestine. However, digestive difficulties can also be due to other elemental imbalances, so do not assume that the small intestine is always the culprit. There are many fine clinical distinctions that a trained practitioner of Chinese Medicine takes into consideration before deciding on a diagnosis of a small intestine problem.

Psychological Problems

The emotion associated with the Fire Element is joy. Laughter is the expression of this joy, but when the Fire Element is hyperactive, there may be excessive talking and laughing. If unchecked by the Water Element within, fire energy can flame out of control, causing mania and psychosis. Have you ever known someone who seemed to giggle or smile inappropriately at a time when there was something serious happening? This is a Fire Element imbalance.

Fire Element People

Fire Element people are charismatic leaders who have the innate ability to motivate and spark others into creating new growth. They are highly creative, keenly intuitive, and exceptionally passionate. They tend to not follow through with their creative endeavors, become bored easily during lulls, and are greatly challenged when in long-term relationships, as they are initiators, and they thrive on initiating lots of relationships. They tend to feel their creative flames dwindling if the relationship becomes too watery. Some famous Fire Element people are: Robert Downey Jr., Julia Roberts, Danny Bonaduce, President Bill Clinton, Patty Duke, and Gengis Khan.

Dream Associations

Images in dreams that are associated with the Fire Element are fires, sparks, red objects, bloody drainage, and creative endeavors. Southern locations, feeling hot, or having passionate sex can also be related to the Fire Element. The terms "fiery passion" and "worked into a frenzy" are terms relative to fire.

For more image correspondences see the glossary in the back of the book.

EARTH

The earth energy is that all-sustaining energy that nurtures everything in nature. The ancients viewed the Earth Element as the procreator or mother of all the other elements. One of the basic four elements identified by the Greeks, the Earth Element was given her right place in the universe by the Chinese: at the center. Chinese scholars identified and extracted two vital energies from out of the earth, wood and metal, and gave them their own identities. The true essence of the Earth Element is loyalty, nurturance, and support.

External Correspondences

"Mother Earth" is the cliché we all use when speaking of the Earth Element. She nurtures us and bears fruits to feed and sustain all her children. She is vast and all encompassing, providing home and hearth to every creature. Some words associated with this element are: soil, nurture, ceramic, brick, mortar, adobe, feed, nutrition, and sharing.

The season associated with this element is late summer, the pause at the end of summer when nature's growth has reached climax and is ready to make the cyclic transition into harvest season. It is the time when heat, mugginess, and dampness abound. Think of August in a hot and humid climate. There is lack of movement. Air stagnation makes vision cloudy and turbid. Sometimes the air is so thick you feel you can cut it with a knife. You wish for breezes to counteract the stuffiness.

If you examine late summer in relation to the other seasonal cycles from a yin/yang perspective, you can see that it is a time where Qi remains still. In spring and summer the movement of Qi waxes. In late summer it halts before turning around and marching in the opposite direction. In spring the wood energy reaches upward and outward, like the inspiratory phase of breathing as we fill our lungs with air. This is a yang movement. In summer, the yang fire energy continues moving outward, like the continued inspiration, reaching into all the nooks and crannies of our lungs. Mother Nature is passionate to display all of her creations. Then, in late summer, she says, "It's time to stop doing so many things and slow down." Her creative prowess has waxed to her fullest potential. During this time of change, however, there is an energetic struggle, similar to the struggle that exists when one cannot make a decision to go one way or the other. Mother Nature's mood is changing. Her yang energy desires to remain active, so more heat is produced; yet the moist, humid yin energy has already come into play. Because of this, we might see many harsh atmospheric changes. Hurricane season flourishes at this time. This season is when we see the repolarization of yang turning into yin. Then the Mother succumbs to the desires of the stillness and the wetness. She embraces the dampness to wet her parched surface, because she has felt the pangs of dehydration from all her productivity over the summer season.

The colors associated with the Earth Element are yellow and orange. Yellow is more associated with the yang earth activity, and the sunset orange color with the yin activity. The direction associated with the Earth Element is the center.

Internal Correspondences

The Earth Element within is demonstrated in the stomach and spleen. Just like Mother Earth, the spleen and the stomach together, as yin/yang paired organs, produce the blood and the Qi necessary to sustain life. Their job in the body is to take the basic substances of water and food and transform them into nutrients, vital fluids, blood, and ultimately tissue. Other body parts related to this element are: blood, connective tissue, fatty tissue, flesh, muscles, esophagus, pancreas, mouth, and lips. The tactile sense and the sweet taste are also Earth Element correspondences.

Physical Problems

The following are possible manifestations of Earth Element problems: obesity, malnutrition, digestive disorders, bleeding tendencies, hernias, organ prolapse, edema, chronic loose stools, loss of muscle tone, and loose flesh.

Psychological Problems

Meditative, contemplative, and mindful are descriptors of a healthy earth psyche. When earth energies are imbalanced they can become overbearing, enmeshed, controlling, clingy, scattered, and wishy-washy. Their weakness is in putting others before self.

Earth Element People

Earth Element people are characteristically warm, nurturing, caring people. They reach out to everyone, making friends easily, and always remaining loyal. They are the perpetual peacemakers, striving to establish harmony in family and community. "Touchy feely" is the nickname often given to these people. They are sensitive, and have great "gut-level" intuitive powers. In the animal kingdom, elephants exemplify earth energy. They are seen as always faithful and never forgetting. Adjectives that describe psychologically healthy earth people are: supportive, empathetic, considerate, and centered.

A strong Earth Element can be recognized by appearance. In general, Earth Element people just look huggable. They have captivating smiles, usually with large mouths. Earthy women often have large breasts, hips, and hands. Earthy men have rugged hands and leathery skin; they may enjoy gardening. Both earth men and earth women are animal lovers.

Some famous Earth Element people are: Willie Nelson, Barbara Bush, Gene Hackman, Dan Blocker, Kathy Bates, and Oprah Winfrey.

Dream Associations

Some dream images related to the Earth Element are: landscapes, caves, houses, marshy areas, singing, heavy feelings, sticky sensations, dogs, horses, elephants, and food.

For more image correspondences see the glossary in the back of this book.

METAL

In some ancient cultures, the Metal Element was not recognized as one of the basic elements. As mentioned in the introduction to this chapter, several cultures around the globe developed elemental theories simultaneously. Most of them had identified four elements: fire, water, earth, and air. Air, however was not considered a basic element to the Chinese, because it was invisible and nontangible. It was just considered to be the space and the void in which the physical world existed. The ancient Chinese were chiefly concerned with identification of material things. They believed that all things visible and tangible derived from the yin substance of earth, so they initiated the analysis of the earth by breaking it down into four basic elements: wood, fire, metal, and water. Earth was kept as a basic element itself, thus making five elements. When cross-referencing the Chinese Five Element theory with the four-element theories of other cultures, the Metal Element is most closely associated with the energetics relating to the air element. However, it is hard in some circumstances to see a direct relationship.

External Correspondences

Pure metals are chemical elements. This means they cannot be broken down into other substances. There are more than a hundred chemical elements known; about eighty of these are metals. A few metals, such as gold, platinum, silver, and sometimes copper, are found in the earth in their pure state; however, most metals are not found free in nature. They are found only in chemical combination with other elements. By definition, a metal is a chemical element that has a shiny surface, has good electrical conductivity, and can be melted or fused. Unlike nonmetals, metals form positive ions and basic oxides and hydroxides. Upon exposure to air, many metals react chemically with the oxygen of the atmosphere to form a metallic oxide such as rust on exposed iron.

Metals are a large part of our world. We use them in everyday life all the time. Whether writing with a pencil, typing on a computer, driving an automobile, or cooking a meal, many people depend on the different forms and compounds in which metals come. Some could not even live without certain machines made from metal, such as those used in hospitals. Current trends in medical biological research is to find mechanisms by which organisms control transition metal ions and the roles of these metals in cellular regulation and cell-to-cell signaling. The National Institutes of Health recently solicited new projects focusing on the role of metals in the body's chemistry and the interactions of metal-containing compounds with enzymes.

Below are just a few uses of metals, listed by category:

• Transportation—cars, buses, trucks, trains, ships, and airplanes.

• Aerospace—unmanned and manned rockets and the space shuttle.

- Computers and other electronic devices that require conductors—TV, radio, stereo, calculators, security devices, etc.

- Communications—wireless and wired communications, and satellites that depend on a tough but light metal shell.

- Food processing, preparation, and preservation—pots, pans, microwave and conventional ovens, refrigerators and freezers.

- Construction—nails in conventional lumber construction and structural steel in other buildings.

- Biomedical applications—artificial replacement for joints and other prostheses.

- Electrical power production and distribution—oilers, turbines, generators, transformers, power lines, nuclear reactors, oil wells, and pipelines.

- Farming—tractors, combines, planters, and other equipment.

- Household conveniences—ovens, dish and clothes washers, vacuum cleaners, blenders, pumps, lawn mowers and trimmers, plumbing, water heaters, heating/cooling, etc.

Metal Element energy is a consolidating and solidifying energy. When the earth's ores are transformed, metal is created. Metal is the strong, compact energy contained deep within the earth that is associated with completion.

According to the Five Phase cycle of elemental interrelationships, metal is produced by earth, it produces water, and it controls wood. Think of it this way. Metals are contained within the rocks and ores of the earth (earth producing metal). Metals are transmutations and become liquids in certain circumstances (metal producing water). Metal implements can be sharp, like an axe, and can cut wood (metal controlling wood).

Metal energy descends, as opposed to its counteracting element, wood, which ascends. Within nature, the harmonious relationship between these two opposing energies is important for maintaining balance in the physical world.

The season of the Metal Element is autumn, a time of decreasing light, increasing cold, and shorter days. Trees lose their leaves as they withdraw their energy internally. The Qi within a tree during autumn begins its decent downward, where it will find a resting place down in the roots for the long winter.

The colors associated with the Metal Element are gray and white. The climatic correspondence is dryness, and the direction is the west. Things pertaining to the west and to the desert regions all correspond with the Metal Element.

Internal Correspondences

One of the ancient Chinese sayings used to describe the relationship between the physical external world and the internal world of the human body is this: "As without, so within." In other words, for whatever we can describe in the environment, we can find a similar counterpart within the body. Since the Metal Element is the topic of discussion here, we can say, "Metals without, metals within." As stated previously, metals are pervasive in the environment and are used in producing necessary products for daily use. In the body there are three metals that are vitally important for our internal manufacturing process: iron, copper, and zinc. A molecule of iron, for example, is necessary to form hemoglobin, the oxygen-carrying molecule in the blood. The iron in the blood meets the oxygen in the lungs and is circulated throughout the entire body. Oxygen has no transporting capabilities on its own, and without iron we would surely perish. Copper, another necessary metal, is required in the body for embryo development, connective tissue formation, temperature control, and nerve cell function. Zinc plays a crucial role in growth and cell division, where it is required for protein and DNA synthesis, in insulin activity, in the metabolism of the ovaries and testes, and in liver function. It is also vital for maintaining a healthy immune system. Research has shown that zinc is needed in more than one hundred enzymes and is involved in more body functions than any other mineral.

The ancient Chinese were not privy to all the fine details of how metals were used in the body. They merely identified the Metal Element within from an energetic perspective, and they assigned two yin/yang paired organs, the lungs and the large intestine, as belonging to the Metal Element category. There are many ways we can bridge the concepts of modern medicine with ancient Chinese Medicine on the topic of the Metal Elements within, but that would fill an entire book. The reader will fill in those gaps of how the metals we know today are energetically related to those Metal Element organs identified by the classical authors of the Chinese medical texts.

In addition to the lung and the large intestine, other body parts related to the Metal Element are: the nose, sinuses, bronchial tree, skin, mucous membranes, and body hair. The sense of smell and the spicy taste are Metal Element associations. The sound of the Metal Element is weeping or crying. Identification of a Metal Element imbalance can be heard in one's voice that cracks as if on the verge of tears, and one that carries a nasal tone. The odor associated with metal is rotten. This smell arises when the metal person fails to let go of useless by-products and garbage—the smell of food or waste gone bad by holding on to it too long.

Physical Problems

Health conditions related to the lung and the large intestine are indicative of Metal Element imbalances. The following are some examples: chronic sinusitis, asthma, allergies, urinary retention, spontaneous sweating, frequent colds and flus, constipation, diarrhea, edema, and skin problems.

Psychological Problems

The Metal Element corresponds to the season of autumn, a time of dying and letting go. It allows a person to be present in the time of farewells, tears, grief, and loss. This element allows acceptance to what is inevitable, including death. Through the lungs and the breath, we are connected outwardly to heaven and inwardly to our spiritual essence. With our first breath the soul connects to physical life and form, and with our last breath the soul returns to pure spirit and the formless. Often people die in the early morning hours. According to the Chinese clock, these hours are the time of metal.

In the individual, the Metal Element represents internal resolve and strength, self-worth, self-esteem, vitality and endurance, as well as the ability to let go of emotional upsets and grudges. When the Metal Element is out of balance, there can be depression and sadness, an inability to recover from loss, lack of inspiration, rigidity, poor self-esteem, excessive materialism, and emotional withdrawal.

The emotion of metal is grief. This is the by-product of an inability to let go of something valuable. The emotional state of one struggling with a Metal Element imbalance is the inability to let go of loss. When the energy of metal is blocked or imbalanced within us, our expression of grief likewise becomes imbalanced and inappropriate. It may become excessive and ongoing. Or, in the other extreme, it may be absent, as in those who cannot express their grief. Regret is another manifestation of grief. It is the inability to let go of the past. Regret can become so paramount that the person with a Metal Element imbalance may have difficulty forming bonds with other people out of fear of being regretful for the development of the relationship, or out of fearing its inevitable loss. This melancholy, or lack of inspiration resulting from constantly looking backward, is at the heart of the Metal Element.

Just as metals give value to the earth (gold and silver, minerals, and trace elements), the Metal Element within us gives our sense of self-worth. Each of us is a miracle of creation, more valuable and special than anything we could ever pursue. Each of us has a unique and priceless contribution to make. Yet when our metal energy is imbalanced, we cannot sense our value. We compensate by seeking what we think will add to our worth: status, money, power, and conquest. None of these are bad or wrong of themselves, but our excessive pursuit of them can be a symptom of a Metal Element imbalance. Once we have acquired these things, however, we remain strangely unfulfilled. Persons with a metal imbalance seek respect, quality, and recognition from outside themselves because they feel the lack of worth within.

Metal Element People

People with strong Metal Element qualities are like metal itself and are electrically conductive. They have strong impulses and generative powers. People who come into contact with metal people feel this current generated, for metal people inherently have the ability to bring about the changes and transformations they desire. According to the Chinese calendar, people who are born in Metal Element years tend to be rigid and resolute in their expressions. They are guided by strong feelings and will pursue their objectives with intensity and little hesitation. Sustained by their ambitions, they are capable of a prolonged effort to get what they want. They are very resourceful and unwavering in their determination. Metal people are not easily swayed or influenced to change a course of action once they have decided on it, even by hardships, drawbacks, and initial failures. They prefer to sort out and solve their problems alone and generally do not appreciate interference or unsolicited assistance from others. They map out their own destinies, clear their own paths, and visualize their own goals without outside help.

People with Metal Element qualities have strong monetary and accumulative instincts and will use these traits to support their strong tastes for luxury, opulence, and power. In order to maintain balance, they must learn to compromise and not to be overly insistent on always having their own way. Often they are unbending and opinionated and will break off a good relationship because others do not heed their wishes or conform readily to their will.

Some Metal Element celebrities are: Kate Winslet, Shania Twain, George Clooney, and Madonna. Famous historical figures with strong but excessive Metal Element qualities are: Adolf Hitler, Atilla the Hun, Mussolini, and Alexander the Great.

Dream Associations

A few examples of dream images associated with the Metal Element are cars, planes, trains, swords, guns, falling leaves, experiencing strong odors, white or shiny objects, crying, flying, desert scenes or animals, and orientation of images facing west.

For more image correspondences see the glossary in the back of the book.

WATER

The Water Element is probably the easiest element to comprehend. It is natural to associate lakes, rivers, oceans, and rain with this element, for they are the personification of water; however, some associations, such as the darkness, the moon, and the colors blue and black are indirect correspondences.

External Correspondences

We live on a water planet—approximately 70 to 75 percent of the earth's surface is water. It is interesting to note that those are the same percentages of water in the human body. Water is mutable, and is both visible and invisible. It moves in the four major directions, from the interior toward the exterior, and from the exterior toward the interior. Like the human heart pumps its vital fluid, blood, the earth pumps its vital fluid, water. The earth contracts inward, sending water to the core of magma, where the dance of fire and water take place. Water then expands outward and upward toward the surface of the earth and continues into the atmosphere as a vapor, where it again is met with the sun, and another dance of fire and water take place, eventually culminating in rain and once again beginning a new cycle of contracting and expanding. These movements of water typify the eternal dance of yin and yang in all things.

Despite the fears of many environmentalists who claim we are robbing the planet of this vital substance, scientists tell us that there is the same amount of water on our planet as there was three billion years ago. Because things are never static, we can only measure them as they are in any given moment. Perhaps those fearful observers based their thesis of water disappearing on a few observations that took place during times when the Water Element was in its decreasing cycle, not recognizing that what naturally follows, according to the universal principles of yin and yang, is a cycle of increase.

The Chinese, as well as many other cultures, have understood water to be the universal healer. Anointing and bathing with water to bring about a healing is as old as time itself. Evolutionists say that all life evolved out of the ocean. Although the creationists do not support that theory, the one thing the evolutionists and creationists might agree on is that life evolved from water. It is within the medium of watery fluids that the sperm cell swims to meet the awaiting ovum. Conception takes place, the fertilized ovum evolves into a zygote, then to an embryo, and finally into a fetus. The fetus is then born out of the water, and becomes a human infant. Some fundamental Christians ceremoniously go into the water once again to celebrate a rebirth into Christ.

Water can be calm and serene, like a glassy lake, or it can be turbulent and raging, like a mighty river. It washes away earth, transports drifting wood, and when it comes across a rock or another impediment, it will seek its way around, coursing every path on its journey toward the sea. Water is passive and yielding, but at the same time it subdues everything.

Trees instinctively know how to find water. Deep within the subterranean plates, water is waiting to be found. Roots burrow deeper and deeper until they tap into the water arteries and draw within them the essence that gives them life. The Chinese proposed that the Water Element is the one true source from where all life springs and it holds the root of all knowledge.

Things associated with the Water Element are: puddles, rivers, lakes, oceans, rain, the colors blue and black, the element of mystery, darkness, the void, the great unknown, the northern regions, coldness, the salty taste, and the winter season.

Internal Correspondences

Water is the medium of all internal physiologic actions, and it is the means of transportation of vital substances such as red and white blood cells, hormones, and molecules. Water forms bonds and consolidates other substances and materials. It is an adherent. Notice how you can take a piece of paper and wet it with water, then stick it to a pane glass window. Have you ever watched a raindrop on your window—how it gravitates to another raindrop, then magnetically is drawn to another, until a little stream of water runs down on the window? The ability to draw inward and downward, astringing and consolidating, is accomplished by the energy of this element.

Water comprises about 75 percent of the whole human body. This amounts to approximately forty-five liters, which form the basis for all growth and development. The Chinese associated the kidneys as the officials governing the absorption, usage, and disposal of water in the body. The kidneys are said to be the ocean of the human body. Just as the oceans of the earth are lower than the earth's surface and lower than the rivers and streams, the kidneys are low and deep within the lower cavities of the body. Just as the rivers and streams of the earth drain down to the oceans, all the waters within drain into the kidneys. Their partner in this business is the urinary bladder. Both the kidney and the bladder employ other internal energetic allies to rule over the movement of this water through internal waterways. They monitor hydration and make sure that osmotic pressures are balanced, so that there is neither dryness, nor internal flooding.

The ability to reproduce and mature is governed by the energy of the kidneys. Within the kidney energy and the Water Element is the storage of our life essence from which all of our body's cells originate. The early Chinese called this vital essence *jing*. Modern terms such as "DNA" and "stem cells" are possibly aspects of the jing discussed by those ancient sages. Having plentiful jing is said to be the determinant of fertility and longevity, but when the jing essence is diminished, then degenerative and abnormal cellular processes begin.

In Chinese Medicine, the kidney is a broader concept than just the organ itself. The adrenals, bladder, bones, brain, ears, pituitary gland, spinal cord, teeth, and ureters all are a part of the kidney system and are Water Element associations. When one is first learning Chinese Medicine, it is a real stretch to understand how some of these organs and differing body parts can be so closely related to each other. But the more one bridges the concepts between Chinese Medicine and Western Medicine, it becomes more and more clear why they were grouped as part of the same internal colony.

The brain, which is part of the kidney system, is referred to as the "sea of marrow," and it is within this kidney energy that all knowledge is contained. Good memory and wisdom are the outgrowth of a strong Water Element within. It is interesting to note that we often use the phrase "ocean of knowledge" in psychological circles when speaking of the universal collective conscious and unconscious. We also refer to the unknown as the "watery void," which is that metaphorical place from where all thoughts arise.

Willpower, ambition, and strength are all housed within the Water Element. A strong Water Element must be present for us to achieve our goals, because goal accomplishment is so dependent on will and determination. The hearing sense and the salty taste are also Water Element correspondences.

Physical Problems

Because water is so vital to almost every body function, we can see Water Element imbalances in almost any illness. All life is born out of the water, so when cellular life on any level has gone awry, we can look to the Water Element for assistance in aiding a problem. Let's imagine some well-known images from movie scenes to highlight how we look to the Water Element for resolving various health conditions. Think of the scene of an injured soldier on a battlefield, or of a frail woman fainting, or of someone overcome by fear, heat, or stress. Picture the people who have come to help these fictitious characters. You see a soldier's comrade wetting the parched lips of his dying buddy. You see a passerby who witnesses the lady fainting and places a cold wet cloth on her forehead. You see someone throwing cold water into the face of someone who is screaming uncontrollably from fright. If you contemplate other scenes of people in hospital waiting rooms, doctors' offices, or at airport ticket counters, where people are in states of stress, the first thing that human services industry workers will offer to soothe the frenzied and the frazzled is a glass of water to drink. Water is the universal solvent.

Examples of Water Element problems are: adrenal problems, anemia due to bone marrow suppression, auditory conditions, bony malformations, early graying or loss of hair, edema, reproductive problems, shortness of breath on exertion, neurological dysfunctions, spinal problems, and ringing in the ears.

Psychological Problems

One of the characteristics of water is that it has an amazing ability to maneuver around any obstruction. It exerts strong willpower to achieve its goal to fulfill its destiny of reaching the seas. People who have strong Water Element qualities are therefore very adaptable. They also have great capability of finding their way around obstacles. Water Element people are introspective, tend to do a great deal of reflecting, and are very observant.

The emotion associated with the Water Element is fear. Because the kidney contains the seat of all knowledge, it is acutely aware of dangers lurking in the deep unknown. When the Water Element energy is imbalanced, an early indicator is becoming a little forgetful. The forgetfulness may only be for a time when water supplies are deficient. Other indicators, such as the lack of foresight or the lack of taking precaution or failure to be proactive, can also point to a malfunction in the kidney system. Extreme fear, such as panic disorder, is related to Water Element deficiencies.

The brain and spine together are about 76 percent water. The total volume of the cerebrospinal fluid is about 125 to 150 milliliters. The loss of just a few drops of spinal fluid during a lumbar puncture can produce the worst headaches known, so you can imagine the importance of hydration on these vital water element organs. When a person has sudden mental status changes, or if he exhibits restlessness, agitation, or insomnia, he may be in need of Water Element nurturing.

Depression, paranoia, and lack of will or desire to live are all other indicators of Water Element issues.

Dream Associations

Dream images related to the Water Element are those that have observable water in them, or that possess qualities of water, such as feelings of wetness, coldness, and darkness. Objects and animals such as boats and fish are also related. Dream scenes containing fear, mystery, sexual encounters, or lack of knowledge are all relative to the Water Element.

For more image correspondences see the glossary in the back of the book.

Now that you are familiar with the Five Elements, try the following method for interpreting your dreams.

Five-Step Five Element Dream Study Process

STEP 1: RECORD YOUR DREAM.

Dreams are better analyzed and interpreted when you can examine them from the written word. You are more likely to get results when you can be more objective.

STEP 2: GIVE THE DREAM A TITLE.

You are the creator of your dreams. Think of yourself as a movie producer who has a message to share with the world. As that producer, you select a writer to tell the story of what you want to say. Imagine who the writer of your dream story might be. You, as the producer, also select a location that has the right topographical landscapes to give the viewer a feeling toward the film. You carefully select the props, which themselves convey meaning. You select the actors who are characters in a scene portraying the message in a way that all who watch will be mesmerized by their performances. You, the *dreamer*, are now captivated by the story knowing, perhaps, the special meaning for yourself.

STEP 3: UNDERLINE THE MAJOR CHARACTERS, OBJECTS, AND IMAGES THAT ARE MOST VIVID.

Include action verbs and some descriptive adjectives that you used in the dream recording.

STEP 4: IDENTIFY ONE MAIN CONFLICT IN THE DREAM.

Stay focused on the main conflict, and use only those characters, objects, and images within the sentence or sentences that contain the main conflict. Many dreams are convoluted and lengthy. You will have an easier time deciphering the message in your dream if you extract the main conflict and work with it. If you cannot identify a conflict, begin with a few images that are the most vivid, or are more emotionally charged, even if they do not seem to have conflict.

STEP 5: LOOK IN THE GLOSSARY AND/OR CHARTS AT THE END OF THIS CHAPTER TO DETERMINE WHICH ELEMENT/S THE DREAM IMAGES CONTAINING THE MAIN CONFLICT CORRESPOND WITH.

Remember, many images will have flavors of other elements within them, but usually there is one that is predominant. Use an *impersonal subject* such as "someone," "some energy," "the dreamer," and so on. Impersonal subjects will help you to decode the message more easily. Use the same verb as contained in the conflict, or a synonymous verb. Use an impersonal object as you did with the subject. Remember to use the main elements relative to the subject and object as qualifiers. Use adjectives with your subjects and objects.

For example, an image of a book, which is made from paper, might be a Wood Element image because paper comes from trees. But if the book is an encyclopedia or a biblical text, you might associate it with a Water Element image because the Water Element is said to be the seat of all knowledge.

Use the following sentence structure to decode the dream, using your sentence containing the dream conflict and filling in the blanks. To make it simple, try to organize it into a simple sentence using subject, verb, and object. Once the sentence is written, substitute various mind/body element correspondences into your sentence to help you decipher your dream:

Here is an example of an extracted sentence of one dreamer's dream that contains the conflict:

I was driving a big bus (Metal Element). I had no seat, and feared I couldn't control the floor brake while standing.

Someone (subject)   is driving fearfully (verb)
(use the word "someone"   (add the verb or action clause here)
instead of "I")

about being able to control some Metal Element
(use both mind and body element correspondences)

Here are a few sentences later written containing various mind/body element correspondences:

Someone was driving fearfully about being able to control or put the brake on large intestine energy. (Metal Element organ correspondence)

Someone was driving fearfully about being able to control or put the brake on grief. (Metal Element mental correspondence)

Summary

You will find that the techniques we have given here in *The Tao of Dreaming* will take you to the same fundamental interpretations of a dream as other, Western-oriented dreamwork techniques you may have used. You will probably find that you receive additional insights, especially related to your body and to the interrelationship between your emotional state and your physical and mental states. Regularly using *The Tao of Dreaming* techniques will help you develop a more holistic perspective on your mind/body/spirit well-being. You may become more attuned to physical cues, and then find supporting correlations in your dreams. Your dreams also may serve as an early warning system of imbalances that, left uncorrected, may lead to noticeable physical symptoms.

The Tao of Dreaming is intended to be an aid to self-awareness and is not a primary tool of self-diagnosis. It is important that you consult a medical practitioner with all concerns about your health and to obtain the correct therapeutic help. A practitioner of Chinese Medicine will be naturally oriented to taking your dreams into consideration in evaluating your health.

The Tao is a state of wholeness and balance. Our dreams provide important information for maintaining balance, thus bringing us into the fullness of the Tao.

May your dreamwork help you establish an abundance of blessings and well-being.

Dream Image Worksheet

Use the following sheet as a study guide to use the Five Element Map to uncover some mind/body issues that could be hidden in your dreams.

Samples are in italics. Use with the *"Five Step Five Element Dream Process instruction sheet."*

I. IDENTIFYING DREAM IMAGES AND MATCHING TO THE FIVE ELEMENTS.
To improve recall of images, review them according to your five senses, such as *visual, auditory, taste, tactile, smell.*

IMAGE	WOOD	FIRE	EARTH	METAL	WATER
1. *car*				*	
2.					
3.					
4.					
5.					

II. COMPARING DREAM IMAGES WITH TABLES 1, 2, AND 3, THE FIVE ELEMENT CORRESPONDENCE CHARTS

1. Answer the following questions about each of your identified dream images.
a. What are some image correspondences from the Five Element Charts? *e.g.*—for *metal—lung, smell, crying, sorrow, controlled*

_____

_____

_____

_____

_____

b. Are there any mental/emotional correlations that are similar to these correspondences? *e.g.—for metal you might ask, "Have I been sad lately?"*

_____

_____

_____

_____

c. Are there any physical correlations? *e.g.—for metal you might ask, "Is there a possible concern with an aspect of my respiratory system?"*

_____

_____

_____

_____

2. FREE ASSOCIATE, **using word substitutions that are synonymous with the words found in the Five Element Correspondence charts.** *e.g.—using word correspondences with metal, some free associations or word substitutions for grief could be "loss" or "detachment."*

_____

_____

_____

_____

_____

_____

_____

_____

_____

Five Element Correspondences Relating to Physical Body

	FIRE	EARTH	METAL	WATER	WOOD
Organs	Heart Small Intenstine	Spleen Stomach	Lung Large Intestine	Kidney Bladder	Liver Gall Bladder
Organ Extensions	Arteries Thyroid Veins Face Complexion	Blood Connective Tissue Fatty Tissue Muscle Esophagus Pancreas Mouth Lips	Body Hair Bronchial Tree Nose Sinuses Skin Mucous Membranes	Adrenal Glands Bones and Marrow Brain Ears Head Hair Teeth	Eyes Fingernails Muscles Tendons
Sense Organs	Taste Tongue Speech	Flesh Touch	Nose Smell	Ears Hearing	Eyes Vision
Taste	Bitter	Sweet	Spicy	Salty	Sour
Body Fluid Secretion	Sweat	Mucous	Saliva Urine	Tears	Phlegm Saliva

Five Element Correspondences Relating to Mind/Body/Spirit

	FIRE	EARTH	METAL	WATER	WOOD
Emotions	Joy Laughter Happiness Mania	Pensiveness Overthinking Anxiety	Anguish Grief Sadness Sorrow	Fear Fright	Anger Frustration Indecision Depressed
Behavioral Characteristics	Passionate Creative Charismatic Intuitive Manic Hyperactive Free Spirited Extroverted	Cooperative Peacemaker Matchmaker Nurturer Overprotective People Pleaser Fickle Ruminative Wishy-Washy Obsession	Controlled Meticulous Structured Autocratic Formal Militaristic Self-righteous Petty	Curious Introspective Distant Observer Conservative Reflective Unexpressive Strong Willed Timid Paranoid Suspicious	Decisive Good Planner Assertive Grounded Rooted Seeks New Growth
Human Sounds	Laughing Rambling Voice	Singing Whiny	Weeping Crying	Groaning Moaning	Shouting Snapping
Mental Energies	Consciousness Spirit Will to Live	Thoughts Ideas Inspirations	Animal Spirit Vital Energy Life Force	Willpower Ambition	Soul Spiritual Faculties

Five Element Correspondences Relating to World and Environment

	FIRE	EARTH	METAL	WATER	WOOD
Colors	Red Fiery Yellow	Sallow Yellow Sunset Orange	White Silver Gold Gray	Blue Black	Brown Green Turquoise
Climate	Heat	Dampness	Dryness	Cold	Wind
Direction	South	Center	West	North	East
Season	Summer	Late Summer	Autumn	Winter	Spring

Sample Dream Images Relating to the Five Elements

FIRE	EARTH	METAL	WATER	WOOD
Bloody Drainage	Canyons	Airplanes	Blue or Black Objects	Budding Flowers
Children	Caves	Being Bitten	Boats	Eastern Locations
Fires/Sparks	Eating Food	Coins	Fish	Forced Sex
Heat	Hunger	Crying	Hidden Animals	Forests
Passionate Sex	Heaviness	Flying	Lakes	Green Objects
Red Objects	Houses	Losing Objects	Oceans	Mushrooms
Southern Locations	Ruined Buildings	Metallic Objects	Pools	New Growths
Fear and Laughter	Kitchens	Powerful People	Rain	Paper Money
Towns and Streets	Marshy Areas	Structured Sex	Introverted Sex	Violence
	Oral Sex	White Objects	Drowning	Wooden Objects
	Singing	Cruel Killings of People Crying	Frightful Fears	Being Trapped
	Playing Music			Mountains
	Slippery Paths			
	Weddings			
	Body Heavy			

Five Element Associations

Wood Element

Organs—liver/gall bladder

Extensions of Organs—tendons, muscles, fingernails

Sensory Organ—eyes

Emotions—*weak wood*—indecisive; *strong wood*—decisiveness (clear intent of direction). *Pathology*—anger and rage

Spiritual Associations—knowledge of strategies

Colors—green, turquoise

Taste—sour

Season—spring

Climatic Influence—wind

Direction—east

Examples of Dream Images: new growths, wooden objects, forests, brush, mushrooms, the spring season or anything related to spring such as budding flowers

Fire Element

Organs—heart and small intestine
Extensions of Organs—the vessels
Sensory Organ—tongue
Emotions—*weak fire*—dispassionate; *strong fire*—joyful countenance. *Pathology*—mania or severe depression, bipolar tendencies
Spiritual Associations—the passion for crafting or constructing; free expression of spirit
Color—red
Taste—bitter
Season—summer
Climatic Influence—heat
Direction—south
Examples of Dream Images: heat, fire, or related things such as lightening, red objects, bloody drainage, being in the south

Earth Element

Organs—spleen and stomach
Extensions of Organs—esophagus, pancreas, connective tissue, thyroid gland, blood
Sensory Organs—tongue and discernment of taste
Emotions—contemplation; *weak earth*—anxious, worried; *strong earth*—thoughtfulness, concern. *Pathology*—whiny, vacillating, unable to make a stand or form opinion, fickle
Spiritual Associations—socially connected and adept
Colors—orange, yellow
Taste—sweet
Season—late summer
Climatic Influence—dampness and humidity

Direction—center

Examples of Dream Images: canyons, caves, earth related images, objects that are hues of yellow and orange, damp marshy areas, slippery paths, mucous, heaviness, turbidity, singing

Metal Element

Organs—lung, large intestine

Extensions of Organs—nose, sinuses, bronchial tree, skin

Sensory Organ—nose

Emotions—*weak metal*—inability to accept loss, sad, grieving; *strong metal*—ability to detach from others with ease. *Pathology*—perpetual sadness

Spiritual Associations—ability to detach from earthly matters, seeing ultimate resolve in things pertaining to heaven

Color—white

Taste—spicy

Season—autumn

Climatic Influence—dryness

Direction—west

Examples of Dream Images: metallic objects, crying, weeping, losing objects, loss of friends, flying

Water Element

Organs—kidney, bladder

Extensions of Organs—brain, adrenal glands, reproductive glands, bones

Sensory Organ—ear

Emotions—*weak water*—fear, inability to overcome obstacles; *strong water*—love, or absence of fear, resourcefulness, easily overcomes obstacles. *Pathology*—panic

Spiritual Associations—the will of the individual, ability to hear and to be heard

Colors—blue, black

Season—winter

Taste—salty

Climatic Influence—rain, cold

Direction—north

Examples of Dream Images: lakes, oceans, pools, rain, fish, blue or black objects

Dream Images and Physical Correspondences

DREAM IMAGE	PHYSICAL CORRESPONDENCES
Streets, roads	Acupuncture meridians, blood vessels, nervous system
Mountains	Breasts, liver
Enemies, aliens	Pathogens, infections
Crowds	Congestion in organs or tissue, increased immune responses
Tornadoes	Wind influences, internal heat and stagnation
Drums	Heart rate, hearing, adrenal function
Airplanes	Nose, lungs, sinuses, upper back and chest
Hats	Brain, head
Basements, cellars	Large intestine
Caverns, caves	Uterus, reproductive organs

Shoes . . . . Feet, gait

Ladders, steps . . . . Spine

Kitchens, restaurants. . . Stomach, intestines

Long passageways . . . . . Vessels

Narrow passageways. . . Respiratory system, anus

Flowers. . . . . Sexual organs

Police . . . . Immune system, liver

Towers and tall . . . . Brain, head
   buildings

Clocks. . . . . Heart

Overeating, gluttony . . . Small intestine

Windows, cameras. . . . . Eyes

Gloves . . . . Hands

Tree limbs. . . . . Arms, legs

Water . . . . Kidney, bladder

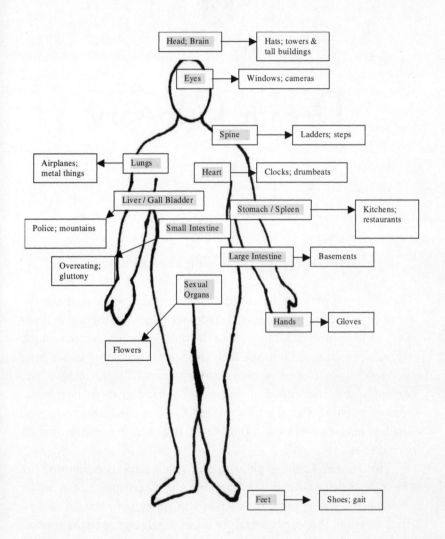

Head; Brain → Hats; towers & tall buildings

Eyes → Windows; cameras

Spine → Ladders; steps

Airplanes; metal things ← Lungs

Heart → Clocks; drumbeats

Liver / Gall Bladder

Stomach / Spleen → Kitchens; restaurants

Police; mountains

Small Intestine

Overeating; gluttony

Large Intestine → Basements

Sexual Organs

Hands → Gloves

Flowers

Feet → Shoes; gait

Dream Glossary

Instructions for Using the Glossary

The following glossary has been included in this work to assist the dreamer in dream exploration. It is by no means all-inclusive; however, we have included hundreds of the most common dream images. The ancient Chinese literature provides little information concerning the yin/yang or elemental associations of most dream images. Accordingly, we have added on our own as many of those interpretations as possible, based on Taoist and Chinese Medicine principles. Readers may discover additional associations in the course of their own dreamwork.

The ancient Chinese philosophies could have been named the "First Theories of Relativity" because the discernment of whether something is yin or yang, or whether something is by nature categorized as wood, fire, earth, metal, or water, is all *relative* to the *context* of any situation or circumstance. For example, a dog, relative to cats, is yang. Dogs are more outgoing in general, seeking social groups, whereas cats are more introspective and antisocial. However, in a given dream, one might dream of a lazy basset hound or a cat who "thinks it's a dog" (in other words, very social and outgoing), and the yin/yang or elemental associations would be different.

The dreamer must be aware of the limitations of a glossary. The assignment of yin/yang associations and elemental qualities to images is a *guideline* to help those who are learning about the basic nature of all things. Dreamers need to further explore their dreams and isolate the predominant quality of an image as seen in context and as relative to other images within the same dream.

We have included brief commentaries on many of the entries where the associations are more vague or where they need more explanation. One thing to keep in mind when reconciling an image with yin/yang and elemental associations is that *images can contain multiple elements*. For example, one could debate whether a snake is yin or yang. A snake certainly possesses both yin and yang qualities, just as do other animals or objects. However, there is usually a preponderance of one basic quality that captures the spirit or essence of the thing we speak of that helped us make the determination.

If you find several possibilities for a dream image, allow your intuition to choose the most appropriate one.

Dream Glossary

abandonment Feeling of being left behind; sense of betrayal; fear of being alone; losing touch with the purpose of life. Abandonment dreams may occur following separation or divorce, or the death of a loved one, especially a parent or spouse. These dreams mirror unresolved grief, anger, resentment, and despair. Facing and working through these feelings is part of the recovery process; abandonment dreams may help make one aware of emotional blockages.
Association: Yin
Element: Water

accident Dreams involving accidents occur during stressful times, especially those involving a major upheaval in one's life, such as divorce or grief. Such dreams are most likely to occur during the first stage of recovery—shock and denial. Typical accident dreams are: losing control in an **automobile** or other vehicle; **falling** off a precipice, out of a boat, or out of a window; being struck and injured; or being caught in a **natural disaster**. Accidents also may mirror catastrophic events that have occurred in life. Or they may reflect the making of others responsible for what happens in one's life.

Association: The yin or yang association is relative to the type of accident. For example, if the accident in the dream involves driving a vehicle and colliding into an external object or going over a cliff, it is yang. The dreamer's yang energy is exhausted or collides with outside forces, depicting an imbalance with nature. If the accident involves being struck by an outside force, the dreamer's yang Qi is severely deficient and cannot withstand external forces. Accidents also depict a deficiency of yin. The body is a solid yin structure, and when it collapses in on itself or is easily broken, it indicates a yin deficient state.

Element: This is determined by specific objects in dream, e.g., auto accident—metal.

acorn Spiritual rebirth; growth; new life. A new phase in life.
Association: Yin
Element: Wood
See **tree**.

actor Role playing in life. Being an actor in a dream or observing an actor (the equivalent to seeing oneself) may point out unfulfilled wishes or desires, or may demonstrate how one is acting out the expectations of others.
Association: Yang. An actor uses creative license to portray a character, a creative action that is yang. This applies even if the char-

acter being portrayed may be yin, such as an actor portraying a depressed person.

Element: Fire

air Creativity; intellect; thoughts; mental effort. Note the quality of the air in the dream—whether it is crisp, clean and pure, and easy to breathe, or fogged, polluted, stifling, stagnant, and difficult to breathe.

Association: Yang
Element: Metal

airplane The intellect and ideas; freedom of thought; open-mindedness; the ability to rise above situations, life, or problems. An airplane also represents a means of fast, but temporary, escape from life's troubles. **Flying** in an airplane is an alchemical symbol of the ascension of intellect.

Dreams involving commercial aircraft have more of a collective symbolism than those involving small, private aircraft. Being a passenger is a symbol of passivity, of allowing someone else or some other force to determine the journey. Being a pilot indicates having control.

Planes that do not or cannot take off indicate ideas that are having difficulty taking shape.

An airplane crash indicates one is soaring too high and needs to return to earth and become grounded. Plane crashes also are a metaphor for stressful periods in life.

Association: Yang
Element: Metal

alcohol A creative or destructive force, depending on context. Alcohol might represent a releasing of inhibitions, social enjoyment, or "mingling with the crowd." Too much alcohol, or its abuse, may symbolize destructive or addictive forces in one's life.

Association: Yin or yang depending on context of dream. Positive aspects of alcohol are yang, while destructive aspects are yin. Alcohol causes dilation of blood vessels. In moderate amounts, it increases circulation, which in Chinese Medicine opens channels for Qi and blood flow. In excess it robs the body of yin substance. The most affected organ is the liver.

Element: Wood

alley A symbol related to life's journey or transitional stages in life. The alley is a type of **path**, a common motif that appears in dreams when one is undergoing a major change of course in life, or a life review.

Alleys have a dark aspect: they are narrow and constricting, almost tunnel-like, and often seem lonely and sinister. They are off the main roads, and may indicate that a sidetracking has taken place. In a more positive aspect, alleys can represent shortcuts. Notice whether the alley is dark and seems dangerous, has a dead end, or seems more like a convenience.

Association: Yin
Element: Water

almond Like all nuts, almonds generally symbolize hidden wisdom. Because of its shape—called *mandorla* or a *vesica piscis*, the almond specifically symbolizes the feminine principle, including sweetness and charm, fertility and pregnancy. Almonds have a spiritual meaning, because they are sweetness (spiritual) concealed by a hard shell difficult to open (the material).

Association: Yin
Element: Earth

altar A place where sacrifices are made; a spiritual center. An altar may symbolize the letting go of something, or the need to let go. It also symbolizes renewal, for through sacrifice comes change and new beginnings.

Altars also may represent a consuming force. For example, an "altar of love" may require the sacrifice of freedom or individuality. Another meaning of altars is thanksgiving.

Association: Yang. Things that pertain to spiritual endeavors are considered yang in nature. The nature of yang is more etheric, and invisible.

Element: Fire

amber *See* **jewels.**

ambush Being ambushed in a dream indicates one may be at an emotional impasse and needs to work through the block. Ambush occurs during stressful periods in life, when one is likely to suffer emotional upheaval and unresolved grief or anger, such as during a divorce or loss.

Association: Yang
Element: The element depends on the type of weapons involved in an ambush. Guns or knives are Metal. Fiery spears are Fire.

amethyst *See* **jewels.**

amputation The cutting off or removal of something no longer desirable, necessary, or healthful. An amputation is forceful, often done under emergency conditions. It may indicate a serious or crisis situation that needs to be addressed.

Association: Yang. The implication when one is amputated, is that there is an external force such as a surgeon's scalpel, or an accident or injury from machinery or such. Any condition caused by external forces is considered yang.

Element: Wood. The limbs on a person are associated with branches on a tree.

See **operation.**

ancestors To dream of being reunited with one's ancestors indicates that a healing process is taking place. Ancestors may be represented by totem animals. Ancestors also may represent attributes from the dreamer's past.

Association: Yin. Our ancestors are our genetic predecessors. Genetic material is considered pure yin substance.

Element: Water

anchor Safety; stability; security. Anchors secure boats, which in dreams are vehicles for navigating the waters of the unconscious. An anchored boat is at rest, secure in a harbor, at a dock, or in shallow water near shore—symbolizing a respite from traveling in the unconscious. Losing an anchor represents fear and feeling adrift in the unconscious.

Association: Yin

Element: Water

angel A messenger of God and an intermediary between God and humankind who has the power to intervene in mundane affairs. Angels in dreams guide and inform. They are messengers from the unconscious or from the Higher Self, bringing something to conscious attention. Figures in white, especially flowing robes, might be interpreted as angels. Dark angels, personified by dark or black persons or persons dressed in dark clothing, perhaps embody a shadow element.

Association: An angel of light is yang. A dark angel is yin.

Element: An angel of light is fire. A dark angel is water.

animals One's primitive, physical, sexual, and instinctual natures; the impulses that reside in the unconscious; the less conscious part of the shadow; spiritual growth. Animals may correspond to physical, sexual, sensual, emotional, and spiritual needs that the conscious mind needs to address. They also symbolize stages of psychic growth and development.

In dreams, as in fairy tales and myths, animals often represent archetypal forces. Animals are close to their instincts and always behave according to their true natures; their positive and negative qualities remain constant. Thus, animals that are domesticated and docile are symbols of those qualities; and animals renowned for their craftiness, stealth, or fierceness are representative of those qualities. In addition, one's personal associations with animals—likes, dislikes, fears, and so on—must be considered.

Common dream animals are **birds**, which are a universal symbol of soul and spirit, and **snakes**, a symbol of transformation and renewal. Animals that exist close to or under the ground, such as lizards and rodents, as well as water dwellers such as fish and turtles, represent the unconscious and instinct. They can also represent the origin of things and rebirth.

The self sometimes appears in dreams as an animal. The most common images are elephants (often representing the highest true self), horses, bears, bulls, white and black birds, fish, and snakes. Less common images are snails, tortoises, spiders, and beetles.

The forces that animals represent sometimes erupt from the unconscious with tremendous power and wildness. Frightening animals are a common motif in dreams; to fight one may indicate an inner battle between the conscious mind and the deeper instinctual nature. To dream of being pursued by a frightening animal may indicate that something has become separated from consciousness and needs to be reintegrated. The pursuit dream is either calling attention to this need or is a signal that the reintegration process is struggling to take place. The more dangerous the animal, the more urgent the need to address reintegration. The type of animal may provide clues to what has become alienated.

Being devoured by an animal is a widespread archetypal motif in legend, myth, and fairy tale; it symbolizes a descent into the underworld, the sinking of the consciousness into the unconscious. Such a descent precedes a spiritual renewal.

Fabulous animals are powerful instruments of psychological projection, for they are primordial and belong to the deepest realms of unconsciousness. They often symbolize the prima materia, the matrix or vessel from which arises all life, and thus represent the beginning stages of individuation. See **dragon; monster.**

Fabulous animals and animals with mythical associations may represent transcendence, higher stages of spiritual consciousness, or the highest manifestation of the self. Spiritual or psychic growth, or the need for it, may be represented by animals with extra legs, wings, or unusual powers; by animals associated with various deities, religious figures, or spiritual systems; or by animals that transform themselves into deities or humans. Such animals typically appear as helpers or guides in a dream.

During pregnancy, dreams of newborn animals—especially puppies, kittens, and seals—and small furry mammals are common among both men and women. They symbolize the vulnerability of the newborn, in anticipation of the birthing of the baby.

In myth, animals are shape-shifted gods and are carriers of the souls of the dead, thus taking on associations with the underworld and unconscious. Important chthonic animals are **dogs**, **pigs**, and pregnant **cows.**

Association: Depends on the type of animal. Animals that are yang are those that move rapidly, such as a cheetah or a gazelle. Birds are yang because they are light and feathery. A hummingbird is an excellent example of yang energy because of its small build and rapid speed. Yin animals have big and solid bodies, such as elephants, hippopotami, and pigs. Other yin animals are those that inhabit watery places, such as alligators, or those that live under the earth, such as groundhogs, moles, and other reptiles.

Element: The elemental quality of an animal is determined by both the characteristics of the animal and by its natural habitat. For example, animals that burrow in the earth are earth, and animals that live in the arctic regions, such as a polar bears, walruses, and penguins, are water. Some animals may be difficult to categorize. For example, a panther is dark and mysterious and thus related to the Water Element, but its jungle abode is associated with the Wood Element. When there are conflicting associations, take into consideration context and other elements in the dream.

See individual listings for animals.

annulment A denial that something intimate, such as a sexual encounter or an emotional confession, ever took place.

Association: Yang. Annulment is similar to rejection that has the energetic function of pushing something away from oneself.

Element: Fire

anointing To be consecrated or made pure or holy; to be initiated or conferred with authority. Anointing is done with water or oil, which both symbolize the primal water. In a dream, anointing may symbolize navigating a spiritual rite of passage.

Association: Yin

Element: Water

ant Diligence, industriousness, organization. Ants are a symbol of collective action or behavior in which individuality is lost. They are stockpilers and tireless laborers; hence they are associated with foresight and perseverance. They possess enormous strength, and are able to bear loads many times their size. Ants also are tiny, fragile, and seemingly insignificant.

See **insects.**

antlers A mark of supernatural power. Antlers also represent power over nature, and fertility. Other meanings of antlers are a trophy of the hunt; and a matter that is sharp and difficult to deal with.

Association: Yang

Element: Wood

anvil Earth; matter; the receptive, passive feminine force; a counterpart to the generative, active masculine force of the **hammer**. Anvils are tools for forging, not only objects, but in mythology, the cosmos. Thunder gods make lightning (creativity, inspiration, and illumination) with hammer and anvil. Another meaning of anvil is stability.

Association: Yin

Element: Metal/Earth

apple Fertility; love; immortality. Apples represent bounteous nature, the Mother Goddess. They are a token of love and desire. In mythology, apples are the fruit of the underworld (the unconscious in dreams). Golden apples, the food of gods, bestow immortality. The round shape of the apple symbolizes totality and wholeness. The red color is desire and ripeness.

Association: Yang

Element: Fire

See **fruits**.

apron A symbol of work. Although aprons may be associated with traditionally masculine work, such as carpentry, they usually are feminine symbols of the mother, motherhood, the home, hearth, and domestic work.

Apron strings generally have a negative symbolism of being tied to one's mother, the home, or domesticity.

Association: Yin

Element: Earth

aquamarine *See* **jewels**.

argument *See* **quarrel**.

armor Protection against others and the world. Armor protects one from harm, prevents others from getting close, and prevents others from seeing one's true self.

Association: Yang
Element: Metal

arrow Irrevocable penetration. The arrow is a masculine, phallic symbol and is associated with the rays of the sun. To be shot by an arrow in a dream is to be forcibly injected by truth, power, inspiration, and illumination (*see* **lightning**), and the fertilizing force of creativity.

The arrow also represents union. A heart pierced by an arrow has associations with love, and with the mystical conjunction of opposites in alchemy.

To be wounded by an arrow may be symbolic of a spiritual initiation (*see* **wound**).

Broken arrows represent broken vows or broken plans.

As weapons, arrows are associated with war, violence, aggression, and the hunt. They represent the element of air or metal.

Other meanings of arrows are movement toward a goal and sense of purpose.

Association: Yang
Element: Metal

art Creativity, beauty, inspiration. Art also represents the expression of the contents of the unconscious, or the release of creative potential.

Association: Yang
Element: Fire

artichoke Sexual feelings and sexuality. Artichokes are considered an aphrodisiac.

Association: Yin
Element: Earth

ash Solidity and stability; holding all things together.
  Association: Yin
  Element: Wood
  See **trees.**

ashes The raw material of spiritual rebirth, of life rising anew after setbacks or devastation. Triumph and victory over adversity.
  Association: Yin.
  Element: Earth. Ashes are the progeny of fire. According to the creation cycle of the five elements, fire generates earth. The ashes from the fire become the new fertile soil.
  See **fire.**

asp *See* **snake.**

asparagus A phallic symbol; sexuality.
  Association: Yang
  Element: Wood
  See **vegetables.**

automobile An archetypal dream symbol that usually represents the ego, the vehicle one uses in getting around the world and in traveling through psychic life. Automobile dreams are common, and may be a warning that something is amiss; lack of control, too much control, traveling too fast or too slow, going down a street the wrong way, taking a dead-end street, needing repairs, having an accident.

A dented, dilapidated automobile might indicate low self-esteem. A big, impressive car that barrels over or through obstacles may indicate that one is running roughshod over others. The presence of a backseat driver, or sitting in the backseat and allowing someone else to drive, may indicate a forfeiture of control over one's life to another person.

An automobile that goes nowhere with its wheels spinning indicates a feeling of powerlessness over circumstances in one's life, or of being stuck in place.

Dreams of automobiles being out of control are symbols of stress and anxiety. These occur during pregnancies (to both men and women), and reflect a feeling of being emotionally overwhelmed. They also occur during major life changes, such as marriage, separation, divorce, any kind of significant loss, and during serious illness, especially cancer.

The automobile also is a common dream metaphor for the body and body parts, and thus can convey information about physical health, as well as attitudes and lifestyles. Associations between automobile and body parts vary according to individual, but the most common ones are:

Body of car: Human body surface.
Brakes: Ability to control one's activities.
Engine or other concealed parts: Inner organs.
Fuel: Energy.
Association: Yang
Element: Metal

axe The liberating power of spiritual light. In mythology, the axe is a symbol of sky gods and is associated with thunder, rain, and lightning, which in turn symbolize fecundity, fertility, inspiration, and illumination. The double axe has particular magical and mystical import, representing the union of sky god and earth goddess, (i.e., opposites), resulting in wholeness.

As a weapon, the axe also represents war, aggression, and violence; separates and cleaves, symbolizing the alchemical process of separation.

Association: Yang
Element: Metal

baby A rebirth of the self; the emergence of something new into the consciousness. New possibilities. A stage of innocence and purity.

A baby wrapped in swaddling clothes may represent an emergence that is being restricted, confined, or tied up before it is allowed to develop.

Dreams of babies are common during pregnancy, among both men and women. Forgetting a baby reflects anxieties about becoming a parent or being able to handle the responsibilities. Violence or injury to a baby, or birth of a deformed baby, reflect fears concerning birth defects.

Babies also represent vulnerability, helplessness, and dependency.

Association: Babies and **children** epitomize rapid, new growth and thus are yang in nature. A sickly child with no energy might appear to be yin in nature, but more likely it should be seen as deficient in yang energy.

Element: Fire

backyard *See* **yard**.

bag A container of emotions, secrets, repressions, hopes, dreams, desires, and so on. Bags denote secrecy regardless of their contents. Releasing the contents may have serious consequences.

Packing a bag might symbolize putting one's self or one's emotional life in order. Putting something away in a bag may symbolize a reluctance to face up to a problem or situation.

A bag also might represent a womb.

Association: Yin

Element: Water, for a bag's function is to hold and consolidate. However, other elements in a dream may weight associations to another element. For example, a small lunch bag may be associated with earth because it is a container for food. A plain, unidentified, empty paper bag is more likely a Wood Element image because paper products come from **trees**. A plastic bag may be more associated with water, because plastic is a petroleum-based product. Sometimes it is helpful to look at the overall function of a bag. If it holds a variety of articles, its function is to consolidate things into one space for protection or for ease of transport. Consolidation is an energetic function of the Water Element.

See **box**; **packing**.

ball Wholeness, completeness. A symbol of the fertile, nurturing Mother Earth.

A ball also represents associations with childhood; something that is not being resolved or decided, the equivalent of a ball being tossed around; relaxation; and a game.

Association: Yin
Element: Earth

baptism An initiation or death and rebirth, especially of a spiritual nature. Baptisms also may represent becoming aware of one's own "dirt" and removal of projections of the shadow.

Baptisms take place in different elements:

Baptism by water represents an immersion in the unconscious and emotions. This is a cleansing and dissolving process. In myth, baptism by water is the creation of a new personality on a higher plane. In alchemy, it is the solution, a rejuvenation of spirit, energy, and viewpoint that transcends the ego. Bath, shower, swimming, sprinkling, and any immersion in water are common dream symbols for baptism.

Baptism by wind represents a blowing away of chaff; air represents the involvement of the intellect.

Baptism by **fire** represents a purging or burning away of what is no longer needed.

Baptism by **blood** is comparable to baptism by fire, since both blood and fire are symbols of intense purging. Blood has the additional dimension of redemption, as seen in Christ's sacrifice of his own blood in order to redeem humanity. Psychologically, baptisms by either fire or blood refer to the ordeal of enduring intense affect that taxes the ego. Successfully enduring this ordeal results in a refinement. (*See* **ashes**.)

Association: Yang.

Element: See above for various types of baptisms.

barley As a grain, barley denotes fertility and the cycle of birth, death, and rebirth.

Association: Yin

Element: Earth

basement *See* **house**.

basket A symbol of the Mother Goddess and the womb, and thus of fertility, abundance, fruitfulness, and everlasting life through birth, death, and resurrection. In a dream, a basket might symbolize the plenty of home and hearth, or might symbolize a spiritual rebirth.

Association: Yin

Element: Earth

bat In Chinese lore, good luck and happiness. The word for bat is *fú* and is phonetically the same as the word *fú,* which means good fortune. Famous Chinese drawings show five bats in a circle representing the Five Blessings: a long life, riches, health, love of virtue, and a natural death.

Western lore associates bats with the opposite: an embodiment of one's fears or the unknown, or one's shadow. Bats are death omens, and in a dream might be a harbinger of the end of a cycle or period in life.

Association: Yin

Element: Water

bath A bath is a **baptism** which represents voluntary death and rebirth or renewal. It is a preliminary to initiation into a new level of consciousness. In the psychic cleansing process, the old is scrubbed away in order to make way for new ideas, a change of mind, or a change of heart.

A bath symbolically purifies both soul and body of contamination, and thus cleanses both for communication with the gods. To bathe in a dream may symbolize the beginning of a healing process.

A bath also may represent getting rid of unwanted emotional or mental "dirt," such as prejudices, resentments and anger, and unwanted relationships.

Association: Yin

Element: Water

battle Warring instincts and inner conflict. Dreams of battles, fights, and **wars** are common and reflect turmoil over decisions and choices. A battle with a single adversary may reflect being at odds with oneself, while a battle with a group of adversaries may reflect feelings of being overwhelmed by outside forces or people. To watch a battle rather than participate in it may indicate an unwillingness to accept responsibility for the matter in question.

Association: Yang

Element: Wood. Most battles that are fought are conflicts over beliefs or territories. Each side of the conflict represents the personal assertion of one's beliefs, or rights to territory. The battle may represent a conflict of an entire nation, but the collective consciousness and ideologies of the people emerge as one cause for battle. The energetic nature of wood is to be bold, confident, and assertive, as it pushes its new growth in the forest upward and outward, battling what it may to accomplish its task of free expression.

beans A symbol of the "vegetable soul," which connects humanity to its roots in the community, earth, and collective unconscious.

Beans are lowly food in the **vegetable** kingdom, and are often scorned.

However, beans have a widespread and ancient association with the underworld and souls of the dead, giving them an exalted status. Beans have been sacred food offered in rituals to feed and propitiate the dead. Beans also are believed to have magical properties and have been used in exorcism rites to banish unwanted ghosts and spirits from homes. These underworld associations link beans in dreams to the unconscious.

Other meanings of beans are fertility; the phallus; erotic pleasure; and wild, unpredictable humor.

Association: Yang

Element: Earth/Water. Beans in general are more Earth Element associations; however, black beans and kidney beans have a strong Water Element inference. When two elements are combined in a dream image, it is helpful to look at the image from dual meanings. For example, if a kidney bean or black bean is in the dream, the dreamer might look at the watery aspect of its earth energy. In nature, the "watery aspects of earth" are the underground aquifers. In the body, this may represent the water passages, or the overall water balances within. If the bean is dry and cracked, this could imply that water is not nourishing the earth. If the bean is soggy and pasty, then this may be an image of earth retaining too much water, such as in the case of edema or swellings.

bear Resurrection, rebirth; initiation into a life passage. Because of its seasonal hibernation and awakenings every spring, the bear symbolizes the cycle of birth, death, and rebirth.

In alchemy, the bear has similar meaning; the darkness that occurs before spiritual rebirth or a new phase in life.

The bear also is a figure in some hero myths, representing the solar, masculine principle.

Other meanings of bears are raw power, primitive instinct, ferocity, and fierce protectiveness.

Association: Yang
Element: Wood
See **animals**.

beard Masculine strength, virility, wisdom, dignity, and authority. A long beard represents the wisdom of the ages. A white beard represents spirituality or saintliness. A bearded man in a dream may symbolize the onset of a healing process.

Beards can also represent a disguise or a cover-up.

Association: Yang

Element: Water. In Chinese medicine, **hair** in general is associated with the kidney. This Water Element organ is also responsible for nourishing the brain. We associate the brain with knowledge, wisdom, imagination, and being the possessor of truths and mysteries. A bearded man in a dream could indicate healthy brain/kidney function, but could also indicate a need to take necessary actions to embrace certain philosophical truths in order to gain wisdom.

See **wise old man**.

beaver Industriousness, meticulous planning. Beavers are excellent engineers and build sound structures.

Association: Yin

Element: Metal

See **animals**.

bed/bedroom Sexual relations; sexual intimacy; marriage; the foundation of a relationship. The size of a bed, and whether it is made up, neat, or unkempt, offer clues to the state of affairs in a relationship. To replace a large bed with a smaller one may reflect an impending separation. To make a bed indicates the paying of attention to a relationship in order to improve it.

Something under the bed represents secrets or issues pertaining to a relationship that has yet to come out in the open.

A bed or the bedroom also can symbolize having to make do with situations one has created in life; accepting the consequences of one's actions.

Association: Yang if the dream image concerns the top of the bed; yin if the image is more about things beneath the bed.

Element: Water. The bed is where one sleeps. When we think of sleep, we think of the night and darkness. Darkness is a Water Element association.

bee Industriousness, organization, cleanliness, and purity. Like the **ant,** the bee is a collective symbol in which individuality is submerged in the group.

In mythology, the bee has divine associations because of its honey, which is the food of gods. Bees are symbols of the soul and the sun and are messengers to the heavens, like **birds.** They are associated with the gift of prophecy. Queen bees symbolize the Mother Goddess.

Bees also are associated with eloquence and poetry. Their hives are sometimes symbols of tombs and resurrection.

Other meanings of bees are having high energy; being too busy and overcommitted; flitting about from one thing to another; drudgery work.

Association: Yang
Element: Fire

beehive *See* **hive.**

bile Bitterness, rage, aggressive anger. Black bile represents depression.

Association: Yin
Element: Wood

birds The soul; higher states of consciousness; transcendence; the embodiment of immaterial things. Birds also symbolize freedom.

In mythology, birds are messengers from the gods, and the carriers of souls of the dead. Thus, dream birds might represent the opening up of the Higher Self or the attainment of enlightenment, or the process of going down into the underworld of the unconscious. Birds also are a widespread means of divination. Dream birds might point to important information overlooked by the dreamer.

In general, birds are solar symbols and thus represent the masculine principle. Large, high-flying birds are symbols of air and intellect. Forest birds have associations with the Tree of Life, the unconscious, and the "vegetable soul." (*See* **vegetables**.) Water birds have associations with the unconscious and the feminine principle. Black birds symbolize death, as in death of the old self. They also symbolize the fear of physical death that comes during serious or life-threatening illness.

Bird claws symbolize the destructive power of the Great Mother.

Association: Yang

Element: Birds are associated with the Metal Element; however, there may be other elemental qualities depending on the species. For example, hummingbirds are more Fire Element in nature, whereas pelicans, penguins, swans, or the mysterious ravens are more Water Element.

See individual bird listings; **egg**.

birth Emergence of a new self or a new aspect to one's life. Such a dream may involve giving birth, witnessing birth, assisting birth, or being born. A newborn who resembles someone known to the dreamer may point to a change in that relationship, or to the dreamer's acquisition of new characteristics observed in the other person. A **baby** born to one's family may represent changes in family relationships.

Anxiety dreams involving birthing also occur to both men and women during a woman's pregnancy. These dreams often involve the woman's birthing of kittens, puppies, or other furry animals, grotesque or monstrous human infants, or human infants that can immediately walk and talk. Anxiety birthing dreams usually reflect fears about the outcome of pregnancy, an individual's ability to cope with the subsequent life change, or the impact of a child upon a relationship.

Association: Yang
Element: Water
See **bubble; cave.**

black *See* **colors.**

black birds *See* **birds; colors.**

blindness/blindfolds/blinders Ignorance; failure to see the obvious, or the right path; narrow viewpoint or focus.

Other meanings are deception; being led astray, and seeing something forbidden.

Association: Yin
Element: Water

blood The emotions, the soul, the vital life-force. Blood is one's essence and is connected to matters of the heart. It represents one's ideals.

Blood also is a symbol of supreme sacrifice. Blood is sacred in all cultures.

To give blood means to engage one's emotions, to give of one's self from the deep core of one's being. To lose blood is to bleed emotionally. To receive blood is to receive emotional support that is vital to one's psychic existence. To make a blood oath is to pledge an unbreakable pact or forge an unbreakable bond. Bloody **violence** in a dream reflects emotional upheaval, or a feeling of being out of control or overwhelmed.

Menstrual blood is a symbol of wisdom, spiritual initiation, and fertility.

Blood figures in **baptisms** (spiritual rebirths) and often has the same symbolism as **fire**.

Association: Yin

Element: Water

See **wine**.

blue *See* **colors**.

boat *See* **ship**.

bog A soggy wasteland that threatens to suck one down into the ooze of the unconscious. Bogs are treacherous territory, their boundaries uncharted, their depths waiting for a misstep. Yet bogs may be likened to an alchemical cauldron of the **vegetable** soul: the putrefaction that precedes the rebirth.

Association: Yin

Element: Water/Earth. An image of a bog or a swamp in a dream indicates a disharmony between the earth element and the water element. By nature, the earth wants to distribute and absorb water; however, the nature of water is to want to store up and accumulate. When these two elements are in conflict with one another, we get "soggy earth." In Chinese Medicine, certain medical conditions are referred to as soggy earth. Examples are Earth Element organs (the spleen and stomach) in conflict with Water Element organs (kidney and bladder). The natural functions of absorption and distribution of water become compromised, and symptoms such as edema, swelling joints, and watery accumulations, such as cysts, can occur. Moisture is trapped and the body can produce spongy soggy flesh and muscles. This is sometimes referred to as a condition of "internal dampness." Dreams of bogs or swamps may alert the dreamer of these organ imbalances.

body/body parts The body and its parts are metaphors for life and expression of human activity. They also represent bodily needs and functions, and may be literal symbols of problems and pathology related to specific parts of the body.

See individual listings for body parts.

bones Structure, especially of an internal and unseen nature. Notice whether the bones are strong or brittle, which may provide clues to inner strength. **Animal** bones may relate to instinct, especially the type associated with a specific animal.

Association: Yin

Element: Water

book A source of wisdom and information. Books are a fundamental source of education by which we learn to make our way in the world. They expand our consciousness and give advice. In a dream, a book may represent something we need to learn, especially about our shadow side. It also can be a "book of life," a retrospective of one's life to date; stories about ourselves and others; a look at paths that were not taken; or perhaps even a look at a possible future.

The condition of a book adds additional shades of meaning in a dream. A tattered, worn, or damaged book may represent something that is undesirable or obsolete, or something in one's life that has passed (or is in the process of passing) from the scene. A new book may have associations with beginnings. Books in excellent condition or in luxurious bindings have positive associations.

Hidden books may represent wisdom we are searching for and have yet to find. Or they may symbolize secrets about ourselves and others. Locations where books are hidden, or where one searches for hidden books, can yield additional insight into the meaning of books in a dream.

Shutting a book and putting it away can signify the closing of a chapter or period in one's life. It also can indicate one's refusal or reluctance to acknowledge something, or even one's fear of learning something about one's self.

Association: Yin. Books are associated with reading and with the storage of information. Reading is a passive activity, one in which the reader sees the printed words and absorbs information.

Element: Water. The nature of the water element is to consolidate, retain, and store. Books by nature consolidate information and act as storage houses. Chinese medicine holds that too much reading will weaken the liver. The Water Element organ, the kidney, which is the mother of the liver, stores and consolidates so much that there is not any nourishment engendered to her son, the liver. If there are images of an overabundance of books in a dream, or an image where the dreamer is overcome by too much to read, this could be a signal that the dreamer's kidney energy is not nurturing the liver. When water does not nourish the wood, the wood becomes dry and brittle. In the body, this can be seen as dry, fibrous muscles and tendons with propensity to having stiff, aching joints and flares of tendonitis. From a mental/emotional level, this could be an indication that the dreamer needs to relinquish old thoughts and stored mental data so that new ideas and new growth can happen.

box Like a **bag,** a box symbolizes containment of the psyche, especially its secrets and repressions. Opening a box can release repressed contents of the unconscious.

Boxes also protect truths.

Boxes are means of organizing one's life and one's emotional life. Packing boxes can represent putting one's life in order.

Another meaning of a box is the womb.

Association: Yin

Element: Water

break-in The forcible entry of someone or something, such as into a home, indicates the intrusion of new or strange elements or circumstances into one's life. Break-ins are often beyond one's control. Fear in the dream may indicate fear of what is taking place in waking life.

Association: Yang

Element: Wood. The gentle nature of wood is to assertively pioneer new territory for its new growth. If the image of a dream is an intrusion of some sort, this implies that the Wood Element may be in excess. By nature, wood knows no bounds and is undisciplined. It is reliant upon the Metal Element to keep it tempered so its overgrowth doesn't intrude. An image of intrusions or break-ins in a dream could be alerting the dreamer that his Metal Element is weak and unable to contain wood. In the body, the liver and gall bladder are the Wood Element organs. When they lose their Metal Element qualities of decisiveness, discipline, and boundary identification, they can become overbearing and energetically intrude on the space of other organ functions. Some symptoms that can reflect these imbalances are: asthma, allergies, and gastrointestinal reflux.

See **robbery.**

bride The lost soul seeking wholeness. On a mundane level, brides may appear in prenuptial anxiety dreams.

Association: Yin

Element: Metal. Brides are often dressed in white, and therefore are by **color** associated with metal. Also, a bride's actions during a wedding ceremony are methodical and ritualistic, which are characteristics of the Metal Element.

bridge Transition from one state to another, such as a state of emotions or consciousness, or a stage of life. Major life changes, such as marriage, divorce, birth of children, death, financial loss, career changes, spiritual growth, and so forth, can be represented in dreams by bridges.

Bridges that disappear into water may symbolize emotions that threaten a transition. A bridge that disappears into the distance may represent uncertainty or fear about the outcome of a transition. High bridges can represent being far removed from transition, or a dangerous transition. Consider the type, construction, and condition of a bridge in a dream. A shaky or poorly made bridge can represent anxieties or fears about changes. Also examine the terrain beneath the bridge: calm water, turbulent or rushing water (emotional states); chasms into the earth (introspection, subconscious); cities (organization in outer life); abysses into nothingness (fears); and so on.

A dream bridge also may represent the inability or unwillingness to plunge into the depths of the unconscious or the unknown.

Association: Yin

Element: Earth. In the body, the Earth Element organs, the spleen and stomach, work to transform Qi and **blood** into the myriad of body cells, hormones, and other nutrients and chemicals. Transformation and transitioning are the main functions of these organs. An image of a bridge in the dream might point to the need to nurture the Earth Element by following healthy dietary guidelines. A rickety or collapsed bridge may be signaling the dreamer that his or her Earth Element organs are having certain problems that should be addressed. On a mental/emotional level, an image of a strong sturdy bridge with no other problems or conflicts may be indicating that the dreamer is very nurturing and supportive toward others. A bridge that is too long, fading into the horizon without seeing the other side, may be an indicator that the dreamer is becoming overprotective and meddlesome, whereas if there is a shaky or collapsed bridge, this may be notifying the dreamer that he or she is too attached, clingy, or wishy-washy.

brown *See* **colors.**

bubble Emerging from a bubble, especially an underwater bubble, is a symbol of **birth.** When such a dream applies to a pregnancy, it usually indicates unresolved anxieties. In a nonpregnancy situation, emergence from a bubble signifies the birth of a new self from the waters of the unconscious.

Bubbles also represent hopes and dreams, and vulnerabilities.

Association: Yang

Element: Water/Metal. A bubble is a fascination. It is light, airy, and, like a moment in time, is short lived. A bubble represents that brief moment when we can witness the perfect balance of yin and yang. On this earth planet, there is always a relative imbalance in all things. The times when we see perfect harmony is always short lived. When we say a person's "bubble has burst," we are speaking about the fragility of emotions. When a person's metal is strong, he or she is able to accept whatever slings and arrows life brings. When the metal is weak, the person becomes very fragile. A bubble in a dream that bursts could signify that the dreamer has weaknesses in the Metal Element organs and functions (lung and large intestine). On a mental/emotional level, the bubble could be a clue that the person needs to be more discerning and scrupulous. If the bubble is sturdy and does not burst, then the opposite is most likely the dream message.

bugs *See* **insects.**

building The self. Different floors may represent different levels of awareness.

Association: If small and more horizontal in shape, this is more yin, but if vertical and tall like a skyscraper, this would be more yang.

Element: Earth

See **house.**

burglary *See* **break-in; robbery; valuables.**

bus A means of transportation and getting to one's destination by a collective, safe, and preplanned route. Buses serve the needs of society. Their routes and schedules are decided by authority figures who determine how the greatest needs will be served. Thus, a bus does not provide the most direct and fastest means to a destination. Riding as a passenger on a bus may indicate that you have chosen a relatively safe, impersonal, or unthreatening path or course of action and have surrendered a certain amount of control to collectivity. It is the opposite of forging your own path through wilderness, for example, and much less direct than driving your own car through traffic.

Association: Yin if the dreamer is a passenger on the bus; yang if the dreamer is a driver.

Element: Metal

See **automobile**. Compare to **airplane; ship; train.**

butterfly Metamorphosis, transformation, especially into something more beautiful. A butterfly also is a symbol of the soul.

Association: Yang

Element: Metal

See **insects.**

buttons Fasteners that hold one's **clothing** (social presentation or facade) together. Tight buttons might represent a social face held tightly together, perhaps out of fear of becoming undone; they might also represent constriction. Loose buttons or missing buttons, or the losing of buttons, might represent a social face in the process of change, one that is becoming undone.

Association: Yin

Element: Water. The nature of water molecules is to bond together. In the body, water forms bonds and draws substances together. Loose or missing buttons might represent the weakness of the Water Element organs (kidney and bladder), whereas tight buttons, or buttons than cannot come apart, might represent excesses in these organs. From a mental/emotional level, a loose button could be associated with being paranoid, pessimistic, or phobic, whereas buttons that are too tight are more associated with a person who is too demanding or too preoccupied with others in social settings.

cabbage Boredom, inactivity, dullness, a state of vegetating. In folklore, the cabbage is one of the lowliest of **vegetables**. In earlier times, its consumption was blamed for depression and dark moods. In modern times, the term "cabbage" is often used to describe a dullard.

Cabbages also symbolize the "vegetable soul," the deep unconscious that connects humanity to its earthy roots.

Other meanings of cabbages are earthiness; a connection to one's roots, home and community; solidity and orderliness (cabbages are planted in neat rows); and an amiable fool.

In Chinese Medicine, the cabbage has a sweet flavor and a slightly cool or neutral quality. It regulates the spleen and stomach and helps to alleviate stomach spasm.

Association: Yin

Element: Earth/Metal. Cabbages that are sweet are associated with the Earth Element. If they are spicy, they are associated with the Metal Element.

cafeteria A collective, public place, institutional, where adequate but uninspired food (spiritual and emotional nourishment) is served. Food is in abundant quantities in cafeterias. Thus, someone who is in need of emotional or spiritual nourishment might dream of selecting from and eating enormous quantities of food in a cafeteria. As an institution, a cafeteria is depersonalized.

cake A common food in rituals, such as sacrifices and offerings to the gods or spirits of the dead. The eating of cakes in a dream may relate to a spiritual initiation or passage.

Association: Yang. Cake is sweet and warm. If it is mildly sweet it is yin/yang balanced. If it is too sweet it will tax digestive functions, and therefore drain yin energy.

Element: Earth

cancer Most dreams of cancer do not concern a real illness, but rather symbolize anxieties over a debilitating, consuming problem or a situation that leaves one feeling ravaged.

Association: Yin. The development of cancer is related to a deficient yin condition in the body. The body's attempt to replenish yin is to create more cells.

Element: Fire. Things related to tangible physical substances, like cells, are yin in nature and might naturally be related to a Water Element. But cancer cells are often rapidly developing and are an abnormal growth out of control. This gives cancer an association with the Fire Element.

candle Spiritual light; faith; the human soul. Candles have been used in rituals since about 3000 B.C. to repel evil spirits. Symbolically, candles push away the darkness of spirit with their own spiritual light.

Candles also symbolize the human soul and the fragility of physical life. In folklore, naturally occurring phosphoresences, sometimes called "corpse candles," are held to be the wandering ghosts of the dead, or harbingers of death. Candles burned at funerals and wakes protect the dead from evil spirits and help light the way of the soul to the afterworld.

In dreams candles are likely to represent light in a spiritual darkness or time of uncertainty. A candle being lit may represent the birth of something new, while a candle being extinguished may represent the passing of something old.

Association: Yang
Element: Fire

cannibalism Consuming the flesh of another person is to absorb their own life force or vital power. The dreamer should identify the attributes or characteristics of the victim that he or she wishes to possess or take into spirit. **Eating** is a symbolic form of taking spiritual nourishment.

cap *See* **hat.**

car *See* **automobile.**

carnelian *See* **jewels.**

carrot An incentive or payoff, especially of taking a risk. Carrots also symbolize novelty, ornamentation, and the surreal. Carrots also are symbols of the "vegetable soul."
Association: Yin
Element: Earth

castration A man's fear of sexual inadequacy; fear of being emasculated; fear of manhood with its attendant responsibilities; repression of deep emotions.

Fear of emasculation also may reflect a conflict between animus (the masculine) and anima (the feminine), with the latter struggling for greater recognition.

Castration also may relate to feelings of guilt, sin, or repulsiveness concerning sex.

Other meanings of castration are fear of impotence in old age, loss of vital energy, and competition with a woman in some arena of life.
Association: Yang
Element: Metal

cat An archetypal image of the feminine principle and the anima, especially aspects of mystery, independence, stealth, and power. Cats are symbols of the Mother Goddess, and represent in particular her chthonic and lunar aspects. Cats also are a symbol of sex, sexuality, and sensuality. Black cats represent bad luck, bad omens, and death (symbolic).

Association: Yin. Throughout history cats have been representatives of the feminine principle. The words "feline" and "feminine" have similar roots from the Latin *felinus* and *femina*. Cats are introspective and are antisocial compared to their domesticated counterparts, **dogs**. Like other creatures who inhabit the night, they are mysterious. All these qualities make them more yin in nature.

Before assigning a dream cat to yin, see what aspect of the animal is predominant. You may need to further explore and ask what is the strong message about the cat. For example, is a dominant image one of the cat's personality being fickle and aloof? These are normal characteristics of cats, but fickleness and aloofness are yang. Does the cat jump high into a tree? This, too, would be more yang.

Element: Before deciding on an element for a cat in your dream, consider first the natural habitat of the animal. For example, a mountain lion who inhabits the regions of the west would be a metal association. Panthers and leopards who inhabit the dense jungles would be more wood, and lions, who come from regions in the hot southern hemisphere would be more Fire Element.

See **animals**.

cave A womb; the unconscious; introspection or the need for introspection. In mythology, caves are a symbol of the Great Mother's womb that brings forth all life; in dreams, this includes the self. Emerging from a cave represents birthing of a new self. Retreating into a cave represents going down into the unconscious, where one connects with earthy emotions and instincts. Living in a cave represents an incubation of a new self.

Caves also occur in pregnancy dreams, and symbolize the pregnancy and birthing.

Association: Yin
Element: Earth

cedar Immortality; strength; durability; the sublime.

Association: Yin
Element: Wood
See **trees**.

celebrities *See* **famous people**.

ceremonial disasters *See* **disasters, ceremonial**.

ceremony *See* **initiation**.

chains Chains can have either positive or negative associations. Negative associations include bondage, slavery, and imprisonment to places, people, jobs, situations, beliefs, dreams, addictions, and so on. Positive associations are anchoring, binding, and communication.

On the material plane, chains generally are a symbol of **marriage**, blood relatives, and comrades-in-arms. On the spiritual plane, chains symbolize the marriage of heaven and earth. They are a form of the spiral, a lunar symbol of the Mother Goddess and of the eternal cycle of renewal.

Another meaning of chains is a succession of events that are linked together in some fashion.

Association: Yin
Element: Metal

chair Support and provision of rest. Chairs also are one's seat or place in the world, an everyday version of a throne. As such, they represent power and authority. A chair being held for you by someone else represents entrusting your power to another.

Sitting on a chair can represent the act of repressing something.

Association: Yin

Element: Wood if wooden; Metal if metal chair.

chanting Chanting utilizes the mystical power of sound to bring body and spirit into attunement. Chanting a word or phrase may be a means of calling one's attention to a matter that needs addressing (reattunement). Chanting by protestors is a way of calling attention to a problem.

Association: Yang

Element: Earth. Chanting involves bringing sound out of the body, which is yin.

chemistry Transformation, especially of an alchemical nature. Participating in versus watching chemistry experiments or procedures indicates the degree of self-responsibility one has assumed in the matter to which the dream relates.

Notice characteristics such as whether the procedure/experiment is risky or safe; whether the chemist knows what he or she is doing; what the purpose is; and what the processes are. Combining solid ingredients into a bowl symbolizes an earthy grounding, or matters pertaining to the mundane or the physical. Combining liquids, or dissolving solids into liquid, brings in the elements of emotions and the unconscious. Vaporizing or burning by fire symbolizes an intense purification process.

Association: Yang

Element: Metal

cherries The feminine principle and female sexuality; fertility. Cherries also are the sweetness of character that comes from good works. Cherries also are a forbidden fruit signifying lust and desire.

Association: Yin
Element: Fire
See **fruits**.

child/children Innocence; naivete; purity; simplicity. Children often represent one's inner child in a dream, and can bear both positive and negative meanings.

Positive meanings include unrealized potential, the process or need for growth, the acquisition and development of skills, the fruits of relationships and of the future. Other positive meanings are the ability to experience awe, wonder, and curiosity; to freely express emotion; to trust; to explore; and to fantasize.

Negative meanings include immaturity, infantilism, and self-centeredness.

The inner child may have emotional or psychological wounds, which can manifest in dreams as physical injuries, personality traits, or activities. To dream of wounded children, especially of saving them, symbolizes a need to heal one's own emotional or physical wounds. This symbol also relates to feeling a loss of one's cultural roots and occurs in dreams of women who are going through menopause.

To dream of your own children may not concern them literally, but may symbolize a part of the self. Children symbolize events in the past or in the dreamer's own childhood. The age of a child should be considered. For example, a three-year-old child may represent something that took place in the dreamer's life three years earlier, or else at age three. Childhood memories often are repressed, and children in a dream may relate to repressed and traumatic memories.

Parents who have suffered the death of a child often dream of finding lost children, or reviving a dead, dying, or fragile child. These dreams usually occur immediately following the death and continue until the loss is accepted.

Association: Yang

Element: Fire
See **baby**.

childbearing One's literal fertility; also, creativity. Being able or not able to have children in a dream also occurs to women who are going through menopause, and reflects unresolved emotions or anxieties about this life change. For women, childbearing may relate directly to self-esteem and self-worth.
Association: Yin
Element: Earth
See **birth**.

chimney Access to the spirit world, or heaven; a means of communicating with the spirit world. Coming down a chimney represents the gifts bestowed by heaven on earth, i.e., the spiritual descending to manifest on the physical plane. Going up a chimney represents escape to heaven. In dreams, chimneys may symbolize the manifestation or germination (depending on direction of movement down or up) of new ideas.
Association: Yang
Element: Fire

church The established order for morals and ethics. Churches in dreams also carry potent personal associations. For example, a church might represent safety; boredom; protection from evil; hypocrisy; truth; salvation.
Association: Yin
Element: Fire. All things that pertain to the spirit or soul of an individual are relative to the Fire Element.

circle A universal archetypal symbol of wholeness, completion, totality, and perfection. The circle is the unmanifest; God without beginning or end, timeless and eternal. It is the symbol of the Mother Goddess and the never-ending cycle of birth, death, and rebirth. It is the radiant spiritual illumination of the sun rolling through the heavens. It is the feminine psyche, the encircling waters of the unconscious.

Circles form mandalas, symbols of wholeness. A circle with a dot in the center represents cyclic perfection. A circle within a square is an alchemical symbol of the integration of heaven and earth, masculine and feminine, spirit and matter. Circles also have a magical potency and are universal protection against evil.

Objects shaped like circles, such as balls or wheels, or containing circles, should be examined in terms of circle symbolisms.

Association: Yin

Element: Earth

circling To go round and round in a **circle** in a dream, whether on foot or in a vehicle, indicates feelings of being stalled. A secondary meaning relates to protection and security. To draw a circle is to define limits and boundaries.

city A collective place that depends upon the collective observance of certain rules, laws, and behavior standards in order to function. Generally, cities are symbols of the masculine/active principle, since their skylines bristle with thrusting buildings and the best technology (a product of intellect). Cities also have their feminine/passive aspect as repositories of a society's greatest cultural expressions, in their museums, performing arts, and artists.

The meaning of a city in a dream depends a great deal upon one's own personal associations with "city." Is a city a desirable place to be, or an undesirable place? And why?

Cities have both positive and negative associations. Positive associations include enterprise, challenge, activity, vitality, opportunity, creativity, fun, accomplishment. Negative associations are over-crowding, stress, confusion, oppression, conformity, authoritarian-ism, crime, inner decay.

Association: Yin if the dreamer relates a city to negative charac-teristics; yang if the city is related to positive characteristics.

Element: If the image of the city is of an urban landscape of tall skyscrapers and precision geographic designs, apply a Metal Element association. If the image portrayed is more of a suburban sprawl, ap-ply an Earth Element association. If the image is of an inner city with a lot of infrastructure breakdown, use Water. If the image is of a new city in its developmental phases, use Wood.

cloak A garment that disguises, hides secrets, hides one's true nature, or renders one invisible.

See **clothing**.

clock Deadlines; running out of time; an acute awareness of the passing of time. Clock dreams often occur when one is faced with se-rious or life-threatening illness, or is close to someone who is in such a situation. Trying to stop a clock, or a clock breaking, can represent a fear of death. Clocks gone out of control symbolize unresolved fears and anxieties.

Another meaning of a clock is a woman's biological clock, that is, her time remaining to conceive and bear children.

Association: Yin if the time on the clock is after noon and before dawn. Yang if the time is from sunrise to noon.

Element: Metal

closet Something being hidden away or hidden from view, such as talents, potentials, or problems. Closets can be orderly storerooms or places where everything one wishes to ignore are kept. Questions to consider about dream closets are: Is the closet secret or locked?

Where is it? What are the contents? Is there fear or anticipation associated with opening the closet? If the closet is opened, do things spill out in disarray? Are there frightening things inside that surprise the dreamer?

Association: Yin

Element: Water

See box; house.

clothing One's social presentation or facade; the appearance or impression a person wishes to make upon the world. Clothes hide shortcomings, flaws, and faults, or they advertise assets. They also represent professions. Clothes can make us appear to be something other than what we are.

The type and condition of garments in a dream may make a statement about one's self-image. A change of clothing indicates a change of direction, a new phase of life, or a reckoning with one's self. Shining clothing, such as the raiment of angels, indicates a conquering of the material. Clothing soiled with excrement indicates a raw creative power from which the alchemical gold or the sun of spiritual illumination emerges.

Association: In general clothes would be a yang association because they are similar to the outer layer of skin on one's body. Their chief function is to provide protection from the elements. In relation to the body, yang energy is the primary protector. In Chinese Medicine the outer layer of yang Qi that protects the body from pathogenic invaders is called the *Wei Qi.*

Element: The elements associated with clothing would be varied, depending on the color, texture, etc. For example, brown leather clothing might be more indicative of the Earth Element, whereas a bright red cloak would be more indicative of the Fire Element.

See costume; excrement; rags.

clouds Confusion, a state of unhappiness, or something being obscured from understanding. In alchemical terms, clouds represent the *nigredo*—especially if they are black—which is the psychological darkening prior to an emergence of a new consciousness.

Clouds also symbolize the unknown, unknowable, and bewildering aspect of the Godhead, the light of which cannot be comprehended unless one is first stripped of every idea and intellectual conception.

Clouds have a positive association when they convey lightness of being, buoyancy and happiness, or being above the anxieties and concerns of the lower, mundane world.

Association: Yin. Although clouds are up in the sky (yang), they are yin manifestations. They are the substantive aspects within the nonsubstantive air. Clouds are somewhat opaque and turbid, and depending on their thickness can block the sun.

Element: Water

club Weapon generally used to beat someone or something into submission. Clubs may symbolize the use of unnecessary force or brutality in some matter in life.

Association: Yang
Element: Wood

cock As the herald of the dawn, the cock represents awakening to spiritual illumination (the **sun**). In ushering in the goodness of the sun, the cock banishes all evil spirits; hence the widespread folk belief that various supernatural creatures and spirits must return to their dwelling places by cock's crow.

The cock also represents vigilance (it does not fail each day to greet the dawn) and activity and renewal and resurrection (the dawn brings the world to new life).

The cock can be both a symbol of good luck and of bad luck,

depending on local lore. It is widely regarded to be a symbol of healing because of its importance in folk medicine.

Other meanings of the cock are fertility, and divining the future.

Association: Yang. In Chinese medicine, chickens are hot meats. Their yang nature will stimulate and produce more yang energy in the body—perhaps the reason why chicken soup is heralded for helping to stimulate the immune system.

Element: Fire

cockroach Furtiveness; hiding in order to survive. Cockroaches are associated with **food** (spiritual nourishment), especially its decay and rotting (an alchemical state of the dying away of the old in preparation for the new). They also are associated with dirt, as in one's psychological "dirt," that is, repressions or projections of the shadow.

Association: Yin
Element: Metal.
See **insects**.

cocoon A womb of spiritual rebirth. Cocoons also represent protected places where one feels secure. They may be associated with fears of leaving relationships, jobs, places, or situations.

Association: Yin
Element: Water

coffin Death of the old; a womb of spiritual rebirth or resurrection. Coffins also can represent an unawakened or "dead" state of consciousness.

Association: Yin
Element: Water

collar In a positive aspect, a collar is a symbol of authority, office, or status. In a negative aspect, a collar represents constraint, bondage, and slavery. A tight collar possibly symbolizes feelings of constraint, restriction, or suffocation in a relationship, job, or situation.

See **clothing**.

colors The most ancient and universal of symbols. Colors represent the forces of light and darkness, the opposites of masculine and feminine, and various attributes. Colors are vibrations of light and thus have an impact upon all levels of consciousness and upon the physical form.

The essential division between the forces of light and dark is expressed in white, the combination of all colors of the spectrum, and black, the absence of color. In Chinese philosophy, the white is yang (masculine) and the black is yin (feminine). In alchemy, the union of opposites is expressed by the colors red (the physical) and white (the spirit). The primary colors, red, yellow, and blue, express primary emotions and forces. Other colors, which are combinations of the primary colors, represent qualities and attributes through natural associations, such as green, the color of vegetation, which is associated with harmony and tranquility.

Specific color meanings are:

Black: The dark aspect of God, nature, or the self; the shadow. Black represents the repressed part of the self, the areas seeking expression and most in need of attention. This dark side can be represented in dreams by black people, people dressed in black, black animals or monsters, and destructive forces of nature, such as storms, tornadoes, hurricanes, and so on.

As the color of mourning, black also occurs in dreams involving unresolved emotions over loss from death, divorce, accident, or other upheaval. If one is suffering from life-threatening or terminal illness, black may symbolize one's fears about physical death. These fears also are expressed in dreams following the death of someone close, especially a parent, when one faces one's own mortality.

Black also represents passive forces, the feminine principle, the unconscious and processes in the unconscious, and the germination of light that occurs in darkness of an unenlightened state. It is the womb of the Great Mother, where all things are born; the descent into hell, or the unconscious; the caves and dark grottoes of the earth; and the inner planes. Black is the measurement of time.

In alchemy, black is the *nigredo,* the initial stage of the Great Work, and also the destructive aspect of the unconscious. The nigredo is the darkness that precedes spiritual light. It is the decay, destruction and death that sweeps away the old order/old self to make way for the new order/new self. Psychologically, the nigredo is depression and dissolution, or the self-reflection that is induced by conflict and depression. When the nigredo is at its worst, a birth of a new self occurs in the unconscious.

Black also is associated with the intrusion of reality, or the Saturnine grounding in the earth, during which one evaluates situations.

Blue: The color of spirit, the spiritual, the heavenly, the numinous, inspiration, devotion, religious feeling, godliness, contemplation and inspiration. Mountains, the abodes of the gods and the symbols of the spiritual ascent, often are shown as blue.

As the color of water and the sky, blue also has associations with the unconscious and the feminine characteristics.

In yoga, blue governs the throat chakra, and is associated with communication, creativity, self-expression, and the search for truth.

Other meanings of blue are enhanced productivity; a sense of well-being; and clear thinking.

According to the Chinese sages, black and blue together are both yin, cool colors and are associated with the Water Element.

Brown: The color of the earth and earthy qualities; renunciation of the material world; spiritual death and degradation. Brown also can be associated with material death, as when vegetation dies and turns brown. Brown is a yin color.

Gold: The sun, divine light, illumination, the highest state of glory; the masculine principle of the cosmos.

In alchemy, gold represents the attainment of the Philosopher's

Stone. It also symbolizes the celestial. Gold is a yang color and associated with the Metal Element.

Gray: Mourning; humility; neutrality; penitence; transformation from material to spiritual. Gray is a yin aspect of the Metal Element.

Green: Green is not a primary color, but is a bridge or transition from one primary color to another. It can be either hot or cool. Its significance in a dream depends upon the context.

In its beneficent aspect, green is the color of growth, hope, renewal, freshness, lushness, health, youth, vigor, harmony, and refreshment. It is the root metaphor of the natural world, and of the way the world is perceived; it holds the secret of all life. Green is the **blood** of the vegetable world (*see* **vegetables**), and thus is part of the fertilizing moisture that flows from the Great Goddess, the maternal consciousness of the cosmos. Green is the color of the soul, the World Soul, and the anima. Green also is a color of passion.

In color therapy, green refreshes and invigorates and is used as an antidote for fatigue and insomnia.

In its destructive aspect, green is the color of rot, mold, slime, overripeness, decay, and death. It is the color of all deities and supernatural beings associated with the underworld and the souls of the dead, and thus is sometimes the color of bad luck and premonitions of death. It is a symbol of suffocation and choking, as in an overgrowth of brush or a dense jungle, or of things neglected and gone wild and out of control, as in weeds taking over a garden. Green also is the color of envy, and of bitterness and unripeness.

Other meanings of green are naivete; innocence; and inexperience.

Green is a yin color and is related to the Wood Element.

See **evergreens**.

Indigo: Advanced spiritual qualities, or wisdom, psychic faculties, intuition. Indigo is more yang than yin, but is associated with the Water Element.

Orange: Pride and ambition, flames, egoism, cruelty, ferocity, luxury. As the color of fire, orange can represent the purifying power of flame, the burning away of impurities. Shades of orange can be seen in both the Fire Element and the Earth Element. Orange is actually a combination of red and yellow. If the shade contains more red, it would be more associated with fire and yang, but if the red is muted and there is more of a pumpkin color, it is associated with earth and yin.

Pink: The flesh, sensuality, emotions, the material. Pink also is associated with the heart center and love from the heart. It is a yin aspect of the Fire Element.

Purple: The color of the gods, royalty, imperial power, pomp, pride, justice, truth; also humility and penitence. Purple is a mixture of red and blue, which are identical yin/yang opposites that are in total balance with each other. Red is fire and blue water.

Red: Blood, life, the life-force, the body, wounds (initiation), and death (transformation). Red is also the color of animal life, and the animal nature in man. It is the color of lust, passion, materialism, and fertility.

In alchemy, red is the sulphuric stage in the creation of the Philosopher's Stone, and represents sublimation, suffering, and love.

Red is associated with fire. It is the color of activity, energy, courage, willpower, war, and ferocity, which are all yang in nature.

Silver: The color of the moon, which gives it associations with magic, Goddess, psychic nature, emotions, and intuition. Opposite gold, silver is the feminine aspect of duality of the cosmic reality. In alchemy, silver is Luna, "the affections purified."

Silver is a yin aspect of the Metal Element.

Violet: Sanctity, religious devotion, knowledge, sorrow, temperance, grief, old age, mourning. Violet also represents power, as well as nostalgia and memories.

Violet is yin and is related to both the Water and the Metal Elements.

White: Purity, holiness, sacredness, redemption, mystical illumination, timelessness, ecstasy, innocence, joy, light, and life. White is transcendent perfection, the brilliance of the Godhead.

White signifies marriage (the union of opposites to form a whole) and death (transformation and renewal).

In the alchemical process of the Philosopher's Stone, white marks the second stage, the beginning of the ascent up from darkness.

White is yang and is associated with the Metal Element.

Yellow: The sun, illumination, light, intellect, and generosity. Like orange, yellow is a color of fire, and thus has associations with the purifying power of flames. Yellow is a point of departure in spiritual ascension, as opposed to the arrival state expressed by gold. Although this color is definitely associated with fire, Chinese medical texts assign yellow to the earth. The earth itself contains a core of hot magma so it can be said to have the Fire Element within.

column Strength and support. Are the columns in the dream solid or cracked? What are they supporting? For example, are they supporting a bridge (transition), a house, or a building (the self)?

composer *See* **music**.

contamination Something or someone that is upsetting. Contamination dreams may also occur to individuals who are suffering life-threatening illness, especially cancer.

corn A totemic member of the vegetable kingdom that is closely bound to the mysteries of death and rebirth, the seasonal dying and reflowering of the earth. Corn is used in funerary rites, and symbolizes abundance in the underworld (the unconscious). It also symbolizes fertility, growth, and abundance in the physical world, and is associated with the sun.

Other meanings of corn are well-being and happiness.

Association: Yang

Element: Earth. Corn is considered a sweet vegetable according to Chinese nutritional medicine, and acts on the stomach and the large intestine.

See **vegetables**.

correspondence Communication with one's self. Correspondence delivers a message about a matter requiring the dreamer's attention, or provides information useful in making a decision.

costume Disguise or facade. Costumes can represent how a person wishes to be seen by others, or what a person really desires to be. Like **masks**, costumes can be liberating, enabling a release of inhibitions to act and behave in certain ways. Or they can be constructing, requiring certain behavior. Costumes also can represent that which a person fears to be.

Another meaning of costume is the inability to see one's self or others clearly or truthfully.

See **clothing**.

couch Healing, rest, and recuperation; a therapeutic process. In certain contexts, a couch may represent laziness or inactivity.

Association: Yin. Couches encourage passivity.

Element: Earth, unless a couch is made of wood or metal.

court A place where justice is meted out by authority figures, and where social order is kept. Courts also may symbolize cause and effect, or reaping what one sows. They may be portents of what might happen if one holds to, or takes, a certain course of action.

courtyard The feminine principle; a womblike enclosure; a place of tranquility and pleasure.

cow The maternal instinct, motherhood, fertility, nurturing, the giving and renewing of life. Cows are universal symbols of the Mother

Goddess, and have associations with the moon (the unconscious) because of their horns. Cows also represent the plenty of mother earth.

By nature, cows are passive and peaceful, and go along with the herd. Cows in dreams may be associated with these attributes.

Other meanings of cows are female sexual feelings, and domesticity.

Association: Yin

Element: Earth. According to the ancient Chinese, dreams of a cow may have many meanings, but often refer to females in a household. Because the cow is a source of power for tilling the land and for agricultural production, the cow can symbolize food and nutritive prosperity. Some texts say that if one sees a cow leading a man in a dream it means that every avenue pursued by the dreamer will meet with success. If a cow in the dream is killed, it can mean disruption of the family.

See **animals**.

coyote A trickster figure; craftiness and slyness. Coyotes are loners who fend for themselves in the wilderness, which in dreams symbolizes the unconscious.

Association: Yang

Element: Metal. This animal's natural habitat in the United States is in the western regions, and the west is associated with metal.

See **animals**.

crab Indirect, sideways movement or behavior; scuttling; unreliable or dishonest behavior. As denizens of water, crabs are associated with emotions and the unconscious. The hard shell of the crab represents one's armor against emotional vulnerability.

Other meanings of crabs are bad moods or irritable behavior, and a tendency to hold on to things, especially too long or in a manner that is painful to one's self or others.

Association: Yin

Element: Water

See **animals**.

cradle A new spiritual life or a beginning of a new phase in life. Rocking a cradle symbolizes nurturing the birth.

See **baby**.

crane In Chinese culture, the crane is one of the many symbols of longevity or immortality, as well as wisdom, and is seen in many motifs in art, clothing, and design. A dream of a flying crane is a symbol that the dreamer will become a high official. There are also some accounts in Chinese folklore where dreams of a crane flying toward you would bring a new birth in the family (most likely the origin of the legend of a stork bringing a child). Cranes on business cards or business signs in China today are used to help one's business have successful longevity.

Association: Yang

Element: Water

crevice An opening into the unconscious. A danger for the unwary.

crocodile Guardian of the gates to the underworld, which in dreams is the unconscious. In a dream, a crocodile may also symbolize the guardian of any kind of threshold, such as an emotional or psychological barrier. To be swallowed by a crocodile or a whale or any large creature of the deep, is to be taken into the underworld, or the unconscious. Dreams of such symbolism may relate to a spiritual initiation, or a need to be immersed in the unconscious.

As underworld creatures, crocodiles also represent the souls of the dead.

In myth, the crocodile swallows the moon and then sheds insincere tears. Thus, the crocodile can symbolize hypocrisy and insincerity.

Because the crocodile lives in both water and mud, it also is a symbol of fecundity (life-giving waters of the Mother Goddess) and vegetation (and thus the "vegetable soul" of humankind).

Other meanings of the crocodile are animal power and viciousness.

Association: Yin
Element: Water
See **animals**.

cross One of the oldest and most universal of sacred symbols. The cross symbolizes the interpenetration of earth and heaven (balance of the yin and the yang), matter and spirit, masculine and feminine; in terms of a dream, it can represent where the conscious meets the unconscious. The cross is a midpoint, the equilibrium, the harmonious center. It is humanity at its peak expression on both the mundane and spiritual planes. The cross also is a symbol of fire and the sun, both masculine principles representing spirit and intellect, respectively.

The four arms of the cross, especially an equilateral cross, represent the four elements, the cardinal points, and the four seasons. Thus, the cross has the magical potency of the number four, which represents foundation and stability (*see* **numbers**). The equilateral cross also forms a mandala, a symbol of wholeness and completeness. A cross within a circle is a mandala, and also has associations with the Mother Goddess (represented by the circle) and the ever-turning wheel of birth, death, and rebirth.

The cross also symbolizes suffering, sacrifice, and a burden to bear; victory over death and the triumph of the immortal soul; and blessings and protection from evil.

On a mundane level, a cross also may represent a **crossroads** where one must make choices.

Objects shaped like crosses, such as anchors, tees, forked trees, etc., should be considered as potential cross symbols in dreams.

Association: The balance of yin and yang.
Element: The type of cross in the dream would determine the element. For example, a wooden cross is associated with the Wood Element, and a metal cross is associated with the Metal Element.

crossroads Choices, especially in relation to momentous decisions or turning points in life. Spiritually, crossroads represent a conjunction of time and space, a place where various forces gather to manifest at once. Like the **cross**, they also are a union of opposites, and thus represent a completeness.

In folklore, crossroads are magical and somewhat dangerous places, because they are a doorway to the Otherworld, a place where the supernatural and the underworld (the unconscious) intrude into the manifest world. Witches, spirits, and the chthonic deities are particularly associated with crossroads.

crow A messenger between heaven and earth, an omen of death, and prophet of the hidden truth or the unconscious.

Like the **raven**, the crow in alchemy represents the *nigredo*, the initial blackening and putrefaction that initiate the process of the Great Work.

Because of its black color, the crow is often associated with evil.

Association: Yin
Element: Water
See **birds**.

crowd Collective action, opinion, beliefs. Pressure, stress, confusion, chaos, emotions running out of control. The individual is at risk in crowds, especially angry ones. One can become lost in a crowd, carried along or manipulated by a crowd, or trampled by a crowd.

Another meaning of a crowd is loss of individuality.

crown Authority; sovereignty; mastery over one's self and one's own "kingdom," that is, one's inner or outer life. Crowns also signify victory, honor, and righteousness. Their circular shape symbolizes the endless circle of time.

Wearing a crown can represent enlightenment, intuition, and highest thinking, all associated with the crown chakra.

Crowns often are associated with father figures.
Association: Yang
Element: Fire
See **father; hat; queen**.

crutches Support; something one leans upon. Crutches in dreams are substitutes for something that dysfunctions in life. They may represent too much reliance upon others, or dependencies upon substances such as alcohol, or upon material things or other values.

Because the foot is often a symbol of the soul, crutches also can symbolize moral "lameness."

crying According to Chinese culture, crying in a dream is a sign of happiness. Dream visions and experiences are what take place during sleep, which is the opposite of thoughts and aspirations that take place during waking states. Waking states and dream states are yin/yang opposites; thus, crying means its opposite, happiness. This way of thinking is part of Taoism, but is not exclusive throughout the entire culture and does not hold true in every dream situation.

In Chinese Medicine, crying is an action that is a physical response to the emotional experience of grieving. Crying is a natural evolution of metal energy's transformative processes. Crying allows the individual to release the dissolving energy of the lung, but when one cannot do this, the lung energy will experience consequences. If crying becomes excessive, this too will meet with similar physical consequences.

When one dreams of crying, it is necessary to see the crying within the context of the rest of the dream to determine its specific implication.
Association: Yin
Element: Metal/Water
See **tears**.

crystal *See* **jewels**.

cube The earth, the material world, the four elements, the foundation of the cosmos. Cubes represent wholeness, and also truth, because the view is the same from every angle. Cubes also symbolize solidity and firmness, and in allegories represent the persistence of the virtues. Chariots and thrones often are represented as cubes.

In alchemy, the cubes is the squaring of the circle, or completion and wholeness. It also represents salt, which in dreams is sometimes a symbol of bitterness.

cup The receptive, passive feminine vessel; the womb; the cosmic center; the heart; the source of all life. Cups symbolize plenty and immortality; they represent the mysteries of the Mother Goddess: birth, death, and rebirth. In mythology, sacred cups are never-ending sources of food, refreshment, and the magical elixir of life everlasting.

Cups are used in many rites of initiation. A cup in a dream may be associated with a spiritual initiation.

Association: Yin
Element: Water

cypress As an evergreen, the cypress symbolizes long life and immortality. Planted as a border around cemeteries, it protects corpses from corruption and banishes evil spirits. Ancients regarded the cypress as a symbol of death, because the tree does not rejuvenate itself if cut down.

Other meanings of the cypress are mourning, endurance, and perseverance of virtue, and the phallus.

See **trees**.

daisy Innocence; purity; freshness; the sun; intellectual light.
See **flowers**.

dancing Connection with, or need to connect with, one's emotions. Dancing represents freedom of movement, creative expression, gracefulness, and a carefree, uninhibited spirit. Dancing also is a form of ritual; ritual marks transitions and passages in life. Dancing in a dream might symbolize a release of creative energy or joy at making a transition from one phase to another.

darkness Death, destruction, dissolution; also chaos, and primordial chaos. Darkness is the *nigredo* stage of alchemy, in which the old is destroyed and dissolved in order to make way for the new. Being lost in the dark or suffering a "dark night of the soul" can be symbols of a psychic reordering prior to the emergence of a new self, or also of the passing of an old stage of life. Darkness is not inherently evil, but rather is the womb of spiritual rebirth; it precedes the light of spiritual illumination.

Darkness also represents the unconscious. Monsters in the dark may symbolize unexpressed or unresolved fears. Exploring darkness or fear of exploring darkness may relate to fears of the unknown, or some issue that has been avoided.

Another meaning of darkness is depression.
Association: Yin
Element: Water
See **light**.

dates Fertility.
Association: Yang
Element: Earth

dawn Emergence into the light of understanding, peace, harmony, a new cycle, or a spiritual state. Darkness, turmoil, and uncertainty are behind one.
Association: Yang
Element: Fire
See **twilight**.

dead people The appearance in a dream of a person who is dead is part of the grieving process. The appearance of the dead restored to youth and vigor, is to give comfort or assurances that they are all right, or to aid the acceptance of death and resolution of grief. Dreams in which the dead appear as angels—which may not occur until a year or more has passed from the time of death—indicate that the healing process is complete or near completion.

Repeated dreams about a dead person may indicate that something concerning one's relationship with or feelings about that person remains unresolved. This unfinished business must be brought into the consciousness.

Association: Yin
Element: Water

death Dreams involving death usually are not literal warnings of impending physical death, but represent the decay and destruction of a stage in life, an attachment, or a neurosis. Death is transformation from one state to another; it is necessary so that rebirth and renewal can take place.

Dreams about death—including mortal wounds and terminal illness—often occur at life passages (especially midlife), which bring stress and upheaval. The death in the dream may be of one's self or a person who is close, but ultimately the symbolism refers to the dreamer's psychological state.

Another meaning of death is angry, vengeful feelings toward others.

Association: Yin
Element: Water

decapitation A split between mind and body. Decapitation may occur in dreams related to midlife crises, menopause, or life-threatening illness, when one feels betrayed by the body or alienated from it.

Another meaning of decapitation is losing one's sense of reason or rationality; decay. A rotting away of a part of life or a part of one's inner self, either from neglect or as part of a transformation that involves the death of something old in order to make way for a spiritual rebirth. In alchemy, decay is the *nigredo*, the blackening phase in which the old is destroyed in order for the Philosopher's Stone (wholeness and enlightenment) to be created.

Association: Yin

Element: Water

deer Swiftness, grace, gentleness. Deer are supernatural beings in folklore and are the divine messengers of the fairies. Fairies live beneath the earth in mounds and burrows in a place where time stands still. Thus, deer in a dream may be messengers from the unconscious. In Chinese folklore, the deer is a symbol for longevity.

Association: Yin

Element: Wood

See **animals**.

defecation A bodily function that is not to be taken literally, but that symbolizes the production of something, typically, out of the center of one's being.

See **excrement**.

deluge *See* **flood**.

demon A source of torment or bedevilment. A representation of weaknesses, vices, and sins. Corrupting or evil influences or persons.

Association: Yin

Element: Fire. However, demons are not universally associated with fire. In Chinese culture, for example, there are demonic spirits associated with other elements. In cultures where Christianity is the main religious belief, demons are considered the devil's workers and therefore have a Fire Element association.

See **monster**.

dentist Dentists in dreams have close associations with the various symbolisms of **teeth**. Dentists repair teeth and improve the appearance and bite of teeth, and in a dream this function may relate to a specific need, such as for sharper teeth (aggression and assertiveness).

Dentists also symbolize personal associations. For many people, dentists represent pain, fear, and a feeling of helplessness. Dentists are authority figures, next to whom one often feels childlike.

desert A stark and harsh wilderness where spiritual transformation can take place. Many mystical traditions call for mystics to withdraw into the desert or mountains to meditate, contemplate, and seek enlightenment by overcoming the darkness within.

Other meanings of desert are lack of emotional, spiritual, or material comfort or nourishment; bleakness; dry emotions or feeling emotionally or spiritually empty.

Association: Yang
Element: Metal

dessert Reward; the treat that comes when we are finished with something, or have accomplished something.

detour A roundabout, indirect way to get to where one is going. Detours take one off the main road of life and postpone accomplishment or completion. Detours that meander and become mazelike may indicate confusion or a feeling of being lost. Perhaps one takes a detour in order to avoid a straight course.

Another meaning of detour is avoidance.

devouring Being devoured alive, either by an animal, a monster, or a shapeless thing, expresses fear.

diamond *See* **jewels**.

diary A place where secrets are kept.
See **book**.

dice Fate. Dice may reflect on one's sense of control over life, especially feelings of powerlessness ("What happens depends on the roll of the dice").

Association: Yang. Random numbers result from the throwing of dice. Energy that is random with no order is associated with yang energy, whereas order and structure are yin.

Element: The elemental association of dice depends on the material that they are made from. Early dice were made from ivory, which is a Metal Element association. Tusks of animals have been associated with strong yang power. For example, the horn of the rhinoceros was used to increase sexual performance and stamina. Black dice are associated with the Water Element; red dice are associated with the Fire Element, and so forth.

digestion The absorption into the psyche of spiritual nourishment (symbolized by food). Digestion is part of the "vegetable soul," our connection to earthy roots. It is the alchemical process of dissolution, the dissolution that is decay and death, from which comes rebirth.

dirt/dirtiness Lack of cleanliness, or impropriety. Dirt, dirtiness, and being dirty can relate to attitudes toward one's behavior, beliefs, or state of mind. Dirt dreams related to sex are not uncommon.

Being dirty also can occur in dreams related to physical illness: the afflicted part of the body may be unclean or dirty. On occasion, these dreams may be early warnings of a yet unmanifested condition.

Association: Yin
Element: Earth

disasters, ceremonial Dreams in which ceremonies, such as **weddings**, social affairs, or business presentations, go awry reflect anxieties about upcoming ceremonies in life. Such dreams involve virtually any mishap that can spoil an event, such as failure to have everything ready, forgetting crucial items, unexpected and terrible food, breakdowns of equipment, and so forth.

Ceremonial disaster dreams are particularly common before weddings, and symbolize natural worries that marriage is the right decision or that the ceremony will go smoothly as planned.

Use anxiety dreams to reexamine emotions and discuss them with others. Perhaps ceremonial disaster dreams reflect one's desire to have a more assertive role in planning.

disasters, natural A common motif of nightmares that expresses profound anxiety over one's ability to survive a major upheaval in life. Such nightmares occur during the inner turmoil of life passages, and also as a result of severe injury or illness, grief, divorce, or loss of job or self-esteem. Natural disasters might be floods, tidal waves, earthquakes, avalanches, fire, etc. Such nightmares can clarify what you need to work on and resolve.

See individual listings for disasters.

discipline Regimentation, order. Self-imposed discipline may symbolize a desire to accomplish, to get something done, or a compulsion. Collectively imposed discipline, such as the rules and laws of society, also represent order but can symbolize limitations, even punishment. Discipline imposed by an individual, an authority figure such as a parent, also can represent punishment.

discovery Dreams of discovery commonly mark the third stage of recovery from an upheaval in life, such as grief, divorce, injury, or loss of job. The third stage is characterized by hope and renewal, and the formation of a new identity that has fully adjusted to the changes.

These are symbolized by dreams of discovery of new rooms in a home or house, valuables or treasures, new clothing, new automobiles, new skills, new lands, etc.

disinfectant Desire to heal or cleanse something, such as the wounds of a bad experience; of emotions, attitudes, or fears; or of relationships or situations.

dismemberment Precursor to spiritual rebirth. Many mystical and spiritual traditions, especially shamanism, have rites of dismemberment that are part of initiation. The old self must be rent asunder and a new self created. In mythology, dismembered gods become the fertilizer for rebirth of crops and nature.

In dreams, dismemberment may in particular relate to a forcible and dramatic change in life.

Another meaning of dismemberment is sacrifice.

Association: Yang

Element: Metal

diving Plunging headlong into something, such as an experience or the unconscious. Diving from a high place, such as a cliff, mountain, or building, onto earth symbolizes a descent from intellect to matter, or things that concern the body or physical plane. Diving into water symbolizes total immersion in emotions or the waters of the unconscious.

Diving is a forcible and sudden descent, and one may have little or no control over the consequences. It may represent the means by which the unconscious forces one to face a situation. It may also be part of a healing process.

doctor An authority figure that often represents one's Higher Self, especially in terms of one's own ability to heal one's self. Doctors in dreams also are associated with a desire to be healed, either physically or psychologically. They are associated with the process of one's own healing.

dog Companion, guardian, and protector in the emotional/instinctual realm. Dogs have both positive and negative attributes. Positive attributes are loyalty, protection, companionship, unconditional love, courage, and sacrifice. Negative attributes are pack instinct, dirtiness, and viciousness.

Dogs act instinctively, and in dreams a dog may show the right way or the right decision despite what the conscious mind thinks. However, a pack of dogs in a dream may indicate actions out of control or blind obedience.

Though domesticated for thousands of years, dogs still retain their wild instincts to defend, hunt, and kill. These instincts are summoned when necessary for survival.

In myth, the dog is a guide to the underworld, or in terms of the dream, the unconscious. The dog, sometimes fabulous, attends chthonic deities and guards treasures and gates of the underworld. The dog also attends gods of magic, healing, dreams, and carriers of the soul to the afterlife. These associations connect the dog to death and rebirth, and to mantic and medicinal powers.

Dogs also represent an animal-like masculinity.

Association: Yang

Element: The element associated with dogs will be determined by the personality, color, and characteristic of the dog in the dream. Black vicious dogs are associated with the Water Element, whereas a yellow friendly golden retriever that is placid and loving to all is Earth Element.

doll Aspects of one's self or others can be projected onto dolls for belittlement or manipulation. Dolls may represent the shadow. The type of doll, its features and characteristics, and what one does with it in a dream, all have significance.

Other meanings of dolls are childhood memories or associations; and future growth.

Association: Yin

Element: Elemental associations for dolls depend on the type of doll in the dream image. A doll that mimics self, such as a ventriloquist's doll, holds the elemental association of the dreamer. A doll that is primitive in character and more folksy is related to earth. A voodoo doll or one that conjures a feeling of being from the dark side is a Water Element association. A baby doll with an angelic quality is Fire Element. Soldiers and action figure dolls are metal.

dolphin Godlike qualities, intelligence, and divine light. In myth, the dolphin is a psychopomp, guiding or carrying the souls of the dead to the afterworld. Thus, in a dream a dolphin may pertain to the unconscious.

Association: Yin

Element: Water

See **animals**.

donkey Stubbornness; stupidity.

Association: Yin

Element: Metal

See **animals**.

door Opportunities and choices; also barriers. Doors may relate to inner processes and growth as well as to external activities.

Being faced with many doors symbolizes being presented with many choices, perhaps confusing ones. Closed doors indicate areas not explored and which may need to be explored. Locked doors may relate to fears about opening into new areas in life. Revolving doors, especially if one is stuck in a revolving door or winds up where one starts, indicate being stuck in a pattern or not making a choice that will lead to a new direction. Glowing doors, golden doors, and doors filled with light symbolize opportunities for spiritual growth. Trap doors to basements indicate openings (perhaps unexpected) to the unconscious. Doors that close or are closing in a dream symbolize the end of something, such as a phase of life or being shut out of opportunities.

Doors also represent states of mind and means of personal expression.

See **house**.

doublet Pairs of identical objects or figures which, when they appear in a dream, indicate the emergence of something into the consciousness. This in turn is closely related to healing.

See **twins**.

dove The soul, the life spirit, the soul of the dead. The dove is also a symbol of the Great Mother and thus of fecundity and the renewal of life. White doves in particular represent purity, innocence, reconciliation, peace, and spiritual salvation. A pair of white doves symbolizes love.

Dark doves are symbols of death and misfortune.

Association: Yang

Element: A white dove is Fire Element; a dark dove is Water Element.

dragon Psychic transformation. Like the **snake**, the dragon represents primordial consciousness, the feminine, the womb, the unformed *prima material,* the alchemical process from chaos to the Philosopher's Stone, and wisdom and knowledge.

A dragon also symbolizes the hero figure, and accompanied by treasure or a **cave** and treasure signifies an ordeal in the life of the hero. Slaying the dragon represents the battle between the forces of light and darkness, i.e., conquering one's own inner darkness in order to master the self. Rescuing a maiden from a dragon is the preservation of purity from the forces of evil.

The dragon also is associated with sky gods, and brings fertilizing rain (the waters of the unconscious), thunder, and lightning.

Other meanings of dragon are one's inner fears, and the negative aspect of the mother figure.

Association: Yang
Element: Fire
See **monster.**

drawer Containment, confinement, or repression; putting something away or keeping it in abeyance; not willing to acknowledge something, wanting to forget something. Drawers often are similar in meaning to prisons or confining rooms.

Other meanings of drawers are a safe place; organization if neat; and lack of organization if messy.

See **prison; room.**

dress *See* **clothing.**

drinking Quenching an emotional or spiritual thirst. Drinking water may symbolize a connecting to the unconscious. Drinking alcohol to get drunk may relate to low self-esteem, or a desire for oblivion or forgetfulness. Drunken drinking also may represent an ecstatic release of repressed emotions.

See **eating.**

driving *See* **automobile.**

drowning Being overwhelmed in an immersion in the waters of the unconscious. Drowning may symbolize a sense of the loss of one's identity or ego, or being overwhelmed by emotions.

Drowning dreams often occur during severe depressions such as following a marital separation, when a person feels unable to cope with emotions.

Drowning dreams also occur during pregnancy, especially the last trimester, and reflect anxieties about **birthing**.

Association: Yin
Element: Water

drum/drumming Beating one's own way in the world, or calling attention to one's self. Drumming also symbolizes the rhythms of life, which may be fast, slow, regular, or irregular.

Association: Yin
Element: Fire. The drum within is considered to be the heartbeat, always maintaining rhythm throughout one's life.

drunkenness. *See* **drinking**.

duck The duck does double duty in dreams. As a bird, it represents spirit and the Higher Self because of its ability to fly into the heavens. The duck also resides in the water, which represents the unconscious. Its swimming along the surface of water symbolizes what is in the conscious mind. By diving beneath the surface, the duck becomes a symbol for probing material that is in the deep unconscious. Its resurfacing, especially with something in its bill, could indicate the drawing up of new or repressed material into consciousness, where it can be dealt with.

Other meanings of duck are superficiality when floating on the surface; and the Great Mother.

In China, the mandarin duck symbolizes married bliss.

Association: Yin

Element: Water
See **birds.**

duel Warring factions within one's self.

dusk *See* **twilight.**

dynamite Explosive emotions or temper. Being injured by dynamite may relate to injuries to one's self in an emotionally explosive situation. Hurling dynamite indicates repressed anger toward an individual, situation, or one's self.

eagle Spiritual victory; the triumph of spirit over matter; the spiritual principle of humanity that is able to ascend to heaven. Eagles also are associated with the sun (illumination) and air (intellect). Since antiquity, the eagle has been associated with kings and royalty (father and authority figures).

Other meanings of the eagle are pride; triumph over adversity; fierceness; liberty; authority; father figure; and inspiration.

Association: Yang
Element: Fire
See **birds.**

ear Receptivity, willingness to listen, not only to others but to one's inner self.

In mythology, the ear also is associated with divine inspiration, the means by which one hears the gods. This, along with the ear's association with the spiral (a symbol of the Mother Goddess), makes it a symbol of birth. In dreams, this might relate to the beginnings of new projects or phases in life.

Association: Yin
Element: Water. In Chinese Medicine the ear is considered the

"flower" of the kidney. It is a physical representation of the whole body because its shape resembles an upside-down embryo. The Chinese mapped the whole body on the external auricle and found that using acupuncture on the ear affects organs that are associated with a certain ear point. Many acupuncture disciplines use the external ear to treat certain conditions such as drug and alcohol withdrawal, allergies, etc.

earth The center of life; the Mother Goddess in her triple aspects of birth, life (nurturing), and death. The earth also represents a cosmic center, and is a symbol of foundation, solidity, and firmness. It is the feminine, passive principle of the universe.

The earth represents the physical plane and materiality, and thus the physical body or physical expression of the dreamer. It may also relate in dreams to too much emphasis on material things, or insufficient attention to them.

The earth also represents the lowest level of spiritual development (earth-bound). A person is purified by ascending through experiences represented by the other elements of water, air, and fire.

Another meaning of the earth is the inexhaustible bounty of nature.

Association: Yin
Element: Earth

earthquake An inner shakeup. Earthquakes, like other natural disasters, occur in dreams during times of emotional upheaval, when one feels there is no firm foundation or stability in life. Earthquakes especially represent the materiality of life, and thus may mirror anxieties in particular concerning changes of residence or finances wrought by divorce, loss, or accident. Earthquakes also have associations with the feminine principle, and maternal nurturing.

Earthquakes occur in dreams of persons suffering life-threatening illness, especially cancer, which threatens to rip the very foundation out from under life.

See **disasters, natural**.

east The direction of the rising sun symbolizes new beginnings, the dawn of spiritual light, the mystical side of nature. The east also represents one's spiritual nature and inner life.

Association: Yin

Element: Wood

eating An attempt to put spiritual nourishment into the body. Overeating or not having enough to eat are symbols of need.

In alchemical terms, eating is the process of *coagulatio,* a grounding process that turns something to earth (the body, the material plane). Eating might represent a need to be more body-conscious or grounded in the material reality.

Consider the type of food being eaten, such as nutritious versus junk, and also the setting. Is the food home cooked, served in a commercial establishment, hot or cold, good or bad? Make personal associations with these aspects of the dream.

eclipse Something being overshadowed or devoured in life.

In many cosmologies, eclipses of the sun and moon are blamed on sky monsters that eat the celestial bodies. Thus, an eclipse in a dream might relate to being devoured by one's inner monsters, or to repressed material in the unconscious.

Eclipses of the sun (intellect, rational thought) might relate more to waking life, while eclipses of the moon (intuition, the unconscious) might relate more to the unconscious or the shadow.

The end of an eclipse signifies a new beginning.

eel A phallic symbol, representing carnality or the penis. Eels also symbolize sperm, especially if swimming in cloudy, milky, or salty water.

Eels also represent slippery dangers lurking in the waters of the unconscious.

Association: Yang
Element: Water

egg Genesis; beginnings. The egg, properly fertilized with the creative force and incubated, germinates new life. In a dream, this might be a new project, a new phase in life, or a new sense of self.

The egg also is a universal symbol of fertility. In mythology, the egg represents the primordial cosmos, the life principle, the undifferentiated totality, wholeness and the womb of the Mother Goddess. This Cosmic Egg is often represented by an egg entwined by a snake or ouroboros.

In alchemy, the egg is the *prima materia* from which the Philosopher's Stone is created. Its white color lends it the association of perfection.

As food, the egg is spiritual nourishment.

Other meanings of eggs are hope and resurrection.

Association: Yin
Element: Earth

electricity Energy, especially creative; the inner driving force.

Association: Yang
Element: Metal

elevator A confined and mechanical means of rising into the realm of the intellect and spirit or descending into the realm of emotions and the unconscious. Elevators are restricted to a certain number and places of stops; thus they present perhaps a more secure but very limited means of accessing different levels of the psyche. One sees nothing along the way. Elevators are, however, swift and direct.

An elevator moving from one floor to another represents a transition between states of consciousness or identity.

Association: Yin
Element: Metal
See **stairs**.

eleventh hour Time running out; final moments. Dreams in which a clock reads eleven a.m. or especially eleven p.m. sometimes symbolize fear of physical death. In some cases of serious or terminal illness, eleventh-hour dreams may appear prior to actual death. However, this symbol should not be read as a literal death omen. Most likely, the eleventh hour reflects stress and pressure, and feelings that one is running out of time to accomplish all goals.
    See **time**.

embroidery Details, embellishments; the finishing touches, especially those that require careful attention.

embryo *See* **egg**.

emerald *See* **jewels**.

entrance A common dream motif symbolizing the beginning of a transition in life. Note the type of entrance, such as to a house (the self), a cave (the unconscious), or a tunnel (a constricted approach to the unconscious). If the entrance is closed off or locked, it might indicate difficulties in making the transition, or decisions yet to be made that will affect the transition. If the entrance is open, the transition has begun and progress may be hastened.

eruption A violent breakthrough of the unconscious into consciousness; a spewing up of repressions.

escalator A variation of the **elevator**. *See* **stairs**.

evergreens Immortality; the eternal, undying soul. Evergreens have funerary associations, as they are planted in cemeteries.

In Chinese art, pine trees are one of the most common designs depicted. Because they remain green throughout the whole year, evergreens symbolize endurance, strength, and self-discipline. Pine trees can have conflicting meanings in dreams. Their use in Chinese culture in burial grounds symbolizes that the deceased lived a long life; thus a pine tree in a dream may symbolize the end of a life.

Association: Yin
Element: Wood
See **cypress; yew.**

excrement The power of a person, the essence of one's being. In many cultures, excrement is highly valued, and is associated with gold and riches. It is the fertilizer of new growth and beginnings.

In alchemy, excrement is the *nigredo,* which in dreams parallels the darkness of the unconscious from which enlightenment arises.

Chinese literature on feces or excrement in dreams is contradictory. Taoism sees dreams as the opposite of waking states, so often dream images will have a meaning opposite the obvious. For example, some Chinese literature states that dreams of feces or dreams of something being dirty or foul smelling is a bad omen. Other literature says it can be a sign of good luck or fortune.

Association: Yin
Element: Earth

executive/executive ability The capacity and ability to take risks, make decisions, and take action. Executive ability is often expressed in dreams in the forms of administrators, officials, managers, pilots, sailors, guards, explorers, caretakers, and riders. Dreams with these imageries might indicate willingness or avoidance in terms of taking responsibility in one's own life.

explosion Something gone out of control; a destructive, unpredictable force ravaging life.

Dreams involving explosions also occur when individuals suffer from epilepsy; the explosions seem to mirror the effects of seizures.

Association: Yang

Element: Fire

eye An archetypal symbol with numerous meanings. The eye is the soul, the heart center, a symbol of the consciousness that resides within the unconscious.

In mythology, the eye is sacred. It is a solar symbol that provides access to heavenly realms. It symbolizes wisdom, knowledge, light, enlightenment, protection, and stability. The Eye of God is wholeness, completeness, and sovereignty. The third eye is the eye that looks within to seek transcendent wisdom. In Western mythology, the right eye represents the sun (enlightenment, the spirit) and the left eye the moon (intuition, the unconscious).

Eyes represent the Mother Goddess, especially her aspects of fertility, birth, death, and rebirth. Eyes and related shapes such as circles and spirals decorated ancient goddess temples. Many-eyed deities are all-seeing and protective. Single eyes sometimes are the evil eye, which represents the shadow.

In dreams, eyes may also indicate how one sees things. Eyes that are blind, half shut, crossed, or otherwise vision impaired may symbolize an inaccurate or partial view of one's world. Glasses may symbolize an aid to seeing things clearly; however, if the lenses are colored, then perspective is filtered or skewed.

Association: Yang

Element: Wood/Fire. In Chinese Medicine, the physical eye is associated with the liver, which is a Wood Element organ. The liver meridian goes to the eye, so energetically if there is some imbalance in the liver function, or some problem in the liver meridian, this can manifest as a problem with sight, or dry eyes. The spirit of the person is also manifested in the eye. If a person has poor eye contact with you when speaking to you, or has a suspicious or fearful look in their eye, this is more related to the energy of the heart, and can then be more related to the Fire Element.

eyeglasses *See* **glasses**.

facelift A superficial alteration that does not affect a core essence. Things appear to be different, but remain essentially unchanged. An attempt to cover up or fix a problem.
See **makeup; mask**.

falcon Sharpness of insight, solar consciousness, freedom, aspiration, ascension through all planes of consciousness.
See **birds; eagle**.

falling Feeling out of control, or being emotionally overwhelmed. Falling is a common nightmare motif that occurs during times of great upheaval and stress in life. Falling also is common during the last trimester of pregnancy, and anticipates the birthing process.

Falling into water indicates a need to immerse one's self in a healing in the unconscious, or a fear of being overwhelmed by emotions. Falling through space or air, or falling to the ground, indicates a need to be grounded, to come back to earth, or a fear of failure. Another meaning of falling is lack of support.

Association: Yin. Yin energy moves in an inward and downward direction, whereas yang energy moves in an upward and outward direction.

Element: Metal/Water. In the body, air descends through the action of the lungs. Falling through air is Metal Element. Falling through water is Water Element.

famous people Dreaming of famous people and celebrities usually pertains to personal associations with their accomplishments, personalities, skills, talents, qualities. Usually famous people symbolize qualities and characteristics the dreamer admires or wishes to have.

See **names**.

fan Folding fans are associated with the changing phases of the moon, and thus represent the feminine principle's instinct, imagination, and intuition.

Waving a fan can mean a warding off of evil forces.

Other meanings of fans are the spirit, and the power of the air to infuse new life into the dead (spiritual rebirth, or a resuscitation of emotion, ambition, or situation in life).

Association: Yang
Element: Metal

farmer A nurturer, one who tends to the cycle of spiritual rebirth and regeneration of the **vegetable** soul. Consider whether the farmer in the dream is tilling the soil or planting (preparing the way for change), is tending to growing crops (nurturing change), or is harvesting crops (completing a process or transition). Applications of fertilizer or treatments of pesticides may symbolize characteristics of the change. Crops withered or otherwise in poor condition might point to something that needs attention in life.

Association: Yin
Element: Earth

farsightedness *See* **glasses**.

fat *See* **obesity**.

father Father figures in dreams represent authority, discipline, tradition, morals, law and order, willpower, and ambition. In myth, they are consciousness, the Air and Fire Elements of intellect and spirit, and the opposite of the feminine principle's powers of instinct.

Father figures may also literally represent one's own father, or the father of someone known to the dreamer. Consider the personality traits, attitudes, and behaviors of these individuals, to which the dream may be bringing to attention.

Association: Yang

Element: Elemental association is determined by the personality features of the father in the dream.

feather A symbol of truth, wisdom, and also the soul. Feathers have the power and symbolism of birds. They represent the heavens and access to the heavens (the Higher Self), and the element of air (intellect).

To acquire or be given feathers may represent accomplishment.

Association: Yang

Element: Metal

See **birds.**

feces *See* **excrement.**

feet *See* **foot/feet.**

fence Barrier; territorial boundary. Fences confine, limit, and protect. To be on a fence is to avoid making a decision.

Association: Yin

Element: Metal

fennel A sacred plant with various associations. In herbal lore, fennel is held to strengthen vision; thus it is a symbol of spiritual clear-sightedness. It is associated with magic and with fire, the latter of which gives it associations with illumination and purification.

In lore, fennel also allegedly causes **snakes** to molt, and thus represents the cycle of death and rebirth.

field The feminine principle. If plowed a field can symbolize the womb, especially the fertile womb. If it is not plowed, a field may represent virginity and purity. Fields also symbolize the bounty of nature, and the grounding of one in the element of earth.

Association: Yin
Element: Earth
See **earth**.

fig Eroticism; fertility; abundance; the living force of nature. The fig leaf represents the male generative principle, while the fruit represents the female principle and the Mother Goddess.

See **fruits**.

fingers Expressions of emotions and intent. Fingers in various positions convey a wide range of meanings. A finger pointed at someone can be an accusation or an insult; also, it is a widespread belief in folklore that a pointed finger carries magical power to effect the intent—good or evil—of the one who is pointing. A finger raised to the lips connotes silence or conveys a warning. The third finger raised has been an insult—especially a sexual insult—since classical times. The first and fourth finger raised is a gesture of protection against the evil eye, but is an insult if pointed at another person. The fingers clenched and the thumb thrust between the index and middle finger also is a gesture of protection against the evil eye. Wagging fingers are accusatory or scolding. Beckoning fingers invite. Fingers raised upward with palms together (the benediction) are a symbol of spiritual power.

Fingers have been part of healing charms since antiquity. Healing deities cure by touch; consequently, the fingers are ascribed great generative, creative, and medicinal powers.

fire Purification, transformation, transcendence, and illumination. Fire burns away all impurities, and reduces the old to ashes, from which arise the phoenix (new spiritual life), and in which is found the Philosopher's Stone (wholeness).

The alchemical process begins and ends with fire. The process is likened to a spiritual purgatory that ends with redemption.

Fire also represents passion, fecundity, and sexual power. Like lightning, it impregnates, fuses, and changes things from one state to another. Fire once was the chief method of sacrifice to the gods, and thus was considered the link between the mundane and the divine.

In ritual and myth, fire often is equated with blood. **Baptisms** in both fire and **blood** signify an intense psychological ordeal, which, if navigated successfully, will end in refinement. Psychologically, fire dries up the watery excesses of the unconscious.

Handling fire may symbolize invulnerability to a situation. Being consumed by fire may symbolize vulnerability and loss rather than transformation. Burning may symbolize punishment for sins and wrongdoing, as in the fires of hell. Ordeals by fire are a test of purity, or a spiritual initiation.

Another meaning of fire is divine wrath.

Association: Yang
Element: Fire

fish A fish is the content of the unconscious, which in turn is symbolized by water. Fish especially represent the nourishing influences of the unconscious contents, which require inputs of energy to maintain vitality. Because of its ability to penetrate the depths of its watery domain, the fish in a dream can represent penetration into one's own unconscious, in search of truth. To fish is also a symbol of reaching down into one's own psychic and spiritual depths.

Eating fish is the taking in of spiritual nourishment.

Fish are associated with sex and generative power. They present fecundity because of the large number of eggs fish produce, and the phallus because of their shape.

Association: Yin

Element: Water

fishing Searching for something, especially of emotional significance. An attempt to connect with one's inner depths, intuition, and emotions.

Another meaning of fishing is experimentation.

flames *See* **fire**.

floating A state of passivity and calm in the waters of the unconscious; respite. Floating dreams also are common during pregnancy.

Other meanings of floating are hopefulness; buoyancy; and a need to rest.

Association: Yin

Element: Water

flood The destructive, overwhelming aspects of the unconscious. Feeling out of control. Being consumed by a flood often symbolizes the overwhelming emotions that accompany periods of great stress and upheaval in life.

Floods also symbolize the end of an old phase in life, in preparation for a new phase. In mythology, the flood is a universal symbol for the death of the world (old order) so that a new world can be born; it brings a spiritual cleansing. The consuming waters carry both the power of destruction and death and the power of fertilization and birth.

Association: Yin

Element: Water in excess. A dream of floods can be an indication of excess Water Element energy in the body, e.g. swellings, fluid accumulations, etc.

See **waves**.

flowers Generally, flowers symbolize beauty, transitions, the enjoyment of life, and the receptive, feminine principle. Flowers also are an archetypal symbol of the soul, or the Mystic Center, with petals forming rays that radiate outward. The alchemists called meteors, another symbol of the soul, "celestial flowers."

The opening of flower buds symbolizes potential and manifestation.

Other meanings of flowers are fragility, especially in relation to childhood; growth and flourishing; youthfulness and freshness; and something that is sweet and beautiful.

Individual flowers have their own unique symbolic meanings, especially related to their shapes and colors.

Association: Yang
Element: Earth

fly Dirt and dirtiness; associations with feeling unclean. Something unpleasant or distasteful that spoils a situation. The fly also is associated with sin, pestilence, and corruption.

Association: Yang consuming yin. Flies are small, quick, and short-lived, therefore they are yang in nature; however, they are associated with dirt and decay, which are yin in nature. Flies are attracted to filth and garbage. They serve a valuable function by consuming dead organic matter. But they also are prominent transmitters of disease. Thus a fly in one's dream can indicate presence of a pathogenic influence.

Element: Fire
See **insects**.

flying Dreams of flying are common, and usually symbolize inspiration and the ability to transcend ordinary reality. Flying means one is not stuck or limited. Problems and issues can be overcome by lifting off and flying up and over them. A flying dream signals a capability or readiness to act and make changes.

A dream in which one flies under one's own power may have more significance than a dream in which one flies in a public conveyance, like an airplane or helicopter. Gliders might indicate a particular freedom of movement. Fantastical flight, such as on a magic carpet or in a flying car might indicate a wish for magical solutions.

Another meaning of flying is the desire to escape from one's earthly problems.

Association: Yang
Element: Metal

fog Not being able to think or see a situation clearly; feeling confused, lost, disoriented, uncertain. Something that is obscured from view.

Another meaning of fog is a dangerous hazard.

Association: Yin. Fog is a yin excess. It is considered an unusual amount of moisture in the air.

Element: Water/Earth. Because the essence of fog is heavy water vapors, it is natural to associate fog with water; however, there may be an Earth Element involved depending on the fog in the dream. Fog that descends is related to water, but fog originating from warm ground and rising off the surface of the earth is related to earth. In addition to unclear thinking, fog in a dream could represent excess moisture accumulation in the body, or can be an early indicator of some imbalances in the organs that handle the transportation and transformation of internal waters.

foot/feet Mobility, balance, freedom of movement. Feet support the body; they are the foundation upon which one stands on the world, thus establishing a direct relationship with the earth and grounding on the material plane.

They represent taking steps in a direction in life, whether it be right or wrong.

Feet are a symbol of humility and reverence, from the practice of washing and kissing feet. Another meaning of the foot is a phallic symbol.

Bare feet signify a carefree attitude, or freedom from convention.

Feet in painful shoes signify constrictions and limitations.

Footprints symbolize leaving one's mark on the world, or the path one has taken.

Footwear represents freedom from the bondage of slavery, and liberation. It can also represent status symbols or lifestyle choices.

forest An archetypal symbol of the unconscious. Forests are vast, dark, and mysterious and harbor the unknown. It is easy to lose one's way in the forest.

The forest is the vegetative aspect of the unconscious: growth, life, primitive instinct, Mother Nature. A forest can seem either friendly and protective, or dangerous and threatening.

Wandering through or traveling in a forest can represent a journey into a higher stage of consciousness.

Association: Yin

Element: Wood

fountain The source of eternal life; the fecundating waters of life; the power of purification. Fountains are associated with the life-giving powers of the Mother Goddess. They also represent deep secrets and hidden sources within the unconscious.

Association: Yang

Element: Water

fox Slyness; cunning; craftiness; deceit; trickery. A fox may represent the deceitful actions of others, or the need to be sly and crafty. A fox may also symbolize deceit on the part of the dreamer.

Association: Yin

Element: Earth
See **animals**.

frog Fertility and eroticism. The frog's associations also with water and rain make it a lunar animal (the moon is considered ruler of rains, tides, and all waters), and therefore a companion to the Mother Goddess. In this regard, the frog represents resurrection and the ongoing cycle of birth, death, and rebirth. It also represents forces in the waters of the unconscious.

Association: Yin
Element: Water
See **animals**.

fruits Generally, fruits are transcendental symbols. They represent the abundance of nature (and thus of the Mother Goddess), fertility, prosperity, immortality, self-knowledge, and spiritual essence. Fruits also are symbols of reward, especially of great or prolonged effort.

First fruits are the best, and are used in ritual, sacrifices. First fruits also are offered in rites to the dead, and thus have links to the underworld, or the unconscious.

Forbidden fruits, such as apples, cherries, and grapes, are symbols of temptation, earthly desires, and sin.

Another meaning of fruit is the source of All.

Association: Yin
Element: Earth
See individual entries for fruits.

game Depending on context, games in dreams can represent playfulness, relaxation, or competition. They may relate to a specific situation or relationship, or to the broader picture of life. Factors that should be taken into consideration include the type of game being played (one-on-one or group sports); one's attitude toward the game (enthusiasm, reluctance to play, enjoyment, anxiety); one's skill; and the win-lose outcome.

garbage Waste; something that is useless, used up, or no longer has value.

In alchemy, garbage is the raw material of spiritual transformation. The stink and rot of detritus and garbage is part of the Great Work—the decay that must occur before rebirth can take place; the darkness of the soul that precedes the light of spiritual illumination. From the refuse of life comes fertilizing power for change and new growth.

Association: Yin
Element: Earth

garden The soul; paradise on earth and in heaven. Gardens, especially those filled with flowers, symbolize the ideal, blissful state of being, an attainment of spiritual enlightenment. The fertility and bounty of the garden indicate the state of the soul. A garden in bloom and beauty means spiritual growth has taken place or is occurring. A garden with withering or dead flowers means there are spiritual matters in need of attention.

Gardens also symbolize a refuge, a place where one can be safe and at peace.

Gardens filled with **vegetables** and **fruits** rather than flowers symbolize the vegetable soul of humanity—its roots to the earth and the unconscious.

Gardens appearing in the dreams of terminally ill persons represent heaven and are a symbol of transition from earthly life to the afterlife.

Association: Yang
Element: Earth

gardener A caretaker or one who facilitates growth, removing decay and debris, and keeping out unwanted growth such as weeds.

A gardener also tends to the psyche on a vegetative level, that is, in terms of the vegetable soul (*see* **vegetables**). This figure represents work taking place on a deep level of the unconscious.

garnet *See* **jewels.**

gate The threshold of passage, such as from one phase of life to another, from the old to the new, or from one spiritual level to another. Gates also symbolize entry to levels of consciousness, such as to the unconscious (often represented by a gate to inner earth) or the Higher Self (a gate to the sky, heaven, or bright light). Gates indicate the opening or closing of communication between levels of consciousness.

In mythology, gates between the worlds are guarded by various animals or fabulous monsters. The purpose of such beings is to prevent the uninitiated from entering. Similarly, gates in dreams may be guarded by animals or monsters. **Dogs**, **dragons**, and winged beasts are common guards, and may symbolize challenges associated with the transition.

Association: An open gate is yang. A closed gate is yin.

Element: A gate is an opening in a fence. Fences have the characteristics of the Metal Element: strong, well-defined borders. Gates provide transition from one boundary to another, also a Metal Element quality. If the gate in the dream is wooden rather than metal, it may refer to metal qualities of a wood association.

See **door.**

gatherings *See* **groups.**

gems *See* **jewels.**

ghost The spirit or essence of life.

Other meanings of ghosts are something that belongs in the past; something that can be perceived only by certain persons, and otherwise goes unnoticed; and memories.

Association: Yang

Element: Water

giant Overpowering, primordial force; forces that have gone out of control. Giants often represent obstacles that seem insurmountable or larger than life. They also can represent any aspect of life, or a situation, that seems to be out of hand. Giants often represent the dark side or the unconscious. Giants can be either beneficent or malevolent; in mythology they are usually portrayed as forces of nature (matter, the body), which are the enemies of the gods (spirit, intellect).

gift A blessing bestowed upon one. Something that is free or unexpected; a reward.

The full meaning of a gift depends on the context of the gift itself, the identity of the giver, and the reason for the giving of the gift.

Association: The action of giving is yang, but dream context may involve yin. Energy that moves outward from the center of something is a yang movement. Thus a dreamer giving a gift is yang. Energy that moves inward, from the exterior to the interior, is yin. Thus a dreamer who receives a gift expresses yin.

Element: Fire. Giving is a gesture that comes from the heart, and is associated with the Fire Element.

glasses Something that sharpens and clarifies one's ability to see people and situations for what they truly are. Farsighted glasses enable one to see things close up, that is, situations that should be obvious to the dreamer. Nearsighted glasses enable one to see things in the distance, which may symbolize the future.

Colored glasses indicate emotional qualities or idealism.
See **eye**.

globe Like the sphere, the globe is a symbol of wholeness, and of self-containment. It also represents the world, or the potential that lies beyond one's own environment.

Globes also symbolize sovereignty and dominion. In a dream, this might mean one's rule over one's own world.

Association: Yin

Element: Earth

gloves Law and order; authority; chivalry; civility. White gloves signify purity, purity of heart, and dignity.

Gloves in dreams can have different shades of meaning, depending upon other factors present. Generally, gloves protect and provide warmth; they also prevent direct contact with a person, object, or substance. Work gloves may be associated with fear of "getting dirty," or with an unpleasant task at hand. Children's gloves or mittens may be associated with something from childhood. Kid, suede, or fine leather gloves may be associated with the need to treat something gently. Taking gloves off may represent aggressive behavior.

See **clothing**.

goat Fertility; vitality; creative energy; unbridled sexual powers, especially male. The ability of goats to climb up mountainsides symbolizes human striving toward the divine.

Association: Yang in most cases. However, the goat has an androgynous symbolism. Both male and female goats have horns, but only the males have beards. If the dream imagery displays a placid goat without a beard, it is yin, whereas a goat with a beard, rearing up or climbing on rocks is yang.

Element: Goats possess both Metal and Wood Element qualities. They are sturdy animals and have natural resilience to disease. They are browsers rather than grazers, preferring to feed on trees and shrubs rather than on grass, like cows and horses. Wild goats will graze, however. Goats are avid climbers, which is a strong woody characteristic. They also are shy of water; they run from the rain and avoid putting their feet in mud and puddles. This behavior is metal, avoiding water to avoid corrosion.

See **animals**.

gold Riches; treasure; wealth; luxury. Gold symbolizes the ability to have whatever one wants. If hoarded, gold may symbolize stinginess or warped material values.

In alchemy, gold represents the attainment of enlightenment and wisdom.

See **colors**.

goose Fertility; love; marital fidelity. The goose's laying of eggs gives it the symbolism of primal creator and the Mother Goddess.

Geese also are symbols of agricultural domesticity and humankind's ties to the earth (matter, the body, the physical plane).

Like other **birds**, and the swan in particular, the goose is a messenger from the spirit world.

Association: Yin
Element: Water

grains The cycle of birth, death, and rebirth; fertility; abundance; prosperity.

See **corn; rice; vegetables; wheat**.

grandmother A caretaker figure or guardian. In her good aspect, the grandmother is associated with warmth, nurturing, and happy feelings, perhaps reminiscent of childhood. In her negative or shadow aspect, she may be evil, malevolent, and hurtful.

In myth, the Grandmother or Great Mother figure represents the goddess of individual fate. Thus, in a dream such a figure may symbolize an important change or transition, or a momentous event about to happen.

Any woman with white hair in a dream may be a grandmother figure, or a wise woman who is able to dispense wisdom and advice.

Grandmother figures may also represent real persons; consider the personality traits, attitudes, and behavior of those individuals, and how they might apply to the dream's message.

Association: Yin

Element: Earth

grapes Wisdom; truth. Also, fertility, abundance, life and the cycle of renewal of life, and ecstasy. In dreams, grapes may represent one's harvesting of the bounties of life, or reaping the intoxicating fruits of one's labors.

Wine grapes are associated with sacrifice and the blood of Christ. To have sour grapes means to offer an implausible excuse for not achieving a goal, or to be bitter about someone else's success.

Association: Yang

Element: Wood. The taste of sour is said to belong to the Wood Element category.

See **fruits; wine.**

grass Submission to others, or allowing one's self to be walked on. Being taken for granted.

Grass also can mean the ability to bend and be flexible.

grave The past that is dead and buried. Graves also represent thoughts of **death**, the dying of something to the world, and spiritual or emotional withdrawal. Individuals under severe stress may dream of graves as an expression of their sense of emotional or psychic death.

In alchemy, the grave is a symbol of the *nigredo,* the blackening phase that represents the death and destruction of the old in order to make way for new spiritual growth.

Association: Yin

Element: Earth

green *See* **colors**.

grocery A place where one can get all the food (spiritual nourishment) that one wants or needs.

grotesquery Dreams involving grotesque human beings often are symbols of anxieties. For example, prior to a **wedding**, a person may dream that his or her partner suddenly appears grotesque. This may reflect natural anxieties that a person has made the right choice in marriage. Prior to **birth**, the prospective mother or father may dream of a monstrous birth, which reflects natural concerns that the baby will be born without defect.

Grotesquery also symbolizes a repressed or unexplored facet of the dreamer's own personality. Such a dream acts like a mirror, forcing the dreamer to look inward.

groups Racial, ethnic, national, and cultural groups in dreams often represent the qualities, attributes, and characteristics the dreamer associates with those groups. The collective associations can be personified by a single individual in a dream.

Groups can symbolize the collective unconscious.

Gatherings of groups of people symbolize collective opinion, action, or influence.

gymnastics Exuberance, liberation, freedom, emotional expression. A sense of being a **child** or childlike; a return to the freedom of childhood. Gymnastics are a holistic experience, connecting body and emotions.

See **dancing**.

hair Strength, vitality, the life-force; also virility. Hair also represents thought, mind, and intellect.

Hair in various states and lengths carries different meanings. Loose hair is freedom, while bound hair is submission. Long hair on men is strength. Long hair on women, if loose, is virginity or whoredom. Long wild hair, or hair tangled with serpents, is a symbol of the destructive power of the Mother Goddess. Disheveled hair is a symbol of grief. Hair standing on end symbolizes fear, or divine possession. To cut hair is to renounce physical powers or civilization, such as the tonsures given to monks. Shorn hair also represents the loss of virility and strength.

Hair on the body represents bestiality or animal-like powers or characteristics.

In dreams, the color of hair may also have significance. (*See* individual listings for colors.)

Association: Yang

Element: Water. In Chinese medicine, hair is the external manifestation of the kidney essence. If one has good strong hair, this is a manifestation of good genetics and substantial kidney/adrenal energy. The ancient Chinese also believed that the kidney energy houses the will, so if a person had long full hair, this was a symbol of might and power.

hall/hallway A connection or route to the unconscious; a means of exploring the psyche, which is often symbolized by a **house**.

Dark, constricting hallways are symbols of the physical **birthing** process, and often occur in dreams during pregnancy, especially the last trimester. On a spiritual level, hallways may represent the birthing or emergence of a new aspect of the self.

Another meaning of a hall is being forced into narrow, limited choices.

Association: Yin

Element: If the hallway is dark—an unknown passage—it is the Water Element. If the hallway is wide and full of light, it is Fire. Hallways can refer to passageways in the body. For example, if a hallway is dark with a musty dank smell, it may refer to the bowels. A hallway with wind or breeze refers to the respiratory system.

See **maze; tunnel**.

hammer   The masculine, creative/destructive force of nature. In mythology, gods of **thunder** and **lightning** forge their lightning bolts, chariots, armor, and other objects with hammers and anvils.

The creative power of the hammer also has feminine aspects, in that thunder and lightning bring life-giving rain.

Other meanings of hammers are justice and vengeance; a practical working tool that is used to both build and to tear apart or crush; a forcible means of insertion; and an effort to make something fit or to acknowledge (integrate) something.

Association: Yang

Element: Metal

hands   Perhaps the most expressive part of the body, especially of emotions and actions. There is little thought or feeling that cannot be expressed solely with the hands.

The hand is a symbol of strength, authority, and power, a meaning perhaps dating to the ancient Egyptians, whose term for the hand also related to pillar and palm. An **eye** associated with a hand—such as a hand pointing to an eye—means clairvoyant vision, or a wise, all-seeing vision. Hands in various gestures, such as a fist clenched with thumb protruding through the index and middle fingers, are ancient and universal amulets against evil and the evil eye.

The hand of God, or divine power or intervention, is often represented by a hand of light reaching down through clouds. The gods of antiquity healed by touch; thus the hand is considered to possess great healing and generative power.

The right hand is the hand of power that gives, transfers, and confers, while the left hand is the hand of receptivity and submission. The left hand also is associated with dishonesty and cheating. In alchemy, the right hand signifies the masculine principle and rational, conscious thought, and the left hand signifies the feminine principle and intuitive, unconscious thought. Thus clasped hands in alchemy symbolize the mystic marriage of opposites to create wholeness and completeness, and also the communication between the conscious and unconscious. On a mundane level, clasped hands also symbolize bonds between persons, marriage, and fidelity.

Other meanings of hand positions include:

Shaking, offering, and clasped hands: friendship, devotion, forgiveness.

Open or palms turned up: receptivity, especially in terms of prayer and divine blessings.

Raised: worship, or amazement.

Raised with palms out: blessing, favor, healing.

Raised or folded hands: submission, surrender.

Raised to mouth: silence, caution, warning.

Raised to head: thought.

Outstretched: welcoming, protection.

Outstretched with palms raised outward: warding off.

Closed: unwillingness, secrets.

Clenched: aggression.

Caressing: love, concern, tenderness.

Laying on of hands: healing, transfer of power or authority, benediction.

Clapping: approval.

The condition of hands also carries symbolic meaning. Soft hands may represent gentleness or care to one's physical self. Rough hands may indicate neglect, or also inconsiderate treatment of others.

Excessively hairy hands have bestial associations. Dirty hands symbolize hard work or an unpleasant task or matter. Clean hands represent purity. Washing one's hands represents letting go or getting rid of something.

Empty hands symbolize lack, loneliness, failure or emptiness, while full hands symbolize bounty, plenty, and success.

Hands also symbolize one's creativity and action in the material world—one's deeds and accomplishments.

See **fingers; gloves.**

harbor A safe port from emotions (water). A resting place for reassessment.

Association: *Yin*

Element: *Water*

hare *See* **rabbit.**

hat One's mental outlook, attitudes, or opinions. Hats cover or enclose an individual's reality. The act of changing hats in a dream represents new thoughts or opinions—a change of consciousness.

As an article of **clothing**, hats also can be interpreted as representative of how one dresses the ego or personality. It could also signify an attitude or idea that fits comfortably with one's current state of mind.

Other meanings of hats are a collection of ideas into a single source, and a mandala.

Association: Yin

Element: The elements depend on the type and color of hat. For example, black hats are related to the Water Element, red hats to the Fire Element, and so forth.

hawk Like the **eagle**, the high-flying hawk is a symbol of royalty, authority, sovereignty and power, and the sun (illumination). Like all **birds**, it is a messenger to the gods.

Other meanings of the hawk are predation; sharp vision transcendence; and freedom.

head The seat of the spirit and the vital force. The head symbolizes wisdom, genius, and rational thought. In addition, it is a symbol of the world, the cosmos, and oneness.

Heads represent fertility, and when associated with pillars or poles, are phallic symbols. Winged heads signify supernatural wisdom. To lose one's head or be beheaded in a dream may symbolize a loss of reason.

A two-headed person or beast symbolizes the duality of nature and the union of opposites. A three-headed person or beast has various meanings, such as the triple nature of the Mother Goddess (Virgin, Matron, and Crone); the eternal cycle of birth, death, and rebirth; past, present, and future; and heaven, earth, and the underworld.

Other meanings of the head are cleverness; common sense; and attitudes.

Association: Yang

Element: Fire

heart Love, especially of a mystical or spiritual nature; the mystic center; the temple of God. The heart has been widely believed since ancient times to be the seat of the soul, the seat of intelligence, and the locus of all emotion and of will.

The sun (illumination) is a symbol of the heart, and conversely, in alchemy the heart is the sun within the person.

A heart surmounted by flames, a cross, a crown, or a fleur-de-lis symbolizes love as the center of illumination and happiness. A flaming inverted heart symbolizes transcendent wisdom, and also religious devotion.

Hearts also may be associated with the keeping of secrets, or with the vital life-force (*see* **blood**), or with bonds to others. A bleeding heart symbolizes emotional wounds. Heart surgery indicates an emotional healing process taking place, or the need to address an emotional issue.

Other meanings of the heart are romantic love; friendship; courage; and resolve.

Association: Yin and yang balance. The heart is the universal icon for the perfection of balance between yin and yang energies. It beats ceaselessly from the moment of birth until the moment of death. In the yang relaxation phase of pulsation it opens its chambers and the yin blood flows through, then the yin contraction phase squeezes out the oxygen-rich blood to the body cells in need of the vital fuel.

Element: Fire

hearth   Home; safety; security; the family unit; domestic affairs and duties. The protection and nurturing of mother and the Mother Goddess.

In mythology, the hearth is akin to the navel: a sacred center; it is especially an omphalos, or center of the earth. The hearth also represents one's inner spiritual center.

heel   *See* **foot/feet**.

hell   A common dream symbol of the *calcinatio* phase of alchemy, in which impurities are burned away. In a dream hell, the dreamer is being subjected to his or her own **fire**, from which there is no light and no escape until the calcinatio is complete.

Other meanings of hell are lack of growth; being trapped by one's own boundaries; and severe trials.

Association: Yin
Element: Fire

helmet Strength and protection, especially in the context of a warrior's or a hero's journey. In mythology, magical helmets confer supernormal powers to the wearer, such as invincibility or invisibility. Helmet decorations, such as shapes, feathers, or horns, have additional symbolic meanings.

See **hat**.

hen Maternal care and nurturing; the safety of a nest.

Other meanings of the hen are picking at or being picked at in an irritating fashion; and gossip and meddling.

See **birds**.

hill An obstacle to any goal. Consider the steepness of a hill and whether it can be traversed by a path, or must be navigated by hacking out a new path. Hills of brushy growth, woods, and forest represent uncharted lands of the unconscious.

Conversely, a hill also may represent a small ambition, something to be achieved by climbing.

See **mountain**.

hive Collective industry and enterprise; an ordered community. Individuality is submerged in the collective society in a hive.

Beehives in particular are symbols of the womb, motherhood, and the feminine earth soul, and also of immortality, because of their tomblike shape.

hole An opening to other worlds, particularly the unconscious. Falling into a hole symbolizes a sudden drop into the unconscious to face matters needing conscious attention. Holes can also access heaven (the Higher Self).

Universally, holes are symbols of the vulva, and thus are ascribed powerful fertilizing and healing properties. A holed stone is believed to be a fertility talisman, and crawling through the holes of megaliths are believed to bring both fertility and healing of illness.

Holes also symbolize an inner emptiness, or errors or pitfalls in one's life.

Association: Yin

Element: Water

holly Health and happiness; special memories of home and family.

holocaust A whole burnt offering; a sacrifice that is totally consumed by flames; annihilation.

See **fire**.

home Security, shelter, and safety. The home represents protection from the ills and troubles encountered in the world. At home, one can let down one's guard and behave as one chooses. One may have childlike feelings of a desire to be nurtured.

Leaving home symbolizes independence, striking out on one's own, assuming risks and responsibilities. Staying at home may represent a withdrawal from the world, a reluctance to face up to problems and difficult situations. However, escape is only temporary, for one must leave home again at some point. Discovering new rooms at home indicates growth or new aspects of personality that are opening up.

Association: Yin

Element: Wood. The Wood Eement conjures thoughts of protection and security. Many of nature's creatures use trees, shrubs, or old logs for their shelter.

See **house; room**.

homeland Dreams of returning to a homeland often occur to immigrants who are undergoing the stresses of adjusting to life in a new country. Like the home, the homeland symbolizes safety and security. It is the place where surroundings are familiar and life is predictable. Depending on culture, it is either the "motherland" or the "fatherland," and, like mother or father, a parental figure that promises well-being.

honey Sweetness; eloquence; the divine word; food for the gods. Honey is also a symbol of wisdom, purity, and immortality (*see* **hive**).

Honey is associated with prophecy. The classical gods and supernatural beings of prophecy, and the great oracles, were propitiated with honey and honey cakes. To not offer honey meant one ran the risk of hearing lies in return.

Honey in a dream may also relate to behavior or words. Too much honey implies insincerity.

Association: Yin
Element: Earth

hood Withdrawal; passing away. Hooded figures are associated with death in mythology. Thus a hood may symbolize death of an old phase of life, or the passing of influences.

Another meaning of the hood is something that is hidden from view.

horns A dilemma; aggression.

In mythology, horns are attributes of the Mother Goddess and are associated with the crescent moon. Thus, they represent fertility and the increase and wane of life. Horns also represent the masculine principle, virility and the vital life-force. Horns are associated with numerous gods, especially of vegetation and nature. A single horn is a phallic symbol. The horn of plenty symbolizes abundance, especially of nature.

Horns also are symbols of sovereign and supernatural power when worn on helmets and headdresses. They are amulets against the forces of evil.

Association: Yang

Element: The elemental association is dependent upon the specific horn in the dream image, e.g. brass horns are Metal Element associations, while the horn of plenty (cornucopia) is an Earth Element association.

horse An archetypal symbol usually representing the human body in dreams. In mythology and folklore, the horse signifies mankind's base animal nature, instinct, nonhuman psyche, and the unconscious. Thus, the horse symbolizes the instinctive, animal life and vitality within the body. Dreams in which a horse suffers injury or destroys itself may serve as an early warning of life-threatening disease.

The horse is a solar symbol, and represents the dynamic power of the sun moving through the heavens. It also has associations with ocean waves, and thus the watery depths of the unconscious. Wild horses or black horses in a dream may symbolize uncontrollable or unruly instinctive drives.

The horse as beast of burden bears close relationship to the mother archetype, a symbol for life at its origin. In myth, fairy tale, and legend, horses often are ascribed clairvoyant, magical, and divination powers. A magical winged horse serves as a vehicle for flights of consciousness into the heavens or into the underworld. Winged horses also symbolize extraordinary powers, and thus may represent extraordinary feats that are possible for the dreamer.

In the book *Interpretation of Dreams in Chinese Culture,* horse dreams are positive omens, for the presence of horses augurs victories. The *Luo Zhong Ji,* an ancient Chinese text, tells how the first emperor of the Tang dynasty, Li Yuan, began his ascent to power following a dream in which he was wearing armor and riding several horses, while other horses were flying through the sky. He asked aloud which army these magnificent animals belonged to and was told, "The first emperor himself, who controls the whole universe." After the same dream repeated itself for several days Li Yuan called his sons and told them the dream was an omen that their campaign would succeed. The fighting continued until Li Yuan finally did control his universe by establishing the Tang dynasty.

Association: Yang
Element: Fire

horseshoe Good luck and protection against evil, misfortune, bewitchment, and illness. The horseshoe is an aspect of the magical nature attributed to horses in myth and folktale.

horse's hoof A phallic symbol, representing creative energy, fertility, and healing power.

hospital A symbol of life passages; a mother figure where birth and death occur; a place of spiritual recuperation and healing. Hospitals also may be symbols of physical health and thus point to health problems. They may symbolize the need for rest and recuperation, or for some sort of healing to take place, whether it be physical, emotional, mental, or spiritual.

Other meanings of hospitals are service to others; sterility; and rules and regulations.

Association: Yin
Element: Water

hotel Transience; a temporary state, a phase of activity or of life. Hotels are collective symbols and are impersonal. They represent a temporary resting place during spiritual or psychic transitions. A hotel may also symbolize not feeling "at home" or comfortable with a situation or relationship.

Association: Yin

Element: Wood. Hotels represent a home away from home, so to speak, and therefore will have the same element association as homes.

See **house**.

hourglass The passage of time and the transitions of life. Also, the impending death (end) of a cycle. Turning over an hourglass represents the end of a phase and the beginning of something new.

Other meanings of the hourglass are time running out; imminent deadlines; the need to make a decision.

house The total psyche, the dwelling place of the soul. The rooms in a house are compartments or layers of the psyche and the soma (body).

Upstairs: the head and mind and related attributes such as logic, will, and self-control.

Kitchen: the alchemical process of transmutation and will; the organs of digestion that transform food into nutrients and blood.

Bedrooms: sexual matters and reproductive organs.

Bathrooms: personal privacy and personal space; creativity.

Basements: the unconscious, and the bowels of the body.

Exterior: the persona, the outer appearance one presents to the world.

Roof: the Higher Self, or spirit.

Doors: barriers to discovery and change, or protection from the unknown.

The condition, cleanliness, furnishings, and activity in rooms indicate various psychological states. Construction, decoration, industry, and maintenance of a house, or a room in a house, indicate a positive psychological state. Houses or rooms that are cold, empty, dirty, tightly locked, and having no open windows to let in fresh air reflect a negative psychological state. The particular conditions of a house in a dream may contain clues for courses of action.

Mysterious, closed rooms that seem to hold monsters or something terrifying may be alerting the dreamer of the need to face a problem or situation and resolve it. Finding new rooms in a house or moving to a bigger, nicer house reflect changes and growth occurring in the inner life. Building a house or entering a new house indicates the emergence of new ego space. Empty rooms, or rooms filled with cobwebs, are symbols of emotional loss, such as separation or divorce, or one's children leaving home.

Houses also represent the feminine aspect of the universe and as the repository of wisdom.

Association: Yin

Element: Wood. In general houses today have wood beams and frames that provide the main structure that gives the house its support and therefore its ability to protect those dwelling within. There will also be other elemental associations with dream images relating to the house. One must examine the dream imagery and see what room in a house is more predominant. For example, bathrooms and bedrooms by basic nature will have a Water Element association; kitchens will be Earth Element; living rooms Fire Element, etc. One must also examine the décor that is in the rooms in the dream image, for although the kitchen is basically an Earth Element association, if the kitchen in the dream has blue everywhere in the interior décor, this is a Water Element association, and might be examined using both elements. For example, the dreamer might examine the Water Element aspects of his or her **earthy** qualities.

See **home; room**.

hunter/hunting The pursuit of material gain; the striving for goals. Victory over one's animal nature. Competition, aggression.

The hunter and hunting also are symbols of impending death, or the end of an old phase of life.

Another meaning of hunting is the search to satisfy insatiable desires.

hurricane. *See* **storm**.

ice Frozen emotion (the waters of the unconscious), and the difficulty or inability to feel or express emotions. Ice represents the absence of love (a cold heart), and rigidity. It also is the hard barrier between the conscious and unconscious; it must melt for communication between the two to take place.

Ice, especially icicles, also symbolizes repressed sexuality.

Thawing ice indicates a release or movement of feeling, or resolution of fears or inhibitions.

Skiing, skating, or walking on ice symbolizes superficial acknowledgement of an emotional block, or the superficial expression of emotions. Thick ice indicates a great deal of work needs to be done on an emotional issue. Thin ice signifies an impending potential emotional breakdown or breakthrough. Falling through ice is an immersion in the unconscious, and a release of emotion.

Association: Yin excess
Element: Water
See **snow**.

iceberg A large emotional blockage. Icebergs indicate small protrusions of the unconscious into the conscious; a much larger matter or issue lies below in the unconscious, awaiting discovery.

identification Driver's licenses, passports, and other forms of identification symbolize a person's identity in the world. Loss of identification indicates confusion or negative feelings concerning self-image or self-esteem; fear of a change in identity, or a loss of connection to one's familial, cultural, or religious roots. The same may be said for the inability to travel or act because of lack of identification. Acquiring new identification, especially a passport, parallels feelings of new or renewed self-confidence. Purses and wallets also may be forms of identification, but are not as universal as passports.

immersion *See* **baptism**.

immobility Inability or unwillingness to resolve a situation. Inflexibility, impassivity. Immobility also can symbolize a vegetative state.
See **paralysis**.

imprisonment *See* **prison**.

inability to catch up The inability to catch up—with a person, vehicle, situation, or time itself—is a frequent symbol in nightmares that points to feelings of helplessness and ineffectiveness. These feelings might concern a relationship, job, living situation, or other matter about which one feels trapped, stagnated, or powerless to change. Examine other elements present in the dream for more information.

incompletion The inability to perform or complete an action or task, or to arrive at a destination, is a common dream reflecting anxiety and frustration concerning a situation faced in waking life or within. Incompletion also symbolizes resistance. For example, the inability to dial a telephone number correctly may indicate the dreamer's resistance to a course of action, an obligation, a change, or a need to change.

indigestion Indigestion, and also nausea, symbolize the inability to accept or process something, or an adverse reaction of one's gut instincts (intuition).
See **vomiting**.

indigo *See* **colors**.

infant *See* **baby**.

infertility *See* **childbearing**.

infidelity Dreams of extramarital relationships mirror anxieties concerning sex, commitment, and health of relationships in life. Such dreams occur prior to marriage, or during times of stress when one feels estranged from a partner, or fears infidelity. These dream images point to a need to confront feelings and issues and resolve them.

Not all dreams of infidelity have overt sexual meaning.

See **sex/sexuality**.

initiation Entry into a new phase of life, which could concern anything of significance to the individual, such as a change of job, home or relationship, or a spiritual transformation. Initiations are characterized by a descent into **hell**, an overcoming of inner darkness that must take place before rebirth can occur. Initiation dreams may reflect various stages of the process of change, such as struggle and turmoil, the battle with obstacles, or the end result of the new.

Initiation dreams often are marked by rites and ceremonies; the bestowal of a **gift**; acquisition of an object with symbolic meaning; **dismemberment, death**, and destruction (which represent the passing of the old life); birth; descent into the underground or underworld; ascent into the sky or heaven; **lightning** strikes; a change of wardrobe or **clothing**; transit across a **bridge**; and **wounds** and bites caused by such **animals** as a **snake** (a symbol of wisdom and renewal).

Persons who appear in initiation dreams are likely to represent archetypes, such as the wise **old man** or wise **old woman; mother** or **father;** hero or heroine; or healer. These figures are forces coming into play in the transition from one phase to another.

Initiation dreams may be confirmation of a change that has already taken place in life, or may be indications of a change taking place within the consciousness.

insects Fear, revulsion, and dirt. Collectively, humankind reviles insects, and fears their ability to penetrate our lives either singly or en masse. Insect dreams are "pay attention" dreams. Things or places that are infested with insects indicate areas of the psyche that have been neglected. Such areas do not wither, but become twisted—bug infested, so to speak, a projection of our fear or revulsion toward that inner part which is not being expressed or acknowledged.

In dreams, insects often are associated with emotional and sexual matters. They can also be larger image manifestations of microbial forms, and could be alerting dreamer to potential infections on the horizon, and therefore to a need to make changes in health habits to bolster immune system.

Association: Yang

Element: Different types of insects express different elements. Insects that come from under the ground, such as an earthworm, are Earth Element. Flying insects are Metal. Wood ticks, some spiders, termites, carpenter beetles, and so forth, are Wood.

intestines The seat of primitive emotions; digestion (absorption) of an idea or situation. Intestines are where food (spiritual nourishment) and the "vegetable soul" are digested and absorbed into consciousness.

Intestines also represent the labyrinth, and thus are associated with the mysteries of death and rebirth.

According to *Interpretation of Dreams in Chinese Culture,* a famous general of the Han dynasty once had a dream of something coming out of his intestines. The general asked several dream interpreters about his dream, but they could not enlighten him. He died on the second day following the dream, and because of this his dream interpreters realized the dream was about the general's impending death.

Association: Yang

Element: Small intestines correspond to the Fire Element; the large intestine corresponds with the Metal Element.

intruder An unwanted, forced, or threatening invasion of a person's life or private space. Vulnerability to intrusion. Intruders can represent either outside forces or inner conflicts.

An intruder—a thief, spy, murderer, or someone who breaks into a place, home, or situation unwanted—is an archetypal figure that occurs frequently as a mythological motif in dreams. As in myth and fairy tale, the intruder seldom is an evil figure, but often turns out to be a friend or benefactor in disguise. When confronted and accepted, the intruder tells or shows how his or her presence or involvement actually will help the "victim."

In a dream, the purpose of an intruder may be to show that a situation or person considered to be a problem, in fact, can be used to one's gain with a change in attitude or action.

invisibility Low self-esteem. Dreams of being invisible may occur after a traumatic event has affected self-esteem, such as loss of face, loss of job, abusive treatment, divorce, or rape.

iris *See* **flowers**.

iron Power, strength, and durability. In occult lore, iron repels evil and protects against it. In alchemy, iron is the metal of Mars, and represents battle and strife, and is associated with **lightning**, a symbol of illumination.

Association: Yin. Iron is one of the sturdy, dense metals, which is a yin quality. The more dense something is, the more yin it is.

Element: Metal

island The conscious mind, the world of the ego, which is surrounded by the sea of the unconscious. Islands often represent the conscious mind in myth as well as in dreams.

Other meanings of island are isolation; loneliness; protection; and contemplation and solitude.

Association: Yin
Element: Water

ivory A feminine symbol representing purity and incorruptibility. Ivory towers symbolize inaccessibility or unworldliness; sometimes arrogance.

Association: Yang
Element: Metal

ivy As an evergreen, ivy symbolizes immortality. It also is associated with the ecstatic nature of the vegetation gods.

Because it clings, ivy can represent dependency, especially of a smothering kind. A single ivy leaf is a phallic symbol, and represents the generative force.

Association: Yin
Element: Wood

jackal Scavenging **animal** associated with death. The jackal is a psychopomp that leads souls to the land of the dead. In a dream, it may be a symbol of transformation; specifically, the death of the old that precedes birth of the new.

Jackals are creatures of the night, and as such represent the dark forces of the unconscious. They represent animal traits, and may be a symbol of dark and destructive forces and a scavenging nature.

Association: Yin
Element: Water

jade *See* **jewels**.

jaguar A chthonic **animal** associated in myth with the underworld and the powers of the moon, and thus with the Mother Goddess. The jaguar is a psychopomp, a guider of souls, or a messenger god of the forest spirits.

A jaguar in a dream may represent certain animal qualities or attributes, such as speed, stealth, power, sleekness, predation, and various characteristics of the cat family.

Association: Yin
Element: Wood
See **cat**.

jail *See* **prison**.

jar A feminine symbol that can represent either death (the grave, the urn) or birth (the womb). A jar may also represent a receptacle (and thus the receiving of or containment of) feminine qualities and attributes.

Other meanings of jar are storage; preservation of something; or keeping something out of sight.

Association: Yin
Element: Water
See **cup**.

jaws Jaws, especially of a monster or large animal, represent the gates to the underworld, to being devoured by the unconscious. Jaws may be likened to gates, passage points that must be negotiated in a trial or transformation.

Another meaning of jaws is something that is overwhelming in life that threatens to consume.

Association: Yang
Element: Wood

jewelry Beautification or the need to make or feel beautiful. Vanity.
See **clothing; valuables**.

jewels Spiritual truths and wisdom; the reflection of divine light. The searching for jewels represents a spiritual quest. To possess jewels is to possess knowledge and enlightenment. The cutting of jewels represents refinement of the soul-in-the-rough through knowledge and wisdom.

Jewels in caves guarded by dragons or serpents represent intuitive wisdom buried deep within the unconscious. Jewels in crowns and necklaces represent the wisdom of the Higher Self. Jewels worn by royalty, especially women, and jewels kept hidden in secret rooms represent superior wisdom.

In occult lore, jewels are ascribed various protective, curative, and magical properties.

In their negative aspect, jewels symbolize the material, greed for riches, and profane love.

Symbolic meanings of specific jewels are:

Amber: A symbol of the sun (spiritual illumination and intellect) and immortality.

Amethyst: An ancient remedy for drunkenness, and thus a symbol of sobriety, clearheadedness, and peace of mind. Amethyst also is associated with enhanced psychic powers.

Aquamarine: Health, youthfulness.

Carnelian: Blood, the flesh, or sexual desire; also, blood bonds, as in family ties and close friendships.

Crystal: Purity, clarity.

Diamond: Spirit, purity, clarity. Something that is indestructible and of lasting value. Like the Philosopher's Stone of alchemy, the diamond also represents the union of opposites—of spirit and matter—that results in a wholeness of consciousness.

Emerald: A symbol of the Mother Goddess, especially in her vegetation aspect; the renewal of the Earth; immortality. Emeralds also symbolize mystical wisdom.

Garnet: Devotion and loyalty.

Jade: Good fortune, prosperity. The soul; also, the vital generative force of the universe. Green jade is associated with the vegetative force of nature.

Jet: Black amber, widely believed to protect against evil and harmful influences. It once was a symbol of mourning.

Lapis lazuli: A stone sacred to the gods; an enhancer of spiritual qualities and inspiration; bestower of divine favor.

Malachite: Great magical and protective powers. The deep and variegated green color of malachite also lends association with the vegetative force of nature.

Moonstone: The unconscious, intuition, and emotion. Moonstone often is associated with romantic love and tenderness.

Onyx: Spiritual strength.

Opal: Foresight and prophecy.

Pearl: The feminine principle. Wisdom, intuition, emotion, and the forces of the unconscious.

Peridot: Lightning bolts, or spiritual illumination.

Ruby: Blood, passion, life, and longevity.

Sapphire: Truth and the values of heaven, and thus protection against bewitchment, the evil eye, sorcery, and all manner of negative influences.

Topaz: Friendship and faithfulness. Also, a symbol of the sun (illumination).

Turquoise: Good luck, success.

Zircon: Knowledge, high ideals, respect, honor.

Association: Yin or yang depending on the brilliance or lucidity of the stone itself. Bright radiant colors are yang, and dark jewels are yin.

Element: The individual element of a jewel is determined by its color. Black or blue stones are Water. Green or brown stones are Wood. Red stones are fire. Orange or yellow stones are Earth. Clear, white, or gray stones are Metal.

job One's role or duty. What one does to get by in the world, or to make a mark in the world, depending on context. Changing jobs or losing a job may symbolize a major transition phase in life that concerns self-definition and self-image.

journey Development of the soul; a spiritual quest for truth and the progress of life. Journeys may represent an initiatory experience, such as transition from one phase of life to another, or from one relationship or activity to another. The heroic journey, involving purification of the soul, typically is fraught with obstacles and dangers.

From a spiritual perspective, the true purpose of a journey is not transit from point A to point B, but self-discovery and enlightenment.

A journey across the sea is navigation of the waters of the unconscious. Mountainous terrain symbolizes intellect, while desert is the spirit. The presence or absence of paths, and whether they are clear or obstructed, may indicate sense of direction and purpose, and progress or lack thereof. A journey in which one wanders or becomes lost may indicate confusion or uncertainty about something in life. The mode of travel also has symbolic significance, such as travel by foot, by animal, by car, boat, or airplane, etc.

Association: Yang

Element: The elemental quality of a journey depends on the mode of transportation. A journey on foot is Earth Element. Riding on a horse is Fire. Traveling by boat is Water. Traveling by plane is Metal.

jug Containment, storage, and holding, especially of liquids, and thus emotional issues. Jugs have narrow openings, making it difficult to see or spill the contents. Consider whether or not a jug is open or closed, or if it is difficult to open.

See **cup**.

juice Like **sap** and **blood**, juice is the life-force, especially of the **vegetable** soul. The type of juice imparts different associations, such as a kind of fruit or vegetable, and whether or not the juice is sweet, sour, salty, bland, and so forth.

Drinking juice is the intake of spiritual nourishment.

Other meanings of juice are physical energy; endurance; sexual vitality and attractiveness; excitement; and enthusiasm.

key A solution to a problem; a means of accessing different layers of consciousness.

In mythology, keys are symbols of initiation into spiritual mysteries. They have the power to open knowledge and wisdom, to let in illumination and enlightenment. Keys are the emblems of both the guardians of heaven (the Higher Self) and of hell (the underworld or unconscious).

Keys also close and shut down, using keys in a dream to lock something may symbolize the locking away of secrets, the repression of emotions, and the repression of the shadow.

Another meaning of a key is happiness.

Association: Yang

Element: Metal

kidnapping Being kidnapped in a dream indicates a desire to escape circumstances. Kidnapping also symbolizes an unwillingness to take action on one's own, or a hope for rescue by outside forces.

kiss Reverence; goodwill; adoration; reconciliation. In lore, the kiss is sacred, an expression of the life-giving breath of the soul and a transfer of power. Kissing objects, hands, and feet are rituals of worship and reverence, and symbolize spiritual union.

Kisses can awaken to new life (as in the fairy tale of Snow White), or can poison or betray (as in the kiss of Judas).

On a mundane level, the kiss is an expression of affection, passion, and sexual attraction.

kitchen A place where spiritual nourishment is created. Dreams set in kitchens indicate the process of psychic transformation. Kitchens are alchemical places where food is transformed from its raw state into cooked and refined dishes for consumption. In dream language, a kitchen represents the process of growth to a new level of consciousness, which then must be integrated or consumed. The kitchen itself is the equivalent of an alchemical vessel in which the transformation occurs.

Association: Yang

Element: Earth. Kitchens are associated with the stomach, spleen, and pancreas, which are organs responsible for transforming food into nutrients and **blood**.

See **house**.

knife Separation. Dreams with knives often occur in nightmares when one is under the stress of a literal separation, such as in a marriage or love relationship.

Knives also are a symbol of the masculine principle of action, rational thought, and intellect, but without the heavy symbolism of the sword. The knife is more a weapon or tool designed to cut, sever, and separate. It has personal significance for the dreamer, for knives, unlike swords, are common implements in everyday life.

Serrated knives or kitchen knives are more feminine, with associations to domesticity (nurturing) and food (spiritual sustenance).

Like the sword, the knife is an alchemical symbol of *separatio*.

Association: Yang

Element: Metal

knight A spiritual initiate, the quest of the soul on its journey to wholeness, facing trials and tribulations. A knight also is a guide of the soul.

In mythology, the **colors** of knights have different meanings. The green knight especially is an initiate, and also represents the powers of nature. The white knight represents purity, innocence, and spiritual illumination. The red knight is the conqueror who has been baptized in **blood**. The black knight represents **death**, and also evil, sin, and expiation.

On a more mundane level, knights are romanticized figures representing high ideals, morals, ethics, and chivalry; they slay dragons and rescue the endangered. Thus, knights in a dream might represent a dreamer's desire to be rescued by outside forces from a situation or circumstances.

Association: Yang

Element: The elemental associations are different depending on the color of the knight. For example a white knight or a knight in metallic armor is associated with Metal; a green knight with Wood; a red knight with Fire, etc.

knot A symbol of either constriction or freedom, depending on context.

Knots drawn tight bind things together, and thus symbolize continuity, connection, fate, and unity. Knots in dreams may represent the dreamer being bound to either desirable or undesirable things.

Knots loosened represent freedom, salvation, and the solution to problems. Cutting knots represents a quick solution to a problem, or a short path to spiritual realization.

Another meaning of a knot is a difficult problem that needs to be solved.

laboratory A place of transformation and experimentation. In the laboratory, the scientist or magus explores formulae and takes risks in order to create something new, or looks for solutions to problems. There is an understanding that many experiments will fail. Yet the scientist or magus is not disheartened, but perseveres.

See **scientist.**

labyrinth *See* **maze.**

ladder Ladders unite heaven and earth, and often represent ascent to spiritual heights or higher levels of consciousness that previously were unattainable. Rungs on a ladder correspond to separate events or markers in spiritual initiation. Jung described climbing ladders as the process of psychic transformation "with all its ups and downs."

Ladders also represent a rite of passage from one plane to another, usually a movement from darkness to light, or lower consciousness to higher consciousness.

On a more mundane level, ladders also represent movement in career or social standing.

Association: Yang
Element: Wood if a wooden ladder; Metal if a metal ladder.

lake The unconscious, the feminine principle, a passive and collective receptacle of wisdom. In fairy tales and myths, lakes are the dwelling places of monsters and supernatural beings, and are places where the mysterious, dangerous, or fatal can happen.

Lakes are associated with the souls of the dead, who either cross lakes to reach the afterworld or go to live at the bottom of lakes after death.

Lakes also are sources of revelation: the future may be glimpsed on their still and shiny surfaces.

Association: Yin
Element: Water

lamb Gentleness; simplicity. White lambs symbolize purity and innocence. In ancient times, lambs were a common sacrificial animal.

Other meanings of lambs are dullness, and a follower of the herd.

Association: Yin

Element: A white lamb is Metal. A black lamb is Water. A "black sheep" of the family is nonconformist, rebellious, and often alienated from relatives. These are Water Element characteristics.

lamp Divine light, wisdom, and guidance. The illumination of a problem or situation that needs to be solved. Lamps also symbolize birth (lighting a lamp) and death (extinguishing a lamp). In a dream, these acts may represent phases of life or influences that are either coming into being or passing away.

Association: Yin if it is an extinguished lamp; yang if it is illuminated.

Element: Fire if the lamp is illuminated; Water if it is extinguished.

lance *See* **spear**.

lapis lazuli *See* **jewels**.

left hand/left-handedness The unconscious. Using the left hand in a dream, especially if the dreamer is right-handed, indicates a need to open up to the unconscious.

lettuce Fertility and rebirth; fragility. Lettuce has a long and distinguished history as a sacred plant. The Egyptians, from the time of the Middle Kingdom, regarded it as a symbol of fertility, its milky sap representing both mother's milk and semen. The ancient Greeks considered lettuce a symbol of the fragile nature of existence. The moist, cool nature of lettuce links it to the moistness of the all-fertilizing

Great Goddess. In astrology, lettuce is linked to the moon, another feminine symbol.

Association: Yin

Element: Water

See **vegetables.**

light Truth, revelation, or illumination, especially as a result of supernatural or divine forces. Light is direct knowledge, a source of goodness. It banishes darkness (uncertainty, confusion) and evil.

Light also represents consciousness, and in a dream may pertain to something being brought into awareness.

Association: Yang

Element: Fire

lightning Inspiration, creativity, spiritual illumination. Lightning is both beneficial (spiritually or creatively transforming) and destructive. To be struck by lightning is to receive spiritual enlightenment, revelation, or initiation. To be struck and killed by lightning is to be transformed directly into heaven.

Like fire, lightning purifies through its destruction.

In its masculine aspect lightning is the tool of thunder and sky gods, and the terrible weapon of justice and vengeance. Lightning is the descent of power from heaven to earth, a forceful, masculine power both destructive and fertilizing. In its feminine aspect, lightning is associated with regeneration and fecundity, for thunder and lightning storms bring fertilizing rain. Thus, lightning also is associated with other feminine symbols of fecundity and regeneration, such as the moon and the spiral.

Association: Yang

Element: Fire

lion Strength and courage; prowess; primitive or "animal" instincts. Lions often are associated with law, justice, and military might, all authoritarian. They also represent the male principle.

The New Collection of Zhou Gong's Dream Interpretations says, "If one dreams of seeing lions, it means he will be noble and rich."

Association: Yang
Element: Metal

lockout Being locked out of a house or building symbolizes a fear of being shut out of something in life, such as a relationship or a career opportunity. It also symbolizes a fear of imminent loss.

loss of identification *See* **identification**.

loss of valuables *See* **valuables**.

lover A lover in a dream can represent a literal lover, but usually represents total involvement and passion—a consuming interest in something. This consuming interest may threaten balance and harmony, or other areas in life that require attention. On the other hand, a beneficial dream lover may represent a state of balance and harmony in life.

Lovers also can symbolize male or female principles—the animus and anima, which are brought to attention in a dream. Or they can symbolize the dynamic tension between opposites, such as the intellect and the emotions, or the conscious and the unconscious.

In addition, lovers also may represent qualities or states of emotion, such as loving, giving, forgiving, passion, or jealousy.

Another meaning of lover is an addiction to ecstasy or physical pleasure.

Association: Yang
Element: Fire

machinery The inner workings of something. Machinery in a dream may represent introspection. However, because of the mechanical, cold nature of machinery, the introspection is likely to be somewhat distant or detached.

Machinery also may symbolize the state of affairs in life: things are going smoothly (as in the running of well-maintained, well-oiled machinery) or things are going poorly (breakdowns, failure to operate). To take machinery apart represents an attempt to find out the inner core of something, or, if there is a problem, to find the source of the trouble. Machinery with missing parts means all the pieces to a solution, or the smooth operation of something in life, are not assembled.

Caretakers of machinery, or the operators of machinery, may represent the dreamer, or persons in the dreamer's life, or qualities or attributes that need to be brought to the dreamer's attention.

In addition, machinery can symbolize one's physical body, and thus may reflect one's attitude toward the body or may point to health problems. For example, trouble in the "guts" of a machine may be a means of drawing the dreamer's attention to the stomach or intestines.

Other meanings of machinery are lack of emotion; and mechanical, automatic behavior.

Association: Yang
Element: Metal

magpie Like other black birds, magpies are harbingers of **death** (transformation), or forewarn of trouble. They also represent vanity and base instincts.

Association: Yin
Element: Water

maize *See* **corn**.

makeup Putting on or taking off makeup in a dream pertains to one's social persona, the face that is presented to the world. Makeup can dramatically alter one's appearance, to enhance, beautify, hide flaws, or deceive.

If one feels exposed without makeup in a dream, it may indicate the dreamer may not feel comfortable presenting himself or herself "as is" to the world. Makeup that is poorly applied or that makes others in a dream stare or laugh, may be pointing attention to feelings of inadequacy or low self-esteem.

See **clothing; mask.**

malachite *See* **jewels.**

manhole *See* **sewer.**

map Directions for navigating through life or a particular situation in life. A map that is not comprehensible indicates confusion. Maps that send one around in circles represent frustration and lack of sense of direction. Losing a map means losing one's way. Finding a new and unknown map represents finding a solution to a problem, or a new direction in life. Requiring a map before making decisions or embarking on a trip may represent a fear of taking risks; one must have the path ahead securely marked first. Maps to buried treasure, or treasure in caves, represent an undertaking into the unconscious (*see* **jewels**). Such journeys are part of the hero's quest toward wholeness.

marching Moving along at a steady pace; steady progress toward a goal. Marching with others represents a collective activity in which one is part of a unit, going along with collective will or the will of an authority figure. Marching alone, or departing from a marching group, means going off in one's own direction. Breaking stride may mean breaking with the expectations of others.

marriage A union of opposites, or a reconciliation of differences. Marriage also symbolizes the attainment of an undivided self, and the union of the material and the spirit.

In a dream, marriage may relate to a resolution of warring factions in waking life, or may relate to a beneficial union of opposing forces within the unconscious, or the union of ego and anima, or the conscious and the unconscious.

In myth, the *hieros gamos* is the sacred, mystical marriage between heaven and earth, and is portrayed as the union of king and queen, bull and cow, and priest and priestess. In alchemy, marriage is represented by the union of sulphur and mercury (quicksilver), sun and moon, gold and silver, and king and queen.

A marriage requires a sacrifice on the part of both forces; each must give up something in order to create a whole. Thus, there is a "death" for each party in order for the birth of the union to occur.

On a more mundane level, dreams of marriage may relate to anticipation of, or anxiety about, an upcoming marriage in life. They also may relate to changes taking place in a marriage relationship that affect the harmony or balance, either positively or negatively. Dreams of marital strife may reflect unresolved problems in marital life.

Association: The union of yin and yang.

Element: In Chinese culture, the bride and groom traditionally dress in white and black, and thus are associated with the Metal and the Water Elements, respectively.

mask Concealment of one's real identity from the world; a facade. Something to hide behind; or, something that protects the wearer.

Masks also symbolize a temporary, liberating spiritual transformation; in sacred ritual, liturgies, theater, and folkart, they are objects of power that transform the wearer into an animal, an ancestor or a presumed image of a supernatural being. By donning a mask, the wearer allows himself to become possessed by the spirit believed to live in the mask or the spirit that is represented by the mask. This enables him to invoke the powers of that spirit.

A mask connects its wearer to archetypal powers residing within the collective unconscious. The mask is a mediator between the ego and archetype, the mundane and the supernatural, the sacred and the comic, the present and the past. In transpersonal psychology, masks help persons identify with archetypal forces and liberate suppressed parts of the self, thus seeing themselves in new ways.

To discover the significance of a mask in a dream, consider the countenance of the mask (pleasant, frightening, funny); the reasons for wearing it (to display, conceal, transform); the emotions associated with wearing it (pride, shame, exhilaration, fear); and the reactions of others to the mask.

masochism Dreams involving masochism are common during stressful periods in life, especially in the early stages following a separation and divorce. The dreamer may be projecting self-blame for everything that went wrong, and thus feels deserving of self-inflicted punishment.

mattress *See* **bed.**

maze A path to the underworld, or the unconscious. In mythology, mazes are associated with the Mother Goddess, and represent initiation into the mysteries of life, death, and rebirth. A maze in a dream may represent initiation into a life passage.

Mazes.also are symbols of mystical quests, and in dreams may represent spiritual attainment after trials and ordeals—a proving of the soul.

In mazes, one meets the supernatural: gods and goddesses who help or hinder progress, monsters that threaten safety. In dreams, these may be aspects of the self, arising out of the depths of the unconscious to confront the dreamer.

Even the simplest maze is not easy to navigate; complex mazes can seem impossible to solve. Mazes thus may represent complex problems in life, the solutions of which seem elusive and hard to reach; the dreamer may be venturing down blind paths.

Other meanings of mazes are difficulty and danger; confusion; and being on a path with limited choices.

Association: Yang

Element: Water. Getting caught in a maze is similar to treading water, exerting activity but not getting anywhere.

meat The sensual and sexual. Meat also may represent animal powers. *See* **animals**.

medicine/medication The giving of medicine and medication is a powerful symbol in Western culture. Western Medicine is largely allopathic, in that it relies on medicine and outside forces to effect healing and pays little attention to the potential healing powers within the patient. In contrast, other medicine systems, such as Chinese Medicine and Ayurvedic medicine of India, take a more holistic approach of mind, body, spirit, and environment. In Western culture, medicine is viewed as having the power to cure. Medicine in a dream may represent any external force that is expected or desired to solve (i.e., "cure") a problem. It may also be a cue to look at a problem from another perspective. The solution may lie within, and the individual may have to use his own inner powers and resources to bring it about, rather than expect rescue from outside intervention.

Association: Yang. Medicine is an external substance that sparks a healing element within.

Element: Fire. Most people associate medicine with bitter taste, which is often regarded as good for one's health. The bitter taste is associated with the Fire Element.

mending Taking corrective action or fixing a problem, such as in the "fabric" of one's life. Mending clothing represents fixing perceived flaws in one's social facade. Mending requires patience and attention to detail.

See **clothing**.

menstrual blood *See* **blood**.

milk Mother's nourishment; also, nourishment from the divine Great Mother. Milk also represents purity, simplicity, rebirth, and the newborn.

Other meanings of milk are childhood and memories of childhood; and semen.

Association: Yin
Element: Earth

mill Something being ground up to bits; something being processed into another form. A mill represents a process of transformation: a raw material is treated and turned into a useful product. A food mill has associations with spiritual nourishment. A lumber or steel mill has associations with building something in life, such as creative ideas, one's psyche, etc. (*see* **house**).

mine A penetration into the earthy depths of the unconscious in order to bring up something of value. The unconscious is the reservoir of emotion, instinct, and intuition, and is associated with the Great Mother. The earth is associated with the body and primitive drives.

Association: Yin
Element: Earth

mirror Self-knowledge, consciousness, and truth; the search for self-realization.

When people look into a mirror, they tend to see what they don't like rather than what they like. Mirrors reveal us as we truly are. Consequently, a mirror in a dream may reveal flaws and shortcomings—things the dreamer feels need correcting. In particular, looking into a mirror signals the need to reflect on one's inner-self. Shattering a mirror is a way of symbolically ridding one's self of a poor self-image. A broken or cracked mirror reflects a distorted self image.

Because of their shiny surface, mirrors are used in divination to look into the future. Thus, a dream mirror may reveal the possible or likely outcome of events in motion. Or it may reveal the dreamer's fears or hopes about the future. A fogged mirror may suggest feelings of uncertainty about the future.

In Chinese culture, to dream of a mirror means that the dreamer is gifted with great insight. If the dreamer gazes at himself, this is an omen of coming death.

Association: Yin
Element: Water

missing transportation Missing an airplane, bus, boat, train, etc. are common themes in frustration dreams. Usually, they symbolize a sense of having missed opportunities, especially by waiting too long. They represent the nagging "I should have . . ." or "I could have . . ." inner voice.

Missing transportation also can symbolize a lack of preparation, a lack of organization, or a sense of low self-esteem.

mist Confusion; inability to see things clearly.
See **fog**.

mixing Stirring things up in life, for better or for worse, depending upon what one is mixing.

Mixing also can represent a synthesizing process taking place, or an integrating process. Trying to mix together incompatible elements or ingredients may symbolize that one is attempting something unfeasible. Mixing together explosive ingredients indicates that one is creating, or contributing to, a volatile situation.

From an alchemical perspective, mixing represents a stage in the process of the Great Work: after ingredients are broken down (the *nigredo* phase), they are recombined and then refined.

mob *See* **crowd.**

mole A destructive force at work in the unconscious. Also, the powers of darkness (and therefore, of potential transformation).
See **animals.**

money Value and worth. Dreams of money can reflect how one values life as well as reveal feelings about an individual's self-worth and self-esteem.

Money also symbolizes psychic energy—the inner resources one is willing or not willing to invest in one's self, one's relationships, career, and so on.

Dreams involving accumulation of money may demonstrate positive growth arising from wise investment of all the resources at an individual's disposal. On another level, a gain or loss of money could represent consequences from past acts.

The amount of denominations of money may have significance in terms of **numbers.**
See **wallet.**
Association: Yang. Money is a physical representation of energy.
Element: Metal if silver and gold coins are the images. If the money is paper, then this is a wood association.

monk Spiritual wisdom, especially pertaining to the animus, or perhaps to a man in one's life. Monks, like nuns, also symbolize withdrawal from the material world. The meaning of a monk in a dream also is likely to be colored by an individual's own religious experiences and attitudes toward religion and church teachings.

monster Monsters in dreams and nightmares are unnamed terrors: the embodiment of repressed emotions, anger, hostility, and fear, or the unacknowledged shadow side of being. To be pursued by a monster in a dream is a signal from the unconscious of the need to confront something in life.

To look into a mirror and see a monster reflected back is to be confronted by one's own shadow. Other people who become monsters may indicate that the dreamer is overlooking or ignoring some flaw or dark aspect of their character. Sometimes others who become monsters in dreams are vehicles for showing the dreamer's own shadow.

Supernatural monsters may be repressed emotions attacking from within.

Monsters are likely to occur in dreams during stressful times in life, such as crises and life passages, especially if the dreamer feels overwhelmed and unable to cope.

Association: Yin or yang depending on the nature of the creature. For example, fire-breathing dragons would be yang, and denizens from the deep would be yin.

Element: The element associated with a monster depends on its characteristics. For example, a flame-shooting dragon is Fire; a creature with tentacle-like arms that is trying to strangle is Wood; a creature in dark waters, trying to drown the dreamer is Water; a blob or slimy creature secreting mucouslike substance is Earth; a creature with horns or spikes, or prehistoric with armorlike hide, is Metal.

moonstone *See* **jewels.**

morning *See* **dawn.**

moth Self-purification and self-sacrifice. Moths commit suicide in light and flame.

mother An archetype of the feminine principle: nurturer, protector, life-giver on one hand, and destroyer, devourer, and death-dealer on the other. The mother figure represents both the beginning and the end of the life cycle, as well as the constant renewal that marks the transition from one to the other. She is wisdom, wholeness, self-mastery, and self-sufficiency. She is also dark and mysterious.

Mother figures come in various guises. The mother, nanny, or nurse shelters and gives love, affection, and approval. The empress or queen is a figure of authority and wisdom. The priestess is a keeper of secrets and mysteries of life. The huntress represents the forces that control or subdue animal instincts and passion. The witch or hag is a destroyer, a depriver, or withholder of all the benefits the Good Mother bestows.

The mother may also be represented by the moon (emotion, intuition, the creative force) and by spiders or webs, as the weaver and spinner of destiny.

Association: Yin
Element: Earth

mountain An archetypal symbol of the self. To climb the mountain—a common motif in dreams, fairy tales, and myths—is to ascend to the realm of spirit. The ascent itself is masculine in nature, and is associated with intellect and rational thought, and with heroes and warriors seeking truth and justice. The spirit at the summit is also masculine: the Divine Masculine, the Father, God.

To descend the mountain is a feminine journey, a return to emotion, instinct, and primitive nature. To enter inside the mountain, such as through a tunnel or especially a cave, is the descent to the unconscious, which also is a feminine realm and is associated with the

Divine Feminine, the Mother, Goddess, the womb. In alchemical terms, the inner mountain is the vessel of transformation.

In dreams, it is significant to note the nature and characteristics of a mountain, and one's ascent or descent. Is the mountain forbidding and distant, a challenge, or an easy climb? What is the terrain? Is the mountain arid, lush, or snow covered? Is there a path, or do you forge one? Is the dreamer confident, or uncertain, or lost? Are there apparent dangers (unconscious fears) along the way? Are guides present, human or animal? Human figures may represent aspects of the self. **Animals** represent instinct; some, such as dogs, specifically are guides to the underworld, the realm of the unconscious. Does the dreamer carry tools or equipment (rational thought, masculine principle)?

Association: Yang

Element: Metal is the basic elemental quality of mountains, but if the images in the dream are of caves within mountains, there will be the Earth Element coming into play.

mouse A primitive aspect of the masculine principle. Mice also represent chthonic or underground powers and forces. Their gnawing and swift, furtive movements may reflect qualities or attributes of someone in a dream. Mice are nocturnal animals. They become active at dusk and during the night, and then get quiet during daylight hours.

Association: Yin. Mice by nature are assertive and always foraging, which is a yang quality; however, because they are nocturnal, elusive, and able to remain fairly hidden, their association is yin.

Element: Metal if white mice; Earth if field mice; Water if sewer mice.

mouth Breath, and thus spirit and creativity. In its negative aspect, the mouth is devouring, and especially represents the devouring, destructive nature of the Great Mother.

Dreams involving the mouth also may relate to constructive or destructive words spoken to others; the ability or inability to keep silent; gossiping; spreading the truth; and so forth.

moving Reflection on a change in life, or of a desire or need to make a change. Moving can refer to changing attitudes or states of consciousness, or even physical changes that have occurred, or are occurring, in life. Moving **house** indicates a change in one's psyche. Moving up to better circumstances represents improvement. Moving down to worse circumstances represents the need to work on something in life.

mud Fertilizing powers. The primeval ooze. Mud germinates new life, such as ideas and creativity. In alchemy, it can be compared to the *prima materia,* the "first matter" that can be shaped into the Philosopher's Stone.

Association: Yin

Element: Earth. Mud implies that the earth is wet and soggy. This can be a signal that the person is accumulating internal dampness, which in Chinese Medicine may indicate a weak digestive system.

murder Committing or witnessing a murder in a dream often represents the **death** of the old self. It also might represent an angry liberation from someone or something. Having murderous feelings in a dream is an exaggeration of repressed anger, hostility, and frustration.

museum One's past life, where memories are on display. Museums are collective places and also represent the collective past of a family or culture.

Association: Yin

Element: Water

mushroom Something kept in the dark. Mushrooms live in the dense, moist parts of the forest, which in turn represents the dark, uncharted territories of the unconscious. One must be careful with mushrooms, since some are poisonous.

Association: Yin

Element: Wood. The Wood Element is dependent on the Water Element for survival. Some mushrooms spring up suddenly after a rain, which typifies the new growth of wood from being replenished by the abundance of water. On a mental emotional level, when one expresses contemplative energy (Water Element), this gives rise to new growth (Wood Element) from new ideas spawned after those contemplative rains.

music The emotions; the soul. Music has tremendous power to influence emotions. The nature of the music reflects the nature and quality of emotions at play in a dream.

To compose music is to open up new emotional areas in one's life.

Association: Yang

Element: The element associated with music is determined by the type of instrument playing the music; however, because the nature of music is to transcend spirit and to transform emotions, it is mostly associated with Metal. For example, a flute or other wind instrument, a piano, and all stringed instruments are Metal. A drum—closely associated with the heartbeat—is Fire.

myrtle Flower of the gods; the living force of nature. Myrtle is a magical plant that symbolizes spiritual initiation, peace, joy, and the feminine principle. As an evergreen, it symbolizes long life and immortality; it is also the breath of life that ensures the ongoing cycle of birth, death, and rebirth. In war, it denotes victory without bloodshed.

Other meanings of myrtle are virginity and love.

nail Piercing, binding. In a positive sense, nails represent the strength to bind and hold together. In a negative sense, they represent a painful binding or wounding.

Another meaning of nails is getting stuck on something or not making progress.

Association: Yang

Element: Metal

nakedness *See* **nudity**.

names The names of persons in a dream usually refer to other people in life by the same name, or to the qualities, attributes, or talents associated with others, especially famous or mythological persons by the same name.

Other associations with names include memories, activities, decisions, fears, hopes, etc. Names may also be plays on words for things going on in life, or may be intended to direct the dreamer's attention to a situation.

To have no name is to be indistinct or formless, or to have no real qualities or attributes.

Another meaning of names is one's secret description of one's self.

natural disasters *See* **disasters, natural**.

nausea. *See* **indigestion**.

navel A center of life, life on earth, and the cosmos. A nexus where all things come together, where heaven and earth are united. As a center, a navel is the source of the outpouring of life energy, and is a refuge and haven.

See **spiral**.

nearsightedness *See* **glasses**.

neck The neck is fragile and a weak point in the body; thus, dreams involving the neck often have to do with weaknesses, vulnerabilities, and risk taking.

To protect the neck is to avoid risks, while sticking it out is to take risks. To be strangled or choked may parallel similar situations in life.

necktie Dreams about tying neckties, or neckties that are askew, too loose, or too tight, often occur as symbols of anxieties, especially related to getting married. Neckties also relate to fears or anxieties concerning job and career, or formal social situations. A necktie that is too tight might symbolize a feeling of being constricted, choked, or suffocated by people or circumstances.

See **clothing**.

needle The power or ability to mend one's problems or life, albeit with some piercing and, probably, some pain.

Another meaning of needle is the ability to pierce through the surface of things to the heart of the matter.

Association: Yang
Element: Metal

nest The home base; safety. Nests symbolize safety and security, especially that afforded by the mother.

Other meanings of nest are the womb; parenthood; and home-making activities.

Association: Yin
Element: Earth

net As positive symbol, nets protect and provide safety—they catch us when we fall from great heights. On the negative side, nets entangle and entrap. In mythology, the Mother Goddess is sometimes portrayed as the goddess of nets; thus, nets can symbolize her destructive aspects.

Association: Yin

Element: Both the negative and positive imagery of a net is related to wood. A net in a dream that catches one when falling is related to the healthy ability of the liver to function in immune system regulation. A net that entraps reflects an excess Wood Element condition.

new year A new beginning; starting fresh. A rebirth of spirit.

night The unknown, which is full of unformed fears. The night is ruled by the Mother Goddess, and can symbolize the terrifying unknown depths of the unconscious. It also can represent the darkness of the womb, which is protective and nourishing.

Night also symbolizes the alchemical darkness that is the destruction of the old, the death that precedes rebirth.

Association: Yin

Element: Water

nightmare The psyche's drastic way of trying to get your attention.

noose Being caught or trapped in a strangling situation.

See **trapped**.

north Primordial chaos; darkness; and night. Ignorance and emotional darkness.

North also is associated with winter, old age, and **death** (as in the ending of a phase of life) and with the Devil's powers (materialism and base pursuits).

Association: Yin

Element: Water

See **night**.

nose Curiosity; meddling. Also, instinct and intuition, especially if an animal nose. The ability to accurately size up a situation.

notebook A collection of memories and records of life. Perusing a notebook may symbolize a review of one's deeds or one's life, a reflection of past events, a toll taking. Consider the emotions associated with notebooks, such as nostalgia, fondness, happiness, sadness, bitterness, etc. Do the notebooks contain any information useful to present situations or events?

Storing a collection of notebooks, especially in a box, drawer, closet, or out-of-the-way place, may represent avoidance or a repression of things in one's past.

nuclear contamination Unresolved anxieties over changes in life that threaten to overwhelm.

See **natural disasters**.

nudity Vulnerability; openness; sincerity; naivete; embarrassment. Dreams of appearing nude in public are common in many cultures. Such dreams are associated with feeling unprepared, or being afraid of exposing emotions.

Nudity as a symbol of vulnerability occurs in dreams related to stage two of recovery, especially from separation or divorce. In stage two, the dreamer feels depressed, angry, and in despair, especially if he or she is the one left behind.

Nudity also may symbolize a change of identity in the making, prior to the acquisition of new clothes.

Association: Yin not protected by yang.
Element: Earth
See **clothing**.

numbers Archetypal symbols representing the self, the dynamics of the psyche and stages of growth and development. Number symbolisms are important to myths, fairy tales, and alchemy, and other esoteric teachings. These meanings can be expressed unconsciously in dreams.

Dream numbers must be considered in a variety of ways. Esoteric meanings may have significance for the dreamer. Numbers may also represent time spans, phases, and ages. For example, the number three might have significance concerning events that occurred three years earlier, or when the dreamer was three years old.

Numbers also can be represented by quantities of people, animals, and objects, by geometric shapes (the square, triangle, cross, etc.), by phases (seasons, months, days of the week, hours of the day), and by repetitions of actions (such as trying twice to accomplish something).

The following are number symbolisms most significant to dreams. Odd numbers have masculine properties and associations, while even numbers are feminine.

Zero: The unmanifest, the nothingness that precedes all things, the Cosmic Egg, which is the container of all life, the Great Mother, who brings forth all life. Zero has associations with the circle, the symbol of wholeness, perfection, and eternity.

Zero also represents emptiness, worthlessness, a waste of time, or "all for naught": "nothing but a big zero."

One: The beginning and end of all things, the source, the Mystic Center, divinity, the spiritual unity that unites all beings. One is auspicious, pointing to creation, unity, light, spirit, and mind.

Though odd, one is not masculine but is hermaphroditic, because one added to an even number makes an odd, and one added to an odd number makes an even one. All numbers, and thus all things, emanate from one.

The ship and the chariot are symbols related to one.

Two: Duality and balance. In alchemy, two is the number of opposites, which are dissolved and recombined to create the Philosopher's Stone. In dreams, two often represents the emergence of something out of the darkness and into consciousness; the dawning of spiritual light. This symbolism appears in myth and fairy tale in the form of twins or two siblings.

Two is associated with horns, which in turn are associated with the moon and the Mother Goddess. Thus two in a dream might also represent birth and nurturing, intuitive faculties or emotions.

Three: The generative force, creative power and forward movement. Three expresses a totality in terms of a beginning, middle, and end, which occurs in myth, folklore, and fairy tales as the triad: three wishes, three sisters, three brothers, three chances, blessings done in threes, and spells and charms done in threes. In the Three Fates of mythology, three has associations with past, present, and future and knowledge of all things. Three is an important number in mysticism, as expressed in the threefold nature of man (body, mind, and spirit).

Four: Wholeness and completeness, which in dreams usually refers to the self. Four is conscious totality. Four also symbolizes the earth (solidity), the physical, the completion of a spiritual evolution, foundations, hard work, toil, and tangible achievement.

Four has a strong association with the square, also a symbol of completeness. The presence of four in a dream can indicate the process of becoming whole or stabilized.

Five: The number of natural humankind, the microcosm, and materialism: the physical body and its five senses; the body with four limbs plus a head; the four cardinal points with a Mystic Center; the four elements plus a fifth element of ether, the universal vitalizing substance. Five also represents equilibrium, because it divides ten, the perfect number, in two.

Five is expressed in the pentagram, a five-pointed star, which in occultism represents the dominion of mind over the lower nature. To the Greeks, the pentagram symbolized light, health and vitality.

The number five is often expressed by five-leaved plants, such as the rose, lily, or vine.

Six: Equilibrium, balance, harmony, health, and time. The six-sided figure, the hexad, and the hexagram, are formed by two triangles in a union of opposites; thus, six is the number of creation, marriage, generation, and evolution.

The Pythagoreans considered six the form of forms, the perfection of all the parts, and associated it with immortality.

Seven: A universal sacred number. Seven is the macrocosm and divinity. It is the number of mystical man, the sum of three (spirit) and four (material), thus making the perfect order. In alchemy, seven metals make up the Work, the creation of the Philosopher's Stone.

Seven also is associated with magical, psychic, and healing powers. In initiatory rites, it represents the highest stage of illumination.

There are seven notes in the musical scale, and seven colors in the spectrum (a rainbow, the mythical bridge between earth and heaven).

When the number seven occurs in a dream, it often indicates the search for wisdom, the growth of spirit, the need to rely upon intuition or the need to meditate on what has been learned.

Eight: A higher order of the number four. Eight represents regeneration and achievement of a spiritual goal. It is associated with the lemniscate (an ellipse), the symbol of eternity, infinity, the Alpha and Omega, infinite wisdom and higher consciousness. Eight also is associated with the spiral, which symbolizes evolution, growth, and flexibility, and with the serpent, a symbol of illumination, and, in dreams, sometimes the self. The octagon, the eight-sided figure, represents a transition between the square and the circle, symbols of completion and unity.

In Chinese culture, eight is auspicious. There is a popular saying: "If you want to be wealthy, don't be without the number eight." In

China, telephone numbers, license plates, and house numbers with the number eight are much sought after. Having multiple eights in them can even command exorbitant prices. The eighth day of the eighth month is considered to be a date for the flourishing of wealth.

Nine: A higher order of the number three. Nine is a powerful number, incorruptible, representing attainment and fulfillment. It is spiritual and mental achievement, and truth. It is also a number of humankind, symbolizing the nine months of gestation before physical birth.

Nine is represented by an inverted triangle within an upright triangle, expressing the union of opposites.

In Chinese culture, the term for the number nine is *jíu,* which is the same word, *jíu,* meaning "forever." Many emperors gave the number nine great importance. For example, the total sum of the buildings in the imperial palace added up to a multiple of nine. In the Ming and Qing Dynasties (1368–1911) the imperial palace was built with nine thousand, nine hundred and ninety-nine rooms.

Ten: The number of perfection, heaven and earth, and the law; the paradigm of creation, for it contains all numbers. The four basic building blocks, one, two, three, and four, add up to ten.

Ten also is a number of completion and a return to origins (10 = 1 + 0 = 1).

Eleven: An unstable and imperfect number, eleven represents transgression and the striving to become twelve. Eleven also represents the last window of opportunity to do or accomplish something before major change takes place.

Twelve: A time symbol, as expressed in the twelve months of the year, the hours of the day and night, and the signs of the zodiac. Twelve turns the wheel of the heavens and represents the cosmic order of things; it is a higher aspect of the number four.

Thirteen: A number widely held to be unlucky and unstable because it exceeds twelve by one.

Thirteen has lunar associations, for there are thirteen full moons in a calendar year. Thirteen also can be interpreted from an alchemical perspective, for $13 = 1 + 3 = 4$. It is not the wholeness of four, but the striving toward it.

Forty: A period of spiritual incubation, trial, and initiation. In alchemy, the initial phase of the work, the *nigredo,* the blackening, takes about forty days to complete.

nun Spiritual purity, relating especially to the anima, or to a woman in one's life. Nuns also symbolize withdrawal from the material world, and healing, especially of the spirit.

In addition, there may be many personal associations with nuns, based upon one's experiences in, and feelings about, religion and religious education.

nurse A healing taking place; or, a desire to be healed, especially spiritually. Nurses may symbolize the dreamer's own anima, or a woman in the dreamer's life who has a capacity to heal a problem.

Another meaning of nurse is the desire to be taken care of.

nut Spiritual wisdom, truth. Also, a symbol of fertility and the generative force. Other meanings of nuts are the heart of the matter; and new life or rebirth.

oak A sacred tree in many mythologies, revered for its strength, durability, majestic size and spread, and its ability to draw lightning (spiritual illumination). The oak is the foundation of the earth and the material.

Other meanings of the oak are wisdom and truth; fertility and the generative force; and the world axis that connects earth to heaven and underworld.

Association: Good, durable yin energy. A healthy mighty oak in a dream reflects ample yin energy in the individual.

Element: Wood

oar Power, with which one plies the waters of the unconscious. Oars also represent skill and knowledge, and are comparable to the rod or wand. They are phallic symbols, and represent the masculine principle of intellect.

Association: Yang

Element: Water

oasis A respite from the harsh world. Emotional sustenance (water) amidst the aridity of intellect and the material.

Reaching an oasis in a dream also may indicate that a rest or a break from routine is needed. The message is to take care of one's self, pay attention to emotion.

Association: Yin

Element: Water

oats Sexual energy or activity.

obesity Low self-esteem; insulation or protection that keeps one from being too close or intimate with others, especially out of fear of rejection. Obesity can symbolize a wall of protection around one's emotions.

Association: Yin excess

Element: Earth excess. In Chinese Medicine, obesity is a condition that arises from the lack of energy in the stomach and spleen to take the nutritive Qi from food and transform it into energy and blood. This condition can be compared to a manufacturing plant with people stationed along an assembly line who either are absent from work, or are lacking ability to assemble the product, package it, and have it be immediately available for distribution. The goods pile up, and may not get packaged at all, or they spew over the edges of the conveyor belt because there is lack of performance at the duty stations along the way. Obesity can also occur when a person is taking in too many foods that are raw or cold in temperature. Cold, by

nature, slows things down, so when people ingest too many cold na-
tured foods, the digestive functions are slowed and can interfere with
the body's manufacturing process of nutrients. Another condition
that causes obesity is the presence of dampness, or excess Water Element influences. A person exposed to a damp environment where
there is an over abundance of water will be prone to having what is
called a "damp spleen." This internal dampness also affects the body's
digestive functions and leads to obesity. Think about a piece of machinery in any manufacturing plant that is overly exposed to moisture, and how that moisture can interfere with the mechanical workings
that are necessary to process the specific products being manufactured. This an example of what happens when there is an overabundance of the Water Element in the body.

observer Detachment or distance from what is unfolding in one's
life. Disconnection from emotions. Passivity.

Observers in a dream who are other than the self—and who may
include **animals** as well as human beings—may represent parts of the
self, including the shadow. One can try to connect with these parts by
role-playing in the imagination.

ocean The unconscious; the primordial waters; the Great Mother.
Oceans represent the unplumbed, mysterious, and seemingly impen-
etrable depths of one's psyche.

Traveling across the ocean symbolizes navigating through life.
Consider the condition of the ocean: smooth, beautiful, placid,
choppy, stormy, tempestuous, etc. Consider also the means of transit:
a raft (little support systems in place), a small vessel, a large boat, a
leaky vessel, etc.

To be pulled down into the ocean is to be pulled into the unconscious. Monsters in the ocean represent unformed or irrational fears
and anxieties. To float on the ocean is to be supported by emotions
and the unconscious.

The ocean also represents the waters of life, and thus is a symbol of the womb, and of birth.

octopus Possessive, clinging entanglements, especially relating to a mother figure. The octopus also may symbolize a desire to be possessive in a relationship.

As a "monster" of the deep, it also symbolizes irrational fears that threaten to drag one down.

Association: Yin

Element: Earth/Water. An octopus has many arms, and can be likened to a mother who is overprotective, possessive, and meddlesome. She has her hands into too many things, and this might mean she is trying to take action on every aspect of your life so that one feels strangled by her presence. An octopus in a dream most likely reflects excessive Earth Element energy, especially if the octopus is not contained within water. However, if the octopus is in dark murky waters pulling one down under, this is an excess water condition. Excess Water Element conditions can be seen in people who are becoming covetous, suspicious, and demanding, and who are exhibiting precocious sexuality.

office One's station in the world; one's career, job, or profession. A collective place where one is judged by others. Offices represent the advancement—or loss—of professionalism, ambition, self-esteem, self-image, and financial security. They also represent planning and organization. A corporate office is a symbol of authority.

officials Authority figures that represent controlling factors in life, or collective influences upon one's choices and actions. Officials also may symbolize specific persons in one's life, such as a parent, teacher, supervisor, or other individual with power.

ogre The Terrible Father, a destructive, oppressive archetypal force that threatens to devour individuality. Ogres often appear in dreams in relation to discipline problems. They may concern father-child relationships or may pertain to self-discipline issues for the dreamer.

oil Lubricant that symbolizes the smoothing out of difficulties and the easing of troubles. Oil is slippery; something covered in oil in a dream may represent a situation that is difficult to grasp.

Oil has played a role in sacred ritual since ancient times and thus has spiritual meanings. To anoint with oil is to bestow new life or confer wisdom. Oil is used in consecrations and dedications. It sometimes is a symbol of the soul.

Association: Yin
Element: Water

old man Mortality, or the passage of time. The appearance of an archetypal old man in a dream may serve as a prompt to action or resolve indecision. The message is that time passes and mortality draws near.

An old man with hourglass and scythe is an archetypal representation of death, and may refer to a phase of life that is coming to an end.

On a mundane level, an old man in a dream may represent a real person in life. He may represent attitudes toward, or fears about, aging held by the dreamer, or characteristics (negative or positive) associated with getting old, such as physical deterioration, illness, wisdom, insight, etc.

Association: Yang
Element: Water

old woman The mature wisdom of the feminine principle or the Mother Goddess. The old woman is an archetypal figure. As the Crone, she is the wise but destructive aspect of the Mother Goddess, the witch, the devourer—that force that brings about the death of the old.

In Chinese culture there is a great respect for elders. It is considered an important Chinese virtue. According to Confucian thought, moral conduct was essential to living a long life. An old woman in a dream can also be a symbol for not just death to the old, but constant renewal, so that longevity can be accomplished.

Association: Yin

Element: Water

olive/olive branch Peace; also, immortality. Olives may symbolize the resolution of conflict in life.

The olive also is a symbol of wisdom.

Association: Yin. The olive is said to be cooling in nature. In Chinese Medicine, the olive is indicated for conditions of heat in the lungs and stomach.

Element: Earth/Wood. The basic taste of the olive is sweet and sour, and so is associated with both of these elements.

onion Layers upon layers that hide or protect a central truth or secret. Onions may represent a probing or a need to probe.

The round shape of the onion lends it a symbolic meaning of wholeness and unity.

In folklore, the onion is sometimes substituted for garlic as an amulet against the powers of evil.

Other meanings of onions are crying and tears.

Association: Yang

Element: Metal. The nature of an onion is spicy. In Chinese Medicine, the spring onion has the property of clearing the surface, which means to help disperse an oncoming cold. It is also used to help rid the body of parasites.

onyx *See* **jewels.**

opal *See* **jewels.**

operating theater Sterility, antiseptic conditions, emergency treatment.
See **hospital**.

operation The need to make a change or get rid of something harmful that is threatening inner well-being or impeding growth. Operations are performed when illness or injury threatens one's physical life or health; they are radical measures.

Operations can be compared to ritual dismemberment, in which an initiate is symbolically dismembered and reconstructed to symbolize the destruction of the old self and the rebirth of a new self.

Individuals who have undergone operations, or who have lost family or friends during operations, associate them with different feelings, states, and conditions, which in turn may have those symbolizations in dreams. These can include fear, helplessness, trust in others, teamwork, salvation, healing, relief, pain, grief, or loss.

orange Fruitfulness, fertility. Juiciness, as in vitality.
In mythology, the orange is a symbol of immortality.
Association: Yang
Element: Earth

orchid Love, luxury, beauty; being in full bloom. Since antiquity, orchids have been regarded as aphrodisiacs and have been ingredients in love potions. In a dream, an orchid may relate to a need for "love magic" to revitalize a relationship, or may symbolize a desire for a love relationship.

In *The Interpretation of Dreams in Chinese Culture*, the orchid represents elegance and nobility, and is believed to drive away evil. The Chinese name for orchid is *lan*. In today's Chinese culture, people still call their best friend *lan you* (orchid friend); an elegant room is a *lan shi* (orchid room); a lucky moment is a *lan shi* (orchid moment); and so on. If a pregnant woman dreams of orchids, she will give birth to a noble son.

Association: Yin

Element: Metal, the element that completes the creation cycle before energy is then transformed, returns to the void, and then is born out of the water once again as a new cycle begins. Persons who achieve such success as to enter the realm of nobility attain the highest status for man on earth. The noble orchids are likened to the emperors and the empresses of the flower kingdom. For this reason they belong to the Metal Element.

orgy Something in life that is out of control, especially pertaining to the physical and material. Orgies represent dissolution and chaos. They also represent regeneration (the sowing of seed), and thus, like the *nigredo* state of alchemy, symbolize the disintegration that precedes renewal, or at least the potential for renewal.

orphan An archetypal symbol that generally represents fears of being unloved, misunderstood, homeless, left out, or abandoned. The fears can pertain to spiritual matters as well as to the mundane.

The orphan is a wounded and needy child, and thus in a dream may be associated with old and perhaps unresolved childhood memories or fears.

See **child**.

ostrich Ignoring (at one's own peril) what is going on in one's life, especially unpleasantries.

Ostrich features symbolize truth and justice in Egyptian mythology.

The ostrich also represents the **dragon**, a symbol of psychic transformation.

See **animals**.

ouroboros *See* **snake**.

oven The womb. The oven is a symbol of the Mother Goddess, where life is created and brought forth; it is associated with the mysteries of life, death, and rebirth. In alchemy, the oven is the athanor in which spiritual transmutation takes place. In dreams, ovens may represent new projects in the making, or new phases of life that are about to come into being.

overweight *See* **obesity**.

owl A symbol of either wisdom or **death**. As a bird, an owl is a messenger from heaven; within the context of a dream, this might represent the presentation of information that needs to be brought into conscious awareness.

In mythology, owls are death omens, and their presence presages a death in a family or household. As a harbinger of death, the owl in a dream heralds the *nigredo*, the blackening stage of alchemy, which represents the death of the old that is necessary for the new to come to life. Such deaths may be of an old phase of life or an old influence.

See **birds**.

ox Toil and hard physical labor. Working very hard toward a goal, but making slow progress. Patience and brute strength.

The ox is a good-natured animal that shares with the bull a symbolism of fertility. In classical and Biblical times, it was worthy of divine sacrifice. Occasionally, the ox is a symbol of Sloth, one of the Seven Deadly Virtues, which is characterized by mental inactivity, melancholia, and creative inactivity.

See **animals**.

oyster Secrecy; or, hidden treasure. Oysters also may represent having a hard, outer shell in dealing with others. An oyster without its shell means having no protection.

The creation of pearls through irritation of the oyster's insides may warn of irritation in one's own innards, such as the stomach or intestines.

In myth, oysters represent the womb and the life-giving forces of the Mother Goddess or feminine principle; they give birth to something of great beauty and value, the pearl. They are denizens of the deep, and thus have associations with the unconscious, particularly the literal "hidden treasure" that lies buried below waking consciousness.

Oysters are considered aphrodisiacs, and thus may represent sexual allure or sexual desires.

In Chinese culture, the word for oyster is *háo*. It is a pun on the phrase *háo shì*, which means "good events."
Association: Yin
Element: Water

packing Putting one's belongings, i.e. inner self, in order. Packing may relate to having too much inner clutter, or too much activity in waking life—things need to be better organized or disposed of. Packing to put something away may relate to repression. Packing in preparation, such as for travel, anticipates change in life. Unpacking may relate to bringing something from the unconscious into light.

paddle *See* **oar**.

paint/painting A desire to enhance and beautify something, or to cover something up. Painting a **house** relates to the psyche. For the painting of objects, see individual entries under **colors**.

The **color** of the paint has symbolic meaning. Gold paint, for example, relates to spiritual or intellectual matters. Black paint signifies the end of something in life.

palm, hand *See* **hands**.

palm tree Victory, valor, triumph, blessings, exultation. In a dream, the palm may symbolize triumph over adversity.

The palm also is a phallic symbol, and represents fertility.

Association: Yang. Palm trees leaves have sharp pointed edges, and the trunk has very hard, spiked outer bark.

Element: Metal

See **trees**.

paralysis A symbol of anxieties over stresses due to major changes in life, especially separation or divorce, or grief. Dreams of being paralyzed characterize the first stage of recovery, shock and denial, when one is still struggling to come to terms with the change and feels overwhelmed.

parents One's real parents; also, caretakers, nurturers, or authority figures.

See **father; mother**.

passport *See* **identification**.

path A course one sets out upon to journey through life or attain a particular goal. Paths typically are small and narrow, often windy, and one travels them alone. The conditions of a path provide clues to the message in a dream. An easy, open path in a tranquil environment reflects a different psychic state than one that is steep and rocky or obscured by overgrowth. Paths through unknown territory that seems frightening may symbolize fears and uncertainties about a direction one has taken or is contemplating taking. Paths that seem to lead nowhere may indicate the dreamer has taken a wrong turn, or is wandering through life and needs a new direction. Paths through familiar environments, either the present or the past, most likely have personal associations, such as to a particular period in one's life that relates to the issue presented in the dream.

See **traveling companions**.

Association: A path implies movement from one place to another, which gives it a yang association.

Element: The element associated with a path will be determined by the condition of the path the traveler is taking. For example, if the borders of the path are clearly well defined, the element is Metal. If a path is a water passageway, it is Water.

pearl In Chinese culture, an omen of nobility or exalted position; wealth and status.

Association: Yin
Element: Water
See **jewels**.

peridot. *See* **jewels**.

physician. *See* **doctor**.

pink. *See* **colors**.

planetary disaster The existence of a threat to one's own world or life. The possibility of major changes; things coming apart.

plowing The fertilizing, creative force. Plowing is a metaphor for sex, especially the impregnating of a woman by a man.

Another meaning of plowing is preparation or making ready for something new to grow, including mental faculties of thoughts and inspiration.

Association: Yang

Element: Earth

plumb line Spiritual balance and uprightness. Knowing that one is right about something.

Another meaning of plumb line is the world axis that connects heaven, earth, and the underworld, and provides a means of accessing those realms.

plumbing The workings of the unconscious; the hidden structure of the psyche (*see* **house**). Leaks, rotting plumbing, or convoluted plumbing indicate that attention needs to be paid to something in the unconscious. The process of repairing plumbing indicates healing work taking place on an unconscious level.

Dreams of plumbing can be associated with some imbalances in the internal waterways, such as the kidney and bladder.

Association: Yin

Element: Water

poison/poisoning Danger, especially to one's physical health. Dreams of being poisoned can occur to people who are suffering "toxic" relationships or situations, and also those who are facing serious life-threatening illness, especially cancer (*see* **contamination**).

Poisoning something or someone in a dream also may symbolize a desire to rid one's self of something troubling.

Another meaning of poison and poisoning is harmful emotions, such as hatred, envy, and greed, which literally poison one's psyche.

police Figures representing the collective authority and body of rules. Police men and women do not make the rules, but enforce them. Mistakes, crimes, and grievances are reported to them for rectification. Their appearance in a dream signifies a reminder or warning that one is overstepping limits, not following proper procedures or behavior, or is going out of control. They also may bring to attention feelings that one "should" do something because it's expected or proper. It may be wise to examine one's motives.

Association: Yang

Element: Wood

potato Simplicity, plainness; a staple of life, especially community life. A provider of concentrated energy.

Potatoes have lowly natures, and, like all members of the **vegetable** kingdom, represent the "vegetable soul." Because of they are shaped liked testes, potatoes also have an aphrodisiacal nature; yet to be likened to a potato is to be insulted, humiliated, or scorned as a lump.

president A supreme authority figure, one who establishes rules and has power over one's welfare and status.

prison Being confined, pinned down, limited in options and activity. Having one's back pressed up against the wall. Dreams of being imprisoned sometimes are a psychic balancing that follows a period of great or improvisational activity.

Dreams of being imprisoned may occur during the first stage of recovery from major upheavals in life that bring a sense of profound loss or disorientation. During the shock and denial of stage one, the dreamer may feel powerless to regain control of life; circumstances have literally created a prison. When the reality of the situation has been accepted, one can move on toward complete recovery.

Other meanings of prison are protection, refuge from the unknown, a retreat from the pressures of the world, and the need to make decisions. Prison life is routine, regular, predictable, and defined. Rules are set by a collective authority. Also, fear or expectation of punishment; and guilt.

Association: Yin

Element: Wood. The Wood Element organ in the body is the liver. The liver's job is to see that Qi is moving smoothly and evenly throughout the body. Whenever the liver Qi itself is constrained, the movement of Qi in other organs is affected. A prison image in a dream may alert the dreamer of a Qi stagnation problem.

prune Anxiety over aging, and showing the effects of aging. Prunes also might symbolize relief for a spiritual blockage.

pumpkin Empty-headedness, foolishness. When double, a symbol of the material world and underworld (consciousness and unconscious). Even as a single gourd, the pumpkin has associations with the underworld, as it plays a role in fall harvest rites and the dying of the natural world.

As a gourd, a pumpkin also may be likened to an alchemical cauldron, especially of the "vegetable soul."

According to Chinese dietary principles, pumpkin has a sweet taste and a warm nature. It has a propensity toward the spleen and the stomach. It helps to dissolve phlegm, promote the discharge of pus, and expel roundworms.

Association: Yin

Element: Earth. Like other **vegetables** in dreams, a pumpkin may send a message to the dreamer to include it in his or her diet, especially if the dreamer is experiencing a condition as mentioned above.

purple *See* **colors**.

purse *See* **identification**.

quarrel Inner conflict, or a disagreement with others in life.

Consider the individuals quarreling in the dream. For example, a quarrel between the dreamer and a woman may indicate a conflict involving the anima, while an argument with a man may represent conflict involving the animus. Men and women, even if strange in a dream, also may represent father and mother figures, siblings, coworkers or supervisors, authority figures, spouses or lovers, etc.

Issues involved in a dream quarrel, if their meaning is not overt, can have symbolic content. An argument over a house relates in some way to the psyche, while disagreement over food relates to spiritual nourishment.

According to Chinese Medicine, a dream about fighting is related to the gall bladder.

Association: Yang
Element: Wood

queen A symbol of the Mother Goddess in her full powers of fecundity and nurturing. The queen is the bounteous earth, the plenty of Nature, the ripeness of fruit and grain. She is the ultimate mother, as well as the ultimate authority, who presides over the mysteries of life, death, and rebirth. Through her, one can attain a higher consciousness.

The queen also rules the night. She is the moon who illuminates the mysterious landscape of the unconscious. In her benevolent aspect, the queen is love, nurturing, guidance, fullness, and generosity. In her malevolent aspect, she is jealousy, vindictiveness, destruction, dryness, and barrenness.

Association: Yin
Element: Earth

quicksand A destructive aspect of the unconscious. Being pulled down by quicksand symbolizes losing one's emotional footing and being consumed or overwhelmed by emotions, fears, and anxieties. Such dreams are common during times of stress and upheaval.

Another meaning of quicksand is a shifting, unpredictable, and potentially dangerous emotional landscape.

Association: Yin. Quicksand's nature is to pull things downward with a strong sucking, negative force. Dreaming about quicksand can reflect a yin excess condition.

Element: Earth/Water. In Chinese Medicine, quicksand is called "soggy earth," which means the Earth Element is deficient and unable to control the Water, and is overcome by Water's negative force. A dream of quicksand can be alert the dreamer to a weak spleen or stomach.

rabbit (hare) Fertility; good luck. In Chinese lore, the hare symbolizes the moon and represents long life and protection. A rabbit or hare forecasts increasing intuitive powers for the dreamer.

In traditional Chinese Medicine, all meat and foods have a basic taste and a basic temperature. The principles of dietary therapy are that each of the five tastes stimulates the five major organ systems. Rabbit is said to be sweet meat and has a cool nature, and therefore has effects on reinforcing the energy of the spleen and stomach.

Association: Yin

Element: Earth/Water. The rabbit's lunar link associates it with water.

rags Material poverty that hides an inner, spiritual wealth. The triumph of the spiritual over the material.

See **clothing**.

rain The unconscious. In dreams, any contact with water symbolizes contact with the unconscious. Rain, which cannot be controlled, often represents something we have failed to recognize or have avoided.

Association: Yin
Element: Water

rainbow A spiritual or idealistic bridge. In mythology, a rainbow bridge connects earth and heaven, humankind and God or the gods. It is the path traveled by the souls of the dead to the afterlife. In mythologies, good souls traverse the rainbow with no problem, while unworthy souls are rejected or consumed by fire.

The rainbow also has mythical associations with a cosmic serpent (*see* **snake**) that encircles the earth.

In ancient Chinese culture, the rainbow was considered to be an evil sign indicating conflict and confusion. *The Huai Nan Zi* text states that the rainbow is the yang inside the yin and indicates that ministers, concubines, and empresses will have difficulty, or will cause difficulty. *The Book of Jin* states that a rainbow was seen to be a symbol of confusion, inner conflict, infidelity, or insurrection.

Association: Yang

Element: Water/Fire. The rainbow is the spectrum of colors that are contained in the sun's light, made visible by water vapors in the atmosphere. Thus, the rainbow is a dance of Fire and Water together.

rat In Chinese lore, a symbol of quick wits and the ability to accrue and hold on to items of value. Rats are considered a symbol of good luck and wealth in both China and Japan.

In Western lore, the rat is associated with disease, illness, misfortune, death, and decay; witchcraft; and malevolent supernatural beings. The rat is deceitful and tricky, and will turn on one when one is unaware.

Association: Yin

Element: A white rat is Metal, because of its association with sacrifice in the laboratory for the benefit of human health. A brown rat is Earth.

See **animals**.

raven Like all **birds**, the raven is a messenger between God and humankind. In particular, ravens are also associated with death and the underworld, and are often considered omens of death because they gather at battlefields and houses where someone is about to die, and symbols of impurity because they feed on corpses. Thus, they are messengers of the dark side of God. However, ravens in mythology and fairy tales are neither good nor evil, but express the blunt truth of the unconscious. Talking ravens are agents of prophecy. In a dream, a raven may be bringing messages from the higher self or from the unconscious.

In alchemy, the raven is the darkness that precedes the light. It represents the *nigredo*, the mortification that represents the dying to the material world that is necessary in order for spiritual purification and illumination to take place.

Other meanings of the raven are warfare and bloodshed; and a magically empowered shape-shifter.

In Chinese lore, the raven is called *wu ya*. Part of this word also means black. Chinese legend has it that the raven is the creature associated with fire that comes down from the sun. According to an old story, there were once ten sun ravens that generated so much heat that mankind was likely to perish, but then the archer named Hou Yi shot down nine of the searing suns, leaving one raven in the sun.

Association: Yin

Element: Water/Fire. Water is always the element associated with blackness, a sense of mystery, and death. In old Chinese lore, however, the raven's link to the sun gives it a Fire Element association.

red *See* **colors**.

retirement The end of a phase of life.

rhubarb Astringency and medicinal qualities. An antidote for spiritual constipation.

The juice of the rhubarb is like sap, and is associated with semen and the generative principle. Rhubarb can go wild, and thus may represent something gone out of control, or which needs to be tended and cut back.

Another meaning of rhubarb is absurd humor.

In traditional Chinese Medicine, the root of the rhubarb plant has cold and bitter properties. According to the Chinese *Materia Medica,* text of Chinese herbs, rhubarb has been used for centuries to combat constipation. The leaf and stalk of the plant are astringent, which has the opposite property of retaining vital fluids during purgation.

Association: The leaves and stalk are yin (astringent). The root is yang (purging).

Element: The root of this plant is Earth; the leaves and stalk are Fire and Wood.

See **vegetables**.

rice A staple of spiritual nourishment; food of the gods. Rice may indicate a need to nourish one's self, especially spiritually.

Rice represents magical replenishment, fertility (the reason it is thrown at weddings), rebirth, and immortality. Rice also is associated with the sun and illumination.

Association: Yang

Element: Metal/Earth. In Chinese Medicine rice is categorized according to its basic taste, which is a little sweet and spicy. Foods that have spicy qualities tonify the lung and large intestine, and foods that are sweet tonify the spleen and stomach. Rice in a dream may indicate a need for attention to these organs.

right hand/right-handedness Rational thought. Using the right hand in a dream symbolizes reliance upon or the functioning of rational thought.

See **hands**.

roadblock Obstacles preventing one from staying on course. A roadblock may indicate the need to change direction.

robbery The loss of valuables, that is, one's identity, self-esteem, or emotions. Robbery dreams can occur during the first stage of recovery (shock and denial) following a major upheaval in life, such as loss, separation, divorce, or serious illness, during which one feels an irretrievable or insurmountable loss in life.

See **valuables**.

roof A covering that separates the conscious from the unconscious. Leaking roofs are a common dream image, and usually represent an invasion of the conscious by the waters of the unconscious. In this way, the unconscious seeks to force attention to something. (*See* **rain**.)

Association: Yang

Element: A tin roof is Metal. A tile roof is Earth. A black tar roof is Water. A wooden shingled roof is Wood. In accordance with the Chinese concept of "as without so within," the roof of the body is the head and its contents. A roof in a dream might relate to physical issues pertaining to the head. The brain belongs to the energy of the kidney, and therefore would be a Water Element image.

room Like the house, the room often symbolizes the dreamer's own person, but narrows the focus to specific areas needing attention. Rooms also are womblike containers and represent protection, separation from the collective.

Interpretations depend on the type of room, the atmosphere in it, the people and objects in it, what takes place in the room, and the emotional tone of the dream. If dream rooms are familiar, such as in a present or former home or school, consider events that occurred there in the past, which might have a bearing on present situations. The presence or lack of objects in a room, and their condition, may reflect the feelings of the dreamer. Objects that are bright, shiny, and in good condition indicate a positive tone, while shabby and dull objects indicate negativity.

The most common room images in dreams are hidden, back, secret, basement, or underground rooms; locked rooms; and closed rooms; locked and closed rooms often hold something frightening. These images often point to the shadow and call attention to the need to acknowledge and integrate repressed material into the consciousness. Basements also can speak about the bowels in the body and can be alerting the dreamer about issues with these organs. Hidden, secret, and inner rooms also symbolize womblike places where one feels safe and protected from the outside world. In addition, hidden rooms symbolize unexplored areas of consciousness, talents, or abilities. (*See* **door; key**.)

Other room associations are:

Classrooms, libraries, and study rooms: learning, growth process taking place.

Family rooms, living rooms, dens, and activity rooms: relationships, dealing with problems and everyday affairs.

Kitchens, dining rooms: relationships in terms of decorum of behavior, role expectations; preparation, digestion of ideas, transmutation. Related to the digestive organs.

Nurseries, childhood rooms: birth and nurturing of ideas and creativity; or, calling attention to events at those periods in life.

Bathrooms: release or blockage of emotions and creative energies; cleansing, release of problems or things no longer needed. Related to the processes of elimination in the body. (*See* **defecation; excrement; urination**.)

Bedrooms: privacy, intimacy, sexual matters. (*See* **bedroom**.)

Upstairs rooms: higher consciousness. Related to mental processes in the body.

Utility and work rooms, garages: basic needs, foundations, fundamentals in life.

Rooms newly constructed or under construction, or newly discovered: new areas of creativity, talent, ability opening up.

Crowded or cluttered rooms: confusion, disorganization, loss of control, overcommittment.

Confining rooms: limitations, boundaries, sense of being suffocated. Also, protection.

Empty rooms: lack of fulfillment, sense of loss, low self-esteem.

Mazes of rooms: feeling lost, disoriented, unanchored, uncertain of one's self; or, journey of discovery.

Holy and sacred rooms: entry symbolizes reentry into a womb, a reversal of the birth process, which in mysticism signifies being spiritually reborn.

Association: The yin/yang association of a room depends on the type of room. For example, a dark basement is yin, and a bright, shiny solarium is yang.

Element: The elemental association of a room also depends on the type of room. A kitchen is Earth, and a bathroom is Water.

See **house.**

roots *See* **tree.**

rose A complex symbol with numerous meanings. The rose in dreams often represents the true, archetypal self, the highest expression of consciousness. Roses in bloom indicate the dreamer is opening to higher awareness, while withering roses indicate that a path to growth is being left untaken.

The rose is a feminine symbol, and thus representative of fertility, passion, creation, life, beauty, love, and the eternal cycle of birth, death, and rebirth.

In alchemy, the rose is a symbol of wisdom; red and white roses together are an alchemical symbol of the union of opposites, part of the process of individuation. It also is similar in meaning to a mandala in Eastern mysticism.

Colors of roses have significance: a white rose represents purity and innocence, a red rose martyrdom and charity, a blue rose the unattainable.

Association: Yang

Element: Roses in general are Fire, for they usually appear in dreams as red. Other colors are related to other elements. For example, a white rose is Metal, and a black rose is Water.

See **flowers**.

ruby *See* **jewels**.

rust An unresolved situation or unresolved emotions; fear or anxieties that are corroding one's life. Rust also symbolizes something that is no longer useful in one's life.

Association: Yin. Rust is the oxidation process that takes place when metal is in transformation from its yang brilliant state of being to its yin deterioration phase.

Element: Metal

salt Purity, incorruptibility, especially of the spirit; moral and spiritual powers. The preservative powers of salt, and its necessity to life, also give it the symbolism of life, immortality, and permanence. Since ancient times, it has been a universal charm against evil.

In alchemy, salt unites water and fire, and is a symbol of the body uniting with spirit and soul.

Salt dissolving in the ocean symbolizes the merging of the individual into the absolute. Salt with food, especially bread, is a symbol of friendship and hospitality.

Other meanings of salt are bitterness in life, and wit.

Association: Yin. Salt is an element that when placed in water precipitates downward, a yin function.

Element: Water

sap The vital life force, especially that which flows through the "vegetable soul." Sap is likened to semen or mother's milk; it is the generative force, the nurturing food. Sap brings strength and vitality.

See **vegetables.**

sapphire *See* **jewels.**

scientist The intellect or rational, logical thought processes. Scientists are thinkers and experimenters.

See **laboratory.**

seal One's soul. Seals live both in the water and on land. Thus, they can represent the emergence of a message from the depths of one's soul into conscious awareness. They also represent one's ability to come out of the depths of the unknown onto dry land to nurture new ideas and to experience new revelations.

In folklore, seals are reputed to save people from drowning. A dream seal may symbolize a healing or rescuing ability within to cope with overwhelming emotions.

Most other mythological sea creatures are considered malevolent, but seals—perhaps because of the kind and sometimes mournful look in their eyes—are associated with kindness and affection. Their affinity to humans has given rise to legends of shape-shifting into human form. Thus, the seal can represent a metamorphosis, especially of a spiritual or emotional nature.

Other meanings of seals are playfulness; good luck; success; spiritual understanding; prosperity; faithful friends; and security in love.

Association: Yin

Element: Water

seminar An educational experience. Attending a seminar means that one has something to learn. Presenting at a seminar means one has something to teach, impart, or disseminate to others.

serpent *See* **snake.**

service station A way station along the journey of life, where one can stop, rest, refuel, revitalize one's self, ask directions, and get assistance. A service station may represent a refuge, or a plateau for reorientation.

sewer The destructive aspects of the unconscious, filled with cast-off waste. In alchemical terms, a sewer is the *nigredo,* the darkness of the soul, the self-reflection that comes with depression and dissolution.

Other meanings of sewers: something that is disgusting or revolting; a place where one does not want to go.

Association: Yin

Element: Water

sex/sexuality Two energies joining together. Dreams of sex and sexuality can represent literal release of sexual feelings and tension. Often such dreams have symbolic meaning. For example, dreams of sexual encounters with persons of the same sex are sometimes mistaken as repressed homosexuality, but they most likely symbolize a need to be more in touch with one's own anima or animus. Sometimes sexual dreams are metaphors for repression of emotion, or liberation of emotion, especially erotic feelings. They also reflect anxieties about commitment (such as prior to marriage) or worries that a relationship has gone stale or is coming to an end. Sexual liaisons with other persons, especially strangers or persons whom we know but have no intimate relationship with, may portray one's own anima or animus.

Dreams of sex with members of one's family are not completely without reference to actual physical desire, but nonetheless must be examined from an alchemical perspective.

Association: The marriage of yin and yang

Element: The dance of Water and Fire.

See **infidelity.**

sexual rejection Fear of being rejected in a relationship, or of being inadequate.

Sexual rejection dreams occur during separation or divorce, especially if the other party initiated the split. They also occur when an infidelity is suspected or discovered. The dreamer feels abandoned, rejected, and vulnerable, and these emotions are reflected in sexual rejection dreams. Sometimes the dream involves the partner, and sometimes it involves old flames from the past.

Sexual rejection dreams are most likely to occur during the second stage of recovery, which involves anger, depression, and despair.

ship An archetypal symbol that is a means of transport across the waters of life or the unconscious. Ships connect one state of conscious or stage of life to another. Consider the size and description of a dream ship, such as whether it is big and comfortable or small and in disrepair. Will it enable the dreamer to travel safely? Is it navigating calm or turbulent waters? Is the dreamer piloting the ship, or is someone else?

Association: Yin

Element: Water

snake One of the most common dream symbols, and one with many meanings depending upon the context of the dream. Generally, the snake is a symbol of great power, indicating change, renewal, and transformation. It is a potent archetype of psychic energy, power, dynamism, instinctual drive, and the entire process of psychic and spiritual transformation. In dreams, the snake may indicate a transformative process already under way, or it calls attention to the need to move to a new level of consciousness. The dreamer may fear it, as he or she may fear change itself, but the snake must be seen as a positive sign and not a negative one. Even a snake bite in a dream can be positively interpreted as being "bitten" by a new awareness.

In mythology, snakes are powerful magical and mystical creatures. They are universal symbols of renewal and rebirth because of their unique ability to shed their old skin for new. The ouroboros, the snake that forms a circle by biting its own tail, symbolizes the eternal cycle of life, death, and rebirth. The snake is a symbol of healing, which is part of the transformation process. In its carnal aspect, the snake represents a phallus and its associations of the life force, sexuality, and sensuality. As a phallic symbol, the snake often is associated with pregnancy in imagery and mythology. In dreams, such pregnancy also may refer to a state of psychic transformation: pregnant with ideas, possibilities, changes, events about to happen. As a creature which crawls along the earth and lives in holes in the ground, the snake has connections to the underworld, the unconscious, and humankind's instinctual drives. Mythical snakes guard the sleep of both the living and the dead; thus, they are creatures at the gateway to new consciousness. The snake also is a universal companion to goddesses, and thus can symbolize the feminine, the anima, the womb, the dark, intuition, emotion, and all the aspects of the Great Mother. (*See* **mother**.)

The coils of the snake represent the cycles of manifestation: life and death, good and evil, wisdom and blind passion, light and dark, healing and poison, protection and destruction. In Kundalini Yoga, a psychic force called the "serpent power" is said to reside coiled near the base of the spine, and in the transformation to enlightenment the energy rises up the spine to the crown.

In alchemy, the snake is the *serpens Mercurii,* the quicksilver that represents the constant driving forward of psychic life forces: living, dying, and being reborn. The snake is the *prima materia,* the unformed and dark chaos, from which order and life spring. Alchemical art often shows the snake wearing a gold crown, gem, diadem, or light to depict its expanded spiritual consciousness, which, like the serpent power of Kundalini Yoga, arises from the same energy as sexuality.

Snakes also are associated with water, the symbol of the unconscious, and trees, the symbol of wisdom and knowledge. A snake climbing up a tree represents the process of becoming conscious, or going through psychic transformation.

The snake is the fifth creature of the Chinese zodiac. It is one of the five noxious creatures. It is regarded as clever but wicked and treacherous. People like this are said to be "snake hearted." A person who has lied or deceived is called a snake. According to West Asian myths, dreams of snakes are interpreted in various ways. For example, it is lucky to dream that a snake is chasing you. A dream of a black snake is a sign of a birth of a daughter, while a dream of a whitish or gray snake tells of the birth of a son. In Taiwan, dreams of a snake mean you are going to lose wealth, and if the snake coils itself around you it speaks of a major change in the dreamer's life. Dragons often carry the same symbolism as snakes.

Association: Yin

Element: Generally, because of the nature of snakes to crawl and slither along the ground, and they represent the transformative process, they have strong earth qualities; however, there may be other elemental associations based on the dreamer's individual snake dream. For example a snake that is tightly coiled and "ready to strike" possesses more metal qualities. It behooves the individual to see what elemental quality is most predominant in the snake image before arriving at conclusions about the snake's meaning in his or her dream.

snake bite Initiation, penetration by a content. A snake bite in a dream is the equivalent of an injection administered by a doctor: one is forcibly administered a substance that will bring about some kind of healing or new spiritual awareness. To be stalked or pursued by a snake intent on biting indicates that the unconscious is attempting to bring something into waking awareness.

See **wound**.

snow Feelings, talents, or abilities that are frozen, buried, or inaccessible. Snow also can represent the absence of emotion. Similarly, melting snow means a cold heart beginning to warm.

Association: Yin

Element: Water

See **ice**.

spear A masculine, phallic symbol; a symbol of the warrior and hunter. The spear is power and strength; it also represents virtue. In myth, the spear is the *axis mundi,* the world axis that connects the physical world to the underworld and the heavens.

Association: Yang

Element: Metal, including knives, swords, and spears. A primitive wooden spear may seem to be Wood Element; however, its lethal point is Metal.

spiral Both the masculine and feminine waxing and waning cyclical powers of the cosmos: fertilization, birth, growth, decline, and death. Spirals come in many shapes, and can indicate a winding up or a winding down. Spirals also are a center of life and a vortex of energy. In a dream they may represent a need for change, a growth process that is taking place, or the withering away of something no longer needed.

Spirals have numerous associations. Mazes, labyrinths, and lightning, navels, S-link chains, fire, and the caduceus are forms of spirals. All life that grows in coils, S-shapes, and spirals represent the symbolism of the spiral, such as seashells, tree cones, serpents, trailing and vining plants, snails, ferns, and octopi. Animals with horns can be interpreted in terms of the spiral, as well as any animal that curls (coils) itself up.

See **labyrinth; maze**.

stairs Access to higher and lower realms of consciousness. Ascending stairs (such as to attics or towers) represent transcendence. Descending stairs (especially into basements or caves) represent going down into the unconscious. Winding stairs represent mysteries; spiral stairs are a symbol of growth, or of the cycle of rebirth.

On a more mundane level, stairs in a dream may represent ascent or descent in career or social standing.

Association: Yang if ascending or if spiraling to the right. Yin if descending or spiraling to the left.

Element: Elements depend on the type of stairs. Wooden stairs are Wood Element; wrought iron are Metal Element; concrete are Earth Element; and so forth.

See **ladder**.

storm A destructive force, especially related to physical things and daily life; also a shadow symbol of the emotions and instincts. Storms may point to a repression of emotions that build to a point where the emotions are released in the fury of a thunderstorm, tornado, hurricane, and so on. Storms that are accompanied by downpours of water may represent being overwhelmed by the unconscious, emotions, instincts, and intuition. One seeks shelter from a storm by going within (reconnecting to one's emotional/instinctual nature), such as to a house, cave, building, or the underground.

Storms also may mirror something horrendous or violent that has happened in life. They can symbolize feelings of being out of control or overwhelmed as a result.

Association: Storms are physical manifestations of the clash of the yin/yang opposites—fire and water, heat and cold, dampness and wind. The natural order in nature is that yang energy predominates for a time, then transforms into yin energy, its opposite. The time of transformation is often met with a struggle, because it is inherent in nature that all things, including energetic forces resist change. This resistance is manifested as storms.

Element: Fire/Water. Storms in dreams represent internal storms. Dreams of electrical storms suggest the presence of internal electrical storms taking place on subtle levels in the brain. For example, there may be chemical incompatibilities between negative and positive ions struggling to rebalance and maintain order. These storms can resolve easily without conscious awareness, but after a time, anxiety, feelings of restlessness, insomnia, and lack of concentration could ensue. The dream, in this case, could be an early warning, alerting the dreamer to take some action to deal with emotional issues or to reduce stress.

In the external world, summer days of relentless heat are broken by storms of thunder and rain—an example of nature's maintenance of order and balance between the polar opposites of fire and water. In the internal world, heat conditions such as feverish or inflammatory illnesses may be present. A dream of a rainstorm could indicate that the Fire Element within is not being controlled, and the need for some Water Element treatment is necessary. A simple example of this might be in a person who has consumed too many hot, spicy foods when he or she already has a hot condition in the stomach, such as gastritis. The dream storm may point to the need for cooling foods, water, and yin activities.

subway A collective symbol of the unconscious, penetrated by planned routes. A subway can represent exploration of the inner self or unconscious; however, the individual does not have control over the route taken. Thus, a subway might represent inner changes that the dreamer feels are beyond control.

Another meaning of subway is safe exploration of the unknown.
Association: Yin
Element: Earth

suffocation Being pinned down, confined, restricted, prevented from taking action. Having one's options limited.

Association: Either yin excess or yang deficiency.

Element: Metal. The breath, which is the movement of yang energy in and out of the body, is often compromised when there is some deficiency or excess in the organs of breathing—nose, sinuses, trachea, bronchi, and lungs. These organs all belong to the Metal Element, so dreams of suffocation could be early indicators of some condition that could ensue if the imbalance is not corrected. Oftentimes, there is another element that is involved, such as the Wood Element. If the Wood Element is in excess, it can counteract the Metal Element. In Chinese Medicine, this is a condition called "Liver Attacking Lung." The energy of the liver is in excess, and rises up and attacks the lung. This can be seen in allergic reactions, asthma, and other acute respiratory conditions that tend to follow emotional upheaval. Dreams of suffocation may alert the dreamer to pay attention to his or her respiratory system, or could send a message to keep emotionally healthy and to not confine or restrict feelings.

swaddling clothes *See* **baby**.

sweater One's total being, body and self.

See **clothing**.

swimming Navigating the waters of the unconscious. Swimming in an ocean or a vast lake indicates an opening up of uncharted territories in the unconscious. The depth of the water, the currents or waves, and the ability of the swimmer all are factors reflecting one's feelings concerning the unconscious. Currents, riptides, or monsters that threaten to pull one under represent fears residing within the unconscious.

Swimming also is a symbol of birthing. It may represent a spiritual birthing of a new awareness or higher plane of consciousness—a new self.

Association: Yin
Element: Water

swimming pool A restricted symbol of the unconscious. Swimming pools are artificial constructions, which gives them associations with collectivity. They have boundaries and known depths and offer relatively safe encounters with water. Symbolically, such safe encounters are with only a restricted part of the unconscious (or emotions), unlike the unbounded depths of the ocean or the great and unknown depths of a lake. A swimming pool at a home takes on a more personal significance than a swimming pool in a public facility such as a gym or school, the latter of which operates under collective rules.

Association: Yin
Element: Water

sword A masculine symbol representing authority, power, sovereignty, truth, and justice. A sword is also a weapon, but does not connote aggression so much as the fight for, or defense of, "right." The sword is the instrument of action, dynamism, and the intellect. It is the symbol of the king, a father or authority figure; the hero, who quests for truth; and the warrior, who seeks justice. It also is a ritual tool of the magician, the intermediary between the heavenly realm of spirit and the earthly realm of instinct.

The sword cuts and separates. It divides right from wrong, good from bad, healthy from unhealthy. As an alchemical symbol, it represents separation, in which the whole is divided into its basic parts prior to recombining or reassembling into a better whole.

Association: Yang
Element: Metal. One of the words for knife or sword in Chinese is *lì*, which is also the word for sharp, and also is the word for profit. In Chinese culture, dreaming of sharpening a knife or sword meant

that profits or riches are coming. Within the context of the dream, if the knife or sword pierces the individual, it could forecast a loss of profit. Because they are weapons, the knife and sword also can represent gaining or losing power. The sword's association with the Metal Element suggests on a physical level that the strong metal energy within (the lung or large intestine) is overpowering and in excess. The most likely targets in this situation are the Wood (liver/gallbladder) and Fire (heart/small intestine) Elements. Dreams of swords could be alerting the dreamer to imbalances involving those organs.

See **spear**.

tears The healing waters of the unconscious. In alchemy, tears are associated with solution, "dissolve and coagulate"—that is, something must be dissolved (eliminated or released) in order for something new to form. In psychotherapy, this occurs when the ego is dissolved (but not obliterated) in a descent into the unconscious and coagulated into a new form.

Association: Yin

Element: Metal/Water. The metal energy that exists within the organ system of the lung is responsible for the process of grieving and letting go. Tears within dreams could signal to the dreamer the need for letting go, or can be an inner vision of the natural process of metal transforming to water. Some Chinese texts say that dreams of **crying** and weeping represent excess energy constrained within the lungs.

teeth One of the most common dream symbols. Teeth have a variety of meanings depending upon the context of the dream.

Teeth can be symbols of attack, hostility, war, and defiance, as in baring one's teeth. While biting is an aggressive act, it also can symbolize sensuality and the act of love. The teeth, representing the male, penetrate the flesh, or the female.

As part of the mouth, teeth are also symbols of speech, and in dreams may reflect the impact of what one says to others. Loose teeth, for example, may represent loose or careless talk, especially speaking without thinking or making wild statements.

As one of the most enduring and indestructible parts of the body, teeth symbolize death and rebirth. Baby teeth being replaced by mature teeth represent the process of psychic transformation.

Losing teeth represents a loss of power or potency, maturation, the process of growing older, or physical or emotional injury. A person may dream of losing teeth when facing situations in which he or she feels powerless.

Association: Yang

Element: Water. In Chinese Medicine, the teeth are associated with the energy of the kidney.

See **dentist**.

telephone Communication with the inner self; the unconscious; one's intuition; or spiritual guidance. Telephones also represent one's communication with others. Dreaming about someone hanging up on you symbolizes fears of abandonment, rejection, or unavailability.

Association: The action of calling someone on the phone is yang. If the dreamer answers a phone, it is yin.

Element: Metal

thieves Someone or something that steals what is valuable to the dreamer, such as money, possessions, relationships, time, and health.

See **robbery; valuables**.

threshold *See* **door; gate**.

thunder The voice of the gods. Thunder denotes creativity and fertilizing power (the rain brought by thunderstorms), as well as divine anger and fury. Like **lightning**, the other great tool of sky gods, it may mean generation, regeneration, or destruction. In myth, thunderbolts are both the weapon and the personification of gods. They also symbolize flashes of divine inspiration and enlightenment.

Another meaning of thunder is a warning of trouble, for thunder often precedes the onset of a **storm**.

Association: Yang

Element: Fire

See **hammer**.

tidal wave *See* **waves**.

tides *See* **waves**.

time Pressure against deadlines. A period allotted one for projects, goals, life in general. Dreams of time running out are anxiety dreams that usually occur when one is under stress or pressure. The dreams may be showing that priorities need to be reexamined, or some projects or activities scaled back or dropped.

Time dreams are likely also to occur during life passages, when one suddenly realizes that important goals have not been achieved. In cases of grave illness, time running out symbolizes a fear of death, and sometimes impending death.

See **eleventh hour**.

tomb *See* **grave**.

topaz *See* **jewels**.

tornado An unpredictable, chaotic change or upset. Tornadoes appear without much advance warning, take uncertain paths, and can leave behind moderate damage to total destruction. Tornado dreams may happen if relationships or health are suddenly upset.

See **storm**.

totem pole The repository of sacred stories, such as of one's life, or of the cosmos; a repository of sacred wisdom.

Other meanings of totem poles are the protective forces of nature; something that must be deciphered; and a phallic symbol.

tower Masculine symbol of the intellect. A repository of wisdom, but isolated from the earth (a feminine symbol of emotions and the physical). Towers also are the exclusive domain or retreat of the select.

Other meanings of towers are a symbol of the father; a phallic symbol, the masculine generative and creative power; and a place to be isolated, or imprisoned and punished.

Association: Yang

Element: Towers are Earth unless made of metal, in which case they are Metal Element. The construction of a tower is the masculine earth energy attempting to connect with heaven. The Higher Self utilizes the image of the tower to alert the dreamer of a need to harmonize mind and body. The body (earth) uses a yang masculine energy to reach for a higher state of wisdom to resolve issues.

train A collective symbol that represents a means of traveling through life by a planned route and schedule. Dreams of vehicles of transportation such as planes, trains, and automobiles often occur during significant life transitions. Trains also have romantic and adventure associations, as they can take a traveler to faraway and exotic places (and thus escape).

Trains jumping the track can symbolize plans or events going awry, or literally derailed. The dreamer may have been "railroaded" by a certain life event that diverts him from an intended path and forces him to take another. Watching a loved one or family member depart on a train symbolizes feelings of separation. Missing a train, like missing a bus or plane, symbolizes fear of missing important opportunities. Being at a train station symbolizes being at a junction in life where decisions and choices are made.

Association: Yang

Element: Metal

trapped Dreams of being trapped mirror feelings of being trapped by people, jobs, circumstances, or situations in waking life.

Being trapped in small spaces is a typical dream motif during pregnancy, especially in the third trimester.

Association: Yin

Element: Wood. According to Chinese Medicine, dreams of being trapped reflect Qi stagnation. Energy is confined and not able to move freely in a part of the body. The organ responsible for the smooth and continuous flow of Qi throughout the entire body is the liver, a Wood Element organ. Dreams of being trapped can alert the dreamer to an energetic imbalance in the liver.

traveling companions The goal of one's journey, and also one's own higher wisdom that will enable one to complete the journey. A traveling companion is a part of the self. The traveling companion is an archetypal representation common to myth and folktale.

Dream traveling companions may be a mysterious or magical person, supernatural being, or animal. The companion may have fantastical or supernatural attributes. It may be silent, or at other times provides guidance and direction.

tree An archetypal symbol of the self and its process of individuation, as represented by growth and branching out. In mythology, the tree is an important symbol of growth, life, and knowledge. Its roots reach deep into the soil and its branches reach toward the heavens. Thus, the World Tree is the *axis mundi* that connects the three cosmic spheres of spirit, earth, and underworld. The fruit of the tree is wisdom.

Roots of a tree symbolize buried or unrecognized potentialities.

Other meanings or trees are a symbol of Mother Nature, the Great Goddess, or the divine feminine; also, family matters, as in one's family tree.

In Chinese culture, trees generally symbolize life and prosperity. Different species of trees have different meanings. For example, pine trees have both positive and negative meanings, and thus need to be seen in context. A dream of a pine tree can symbolize strength and endurance, as a pine is an **evergreen** and is able to withstand harsh climates. But a pine tree growing in front of one's house could be a death omen. This association comes from the Chinese practice of planting pines in graveyards.

A willow tree in dreams portends a move away from home.

Association: A whole tree is yang, because a tree grows upward and reaches toward heaven. Within the tree are parts that are yin, such as the roots and the sap.

Element: Wood. Within the body, there are physical body parts that resemble trees, such as the respiratory tract, which in Chinese Medicine is called the "respiratory tree." A bare tree, such as one in winter after leaves have fallen, resembles the whole nervous system with all the axons and dendrites branching outward in the brain. The spinal cord is the trunk, and the cauda equina, the roots. In Chinese Medicine, the whole tree is a symbol of the liver energy. According to one ancient text, *The Golden Mirror of Medicine,* dreams of forests on mountains, or of lying under a tree and being unable to get up, represent a liver deficiency.

trunk A container for shutting away repressed and unresolved emotions and memories. Opening a trunk in a dream may be akin to opening Pandora's box: whatever is released will have to be dealt with.

tunnel Access to and egress from the unconscious. Tunnels go underground and under water, both symbols of the unconscious. Emerging from a tunnel is a symbol of birthing a new self out of the unconscious. Going into a tunnel symbolizes self-reflection and introspection.

Tunnels may be twisted or dangerous, or filled with monsters, which are symbols of unresolved fears. Twisted tunnels can have associations with mazes and labyrinths.

Tunnel dreams commonly occur during pregnancy, especially the last stages, and symbolize the physical birthing process.

Tunnels are like passageways, paths, sidewalks, roads, and rivers. They take a person to a place that may be unknown, may be safe, or may be dangerous. In some cases, dreams containing tunnels, or other passageway elements, can be indicators of the dreamer having an OBE (out-of-body experience), especially if there are strong somatic sensations attached to it, such as paralysis, numbness, tingling, inner sounds, and itching.

Association: Yin

Element: Water/Earth. In general, tunnels are Water. An underground tunnel suggests Earth as well.

turquoise *See* **jewels.**

twilight A time of uncertainty, when things are not clear and when shadows appear over the landscape of the psyche. Twilight may indicate that one is uncertain, undecided, confused, or fearful about events or states of affairs.

Twilight also is the final stage before entry into the darkness of change and transformation. In alchemy, the *nigredo,* or blackness, involves a dissolution that must occur in order for a reconstruction into something greater to occur. Twilight can symbolize a stage of turmoil and despair that has the potential for transformation into a higher, enlightened spiritual state.

Association: Twilight is the time where the yang is fading and transforming to yin.

Element: Metal/Water. When the clarity and precision of images during the daylight become gray and muted, metal energy is in decline and water (blackness) is increasing.

See **dawn**.

twins The appearance of twins, or people or animals in twos, heralds the emergence of something into the consciousness. Twins and pairs are a common motif in mythology as the start of something new.

The appearance of two of a kind in a dream also may indicate the presence of duality or conflict.

umbrella Protection, especially from the waters of the unconscious when in the form of rain. If the unconscious cannot engage a person through immersion, such as in a body of water, then it may attempt to reach the dreamer from above through rain. Umbrellas prevent, or at least limit, contact.

Association: Yang. Implements and articles that are on the exterior of the body and that protect the body are yang in nature.

Element: Water

unicycle Riding a unicycle symbolizes being on one's own, especially in terms of marital or love relationships.

urination A bodily function symbolizing psychic states and experiences. Urination often represents the expression of deep emotion and feelings. It may harken back to a time in early life when feelings were more fluid and easily expressed. Urination by a child symbolizes the naivety and spontaneity of childhood. Urination in copious quantities, or in great frequency, may parallel a great outflow of emotion taking place in waking life. Urine that spills out of control may mean overwhelming emotions. Hot urine may represent emotions difficult to cope with. The inability to urinate may indicate blocked feelings.

Urination can have other meanings:

Creative output: As a liquid, urine is associated with **water**, which is representative of the unconscious and creativity. In alchemy, both urine and water are names for the *prima materia,* the basic material of the cosmos. In depth psychology the prima materia is the state of conscious chaos at the beginning of the process of individuation.

Psychic waste: A person undergoing analysis might dream of passing enormous quantities of urine, representing the release of repressed material from the shadow.

Transmutation: Urination may symbolize a significant emotional shift or change.

Association: Yang. Urination is an action and therefore is yang in nature.

Element: Water

See **defecation**.

valuables One's identity or emotions. Dreams of loss of valuables, such as money or jewelry, are common symbols of anxieties over major changes in life, such as marriage, separation, divorce, grief, serious illness, or job loss. These dreams especially occur during the first stage of recovery, when one is suffering from shock and denial.

Finding, carrying, and losing valuables are common symbols in the dreams of pregnant women.

Association: Yin. Something of value is something revered, saved, and withheld. In reference to the body, valuables would be related to one's vital essence, the physical substrate with much value for the propagation and continuance of life.

Element: The element will vary depending on the nature of the article of value in the dream. Diamond jewelry, for example, has Fire Element qualities. Family picture albums have a Water Element association.

vegetables The vegetable kingdom is much maligned, and is often used as a metaphor for inactivity, dullness, lack of vitality, low intelligence, absence of emotion, lack of will, melancholy, and bad humor. In fact, the symbolisms of vegetables are much more profound and go deep into the souls of humankind and nature.

The root of the word "vegetable" means the very opposite of dullness and inactivity: to animate, invigorate, enliven, grow, refresh, and vivify. The concept of a vegetable soul that nourishes all living things goes back to classical Greece and passed into the hermetic and alchemical philosophies of the Renaissance. Humankind is viewed as having a tripartite soul, including the vegetable, animal, and rational.

The vegetable soul grounds the rational soul and is the mediator between the conscious and the unconscious. It is dark and downward pulling, connecting us directly and intimately to our ancestral roots and to the roots of the earth and nature. The vegetable soul is part of the anima mundi, the World Soul, that which animates all things.

Physically, the vegetable soul is connected to the human body's autonomous nervous system, the unconscious, unthinking forces that rule metabolism, digestion, and primitive functions. Plants are nourished by the elements, and therefore the vegetable kingdom represents the very deepest level of the unconscious, where one encounters the roots of one's real self and where the fundamental life-energy of all things originates. Vegetative energies can become bound up in people, and their release brings about a state of wholeness.

Because it is elemental, material, of the earth, and in the earth, the vegetable has numerous associations with the mysteries of death and rebirth. Vegetation deities are all associated with these mysteries: that from the vitality of death, rebirth and new growth are possible. Various societies have mystery rites around certain totemic foods, such as corn, wheat, rice, yams, coconuts, breadfruit, and taro root. Such totemic foods are vessels for the gods, representing the complexities of their manifestations in the material world.

Thus the vegetable is the most widespread metaphor for spiritual growth. On a simple level, the vegetable is plain, a staple. It is dark and melancholic. On a higher level, it is the foundation of the animating force of the cosmos.

Within the vegetable kingdom is a hierarchy of symbolisms. The lowly cabbage signifies dullness and solidity, while trees are the alchemists' gold. Nuts are hidden wisdom, the generative principle. Fruits and flowers are transcendental symbols. Some vegetables, such as beans, are ascribed magical properties in myth and fairy tale—they become talismans that take human consciousness into another realm.

In dreams, vegetables are seldom dramatic, but their appearance may have profound meaning. In the broadest sense, vegetables are a connection to one's family, community, and ancestral roots. Vegetables pull us down, bring us back to earth, force us down into the depths of our unconscious.

Eating vegetables signifies the taking in of spiritual nourishment of the most fundamental kind; the subsequent process of digestion is the absorption and assimilation of this nourishment into the psyche. Cooking vegetables is an alchemical process. Growing vegetables indicates fertility and renewal. Rotting vegetables—a symbol of death—are a precursor to renewal and growth. Seeing rows and rows of neatly planted vegetables could mean immobility of fear or a loss of will, or a sense of orderliness and solid organization. Wild vegetables are disorganization, chaos, the vegetable soul out of control. Frozen vegetables show a state of spiritual suspended animation. Processed vegetables have had some or all of their spiritual nutrients removed.

victimization Dreams of being victimized often are a symptom of severe depression, such as the low that follows a separation or divorce. Such dreams indicate self-blame for everything that has gone wrong.

Victimization dreams alas may symbolize a feeling of being oppressed by others or by circumstances in life. Again, the dreamer is projecting self-blame onto the situation.

Association: Being a victim in an act of violence is excess yang. Being victimized in a relationship where the dreamer is unable to speak up or defend herself is deficient yang. The dreamer may also have an excess yin stagnation condition that prevents the movement of yang energy.

Element: The elemental association of being victimized needs to be evaluated according to the context of the dream. For example, a violent act committed against the dreamer with a gun is a metal association.

violence Murder, bloodshed, mutilation of bodies, massacres, and other horrendous physical violence symbolize the alchemical state of mortification, in which ingredients are cut apart and ground to their common elements before being recombined into something better. Thus violence may indicate the beginning stages of transformation, in which the old is rent apart to make way for, and to create, the new.

Dreams of violence often symbolize feelings of being out of control or overwhelmed as a result of major upheavals in life. They may also represent rage and anger toward others.

Association: Yang

Element: The element associated with violence is Fire; however, for the individual dreamer this may need to be evaluated according to the context of the dream. For example, an act of violence using a knife may be Metal. Bludgeoning with a baseball bat is Wood.

violet *See* **colors.**

volcano Like the **mountain,** the volcano is an archetypal symbol of the self. Its potential for eruption, for spewing forth great quantities of material, signals impending or potential drastic inner change.

Association: Yang

Element: Fire.

vomiting Revulsion; a desire to get rid of something unpleasant or poisonous in one's life.

Association: Yang. The movement of Qi that causes vomiting is in an upward and outward direction.

Element: Fire/Earth. An external image association for vomiting is that of a volcano. Fire energy that is contained within the earth moves upward, outward, and overflows. In the process, it is both destructive and productive. The molten lava can destroy that which is in its path, yet as it cools, new earth and rock is created. Vomiting is the fire energy of the Earth Element (stomach) that needs release. Vomiting can damage the stomach and gastrointestinal tract; at the same time, new cells can be born like a phoenix rising out of the ashes of the fire.

wallet *See* **identification**.

walnut Because of its shape, the walnut is a symbol of the brain, and by association intellectual activity. It also represents the general symbolism of nuts as hidden wisdom; the heart of the matter; and fertility.

Association: Yin

Element: Water. The brain, in Chinese Medicine, is said to be a "curious organ" and is related to the kidney/adrenal system.

war Inner conflict, especially one of a serious nature that is not being acknowledged or resolved.

The weapons used in a dream war can shed additional light on the nature of the conflict. Swords and knives are symbols of severance and separation, and may indicate an inability to separate one's self from a situation. Guns, grenades, and bombs are symbols of anger; the latter two may also indicate a threatening buildup of inner pressure. Nuclear weapons (as well as large-scale warfare) are symbolic of great frustration and anger which may be directed at ideas, beliefs, and concepts.

Association: Yang

Element: Fire. Like violence, war has a strong yang/Fire Element association, however, the dreamer must look at the dream in context. The dreamer might feel the weapons of the war are more vivid in the dream, so the element of the individual weapon may be more significant.

washing machine Washing machines may appear in dreams involving one's identity (*see* **clothing**), and relate to changing or improving identity.

Washing machines also are a common symbol in dreams during pregnancy, and represent the watery inner space of a pregnant womb.

Other meanings of washing machines are a purification process going on in the unconscious; and turbulence or agitation concerning something.

Association: Yang
Element: Water

waves Being buffeted or engulfed by waves represents feelings of being emotionally overwhelmed, especially during times of crisis or major life change. Tidal waves reflect extreme upheaval in life. Being lapped by gentle waves or tides represents peace and tranquility in the womblike waters of the unconscious.

Dreams involving waves are common during pregnancy, and represent the womb.

Association: Yang
Element: Water

wedding. *See* **initiation; marriage.**

well The deep layers of the unconscious; contact with the underworld. Nature spirits (the forces of nature) dwell by and protect wells.

Wells also are a source of spiritual refreshment and powers of healing.

Other meanings of wells are a woman's womb; the womb of the Mother Goddess; and emotions that go deep within.

Association: Yin

Element: Water

wellness Dreams of good health and wellness are not uncommon among persons who are terminally ill. Such dreams may symbolize the desire for recovery. They also may symbolize impending death, and recovery in the afterlife.

Dreams in which deceased persons appear well and perhaps younger and more vital—especially if they died of illness or in a debilitated state—are difficult to interpret. They may represent the desire on the part of the living to see the deceased restored to life, or they may be a symbol of one's acceptance of the deceased's transition from life. However, it cannot be ruled out that such dreams may also represent a picture of the afterlife.

Association: Yin/yang balance and harmony.

Element: In general, no one element is associated with wellness. The implication of wellness is that there is balance and harmony in all elements.

wheat A symbol of the mysteries of death and resurrection; the Mother Goddess; fecundity; the bounty of the earth; and prosperity. Wheat is associated with the womb of the earth, which brings forth life and takes in death to resurrect life anew.

Association: Yang

Element: Wood. According to the ancient Chinese theory of correspondences, wheat is correlated with wood, the color green, and the spring season.

wheel Dynamism; change; the relentless turning of time; the course of life; the seasons; the cycle of birth, death, and rebirth; the sun (illumination) rotating through the heavens. Like the **circle**, the wheel also symbolizes completion and wholeness; becoming and passing away.

In alchemy, a wheel represents circulation, the rotation of the universe, the ascension of humankind into God, and the descent of God into humankind.

The wheel also represents the pattern set in motion by the psyche, in terms of the manifestation of inner potential in real events.

On a mundane level, the wheel represents fortune: the ups and downs of life

A spoked wheel should be considered in terms of **numbers** symbolisms.

Association: Yang. A wheel is a representation of perpetual motion.

Element: The specific image of the wheel determines the element. For example, a spoked wheel is Metal, and an old wooden stagecoach wheel is Wood.

whip/whipping Domination, superiority, authority; also punishment, degradation, and abuse.

The whip is both a symbol of male virility and the generative force, and female fecundity and the dark aspect of the Mother Goddess, or Terrible Mother. In ancient times, people and fruit and nut trees were whipped to ensure fertility, and also to drive away evil spirits.

In a dream, whips or whipping may represent the germination of creativity or something new. They also may be a form of punishment or self-punishment, and relate to one's relationships, job, or other circumstances.

Association: Yang

Element: The type of whip in a dream determines the element.

white *See* **colors.**

window Consciousness; one's perception or perspective on the world. Looking in a window can symbolize insight. Looking out a window can mean one's outlook on the world.

Windows also are symbols of openings to other levels of consciousness.

Association: Yang. The nature of clarity and transparency is yang.
Element: Water

wine Vitality; truth; the **blood** of the gods. Like blood, wine has a transforming power. It has been used in ritual offerings to chthonic deities, a symbolic connection to the realm of the unconscious. Wine also represents intoxication, divine ecstasy, the vital powers of nature, and the "vegetable soul."

Wine may symbolize sacrifice.

Association: Yin
Element: Water

witch The destructive side of the feminine principle; the Terrible Mother. In dreams, a witch often symbolizes destructive, malevolent acts or nature of a mother, wife, or lover, or of one's shadow.

wolf Devouring forces; diabolic forces; the principle of evil; fierceness; craftiness; gluttony. The wolf frequently appears in mythology and fairy tales as a negative force, but it has positive, spiritual associations as well.

The wolf is a chthonic animal, the companion of gods of the underworld (the unconscious) and a guide or psychopomp of the souls of the dead. Like the **dog**, the wolf has lunar associations and thus is connected to the Mother Goddess, especially her dark aspects.

In its positive aspects, the wolf is a symbol of light because it can see in the dark. It also is a symbol of valor and victory.

Another meaning of wolf is devouring fear.

In Chinese literature, dreaming of a wolf is an omen of unsuccessful travel.

Association: Yin

Element: Earth

See **animals**.

wood Solidity; hardness; the raw material of building and new construction. In alchemy, wood is the first matter, the *prima materia* from which all things are shaped and from which the Philosopher's Stone is derived. It is a mother symbol with associations of protection and carrying. It is a repository of the vital force that animates the universe.

The burning of wood has magical properties in sacrificial rites, signifying wisdom and death; its ashes symbolize rebirth. Wood thus is related to the symbol of **fire**, and to the alchemical process of calcination, or purification through a burning away.

Association: Yin

Element: Wood

See **trees**.

worm Death; decay; dissolution; rotting. Also, the earth, or the material.

The worm kills rather than gives life. In alchemy, the worm is key to putrefaction, the blackening and decay that precede resurrection and light. Similarly, worms aerate rotting compost that becomes the fertilizer of new life.

The worm also is a symbol for the world serpent (*see* **snake**) and for the principle of evil.

Because of its association with rot, decay, and stench, the worm in dreams also may symbolize pollution of one's life, environment, or literally the air.

Other meanings of worms are untrustworthiness and low moral character.

Association: Yin

Element: Earth

wound A symbol of initiation. Also, unresolved emotions, anxieties, or fears.

Dreams of mortal wounds commonly occur during the stresses of midlife crisis, and represent the fears of letting go of the old self to make way for a new self.

Association: Destruction of yin substance, usually by a yang force.

Element: The element is determined by the object or implement causing the wound.

See **death**.

wounded children *See* **child/children**.

yam A phallic symbol because of its shape. Like potatoes, yams are a staple of life and community life. They also are an important totemic vegetable tied to the mysteries of death and rebirth.

Association: Yin

Element: Earth

yard A personal boundary associated with family, home, and security. A place where games are played; a child's world. A yard is a place of innocence: the real world constitutes the yard, and the mysterious and possibly dangerous unknown lies beyond.

yellow *See* **colors**.

yew An **evergreen** that is a symbol of long life and immortality. In folklore, the yew is a magical charm against bewitchment. In its destructive aspect, the yew is a symbol of death and mourning, because its needles and seeds are poisonous.

See **trees**.

yoke Union; being connected or bound to something in a balance.

Yokes also carry negative connotations of slavery, bondage, obedience, toil, and being treated like an animal.

Association: Yin. Being confined or restrained in a dream is a yin energy constraint. This situation can occur in the body when there is a yin excess, or when there is a yang deficiency unable to control the yin.

Element: The element will be determined by the type of yoke.

zircon See **jewels**.

zone A bounded space that implies territoriality, limited access or activity, or sovereignty. Zones are collective symbols, the rules for which are set by collective authority.

zoo Confined or imprisoned animal nature, urges, or instincts. A zoo also represents chaos.

Association: Yin

Element: The element depends on the predominant images of the zoo. For example, a cage with metal bars is Metal. Seeing an elephant in a natural enclosure is Earth.

Bibliography

Beinfield, Harriet and Efrem Korngold. *Between Heaven and Earth*. New York: Ballantine Books, 1991.

Capra, Fritjof. *The Tao of Physics*. Boston: New Science Library Shambala, 1983.

Cleary, Thomas. *The Illustrated Art of War Sun Tsu*. Boston: Shambala, 1998.

Cleary, Thomas. *Practical Taoism*. Boston: Shambala, 1996.

Cleary, Thomas. *Wen-Tzu: Understanding the Mysteries, Further Teachings of Lao Tzu*. Boston: Shambala, 1991.

Connelly, Dianne, M. *Traditional Acupuncture: The Law of the Five Elements*. Columbia, Maryland: The Center for Traditional Acupuncture, 1987.

Edmunds, E.W. and J.B. Hoblyn. *The Story of the Five Elements*. London: Cassell & Co. Ltd., 1912.

Fang, Jing Pei and Zhang Juwen. *The Interpretation of Dreams in Chinese Culture*. New York: Weatherhill, 2000.

Ferguson, Pamela. *Take Five: The Five Elements Guide to Health and Harmony*. Dublin: Newleaf Gill & Macmillan, Ltd., 2000.

Guiley, Rosemary Ellen. *Dreamwork for the Soul: A Spiritual Guide to Dream Interpretation*. New York: Berkley Books, 1998.

——. *The Encyclopedia of Dreams: Symbols and Interpretations*. New York: Berkley Books, 1995.

——. *Harper's Encyclopedia of Mystical and Paranormal Experience*. San Francisco: HarperSanFrancisco, 1991.

Ong, Robert K. *Interpretation of Dreams in Ancient China*. Munich: Bochum, 1985.

Pei, Fang Jing and Zhang Juwen. *The Interpretation of Dreams in Chinese Culture*. Trumbull, Connecticut: Weatherhill, 2000.

Plambeck, James. "Concept of the Four Elements," in *University Chemistry: Introduction: Greek Theory and Roman Practice*. Available online. URL: http://www.psigate.ac.uk/newsite/reference/plambeck/chem1/p01012.htm. Downloaded on May 27, 2004.

Rinpoche, Tenzin Wangyal. *Healing with Form, Energy and Light*. Ithaca, New York: Snow Lion Publications, 2002.

Sheikh, Anees A. and Katharina Sheikh. *Healing East & West*. New York: John Wiley & Sons, 1989.

Siu, R.G.H. *The Tao of Science*. New York: John Wiley & Sons Inc., 1957.

Strickmann, Michael. *Chinese Magical Medicine*. Stanford: Stanford University Press, 2002.

Too, Lillian. *The Illustrated Encyclopedia of Feng Shui*. New York: Barnes & Noble Books, 1999.

Unschuld, Paul U. *Medicine in China*. Berkeley: University of California Press, 1985.

Wagnan, Doris Jeanne. "Elementary Particles," in *Microsoft Encarta Encyclopedia*, 2002.

About the Authors

Rosemary Ellen Guiley, Ph.D.

Rosemary Ellen Guiley is a bestselling author whose work includes self-help books on dreams and intuition development. She is president of her own company, Visionary Living, Inc. A noted expert on lay dreamwork, she conducts dreamwork groups, classes, and workshops. She is a former member of the board of directors of the International Association for the Study of Dreams.

Her other books on dreams and intuition are *The Dreamer's Way: Using Proactive Dreaming for Creativity and Healing*; *Dreamspeak: How to Understand the Messages in Your Dream*; *Dreamwork for the Soul: A Spiritual Guide to Dream Interpretation*; *The Encyclopedia of Dreams: Symbols and Interpretation*; and *Breakthrough Intuition: How to Achieve a Life of Abundance by Listening to the Voice Within*. All are published by Berkley Books.

Guiley has authored books on other subjects, including prayer, mysticism and mystical experience, saints, angels, ghosts, sacred sites, and more.

Her work is translated into thirteen languages, selected by major book clubs, and cited for excellence.

Her Web site is Visionary Living, at www.visionaryliving.com.

Sheryl Martin, OMD, L.Ac., RN

Sheryl Martin is a Doctor of Oriental Medicine, Licensed Acupuncturist, and Registered Nurse. She graduated from the Pacific College of Oriental Medicine in San Diego, California, and received her doctorate from Samra University of Oriental Medicine in Los Angeles, California. She has been practicing traditional Chinese Medicine for more than seventeen years and teaches both locally and nationally on health topics such as infertility, natural hormonal regulation, and how to integrate Chinese Medicine in daily life. She conducts dream workshops and facilitates self dream interpretation using the principles of Chinese Medicine with her patients. She practices in Baltimore, Maryland, at the Maryland Center for Integrative Medicine.